The Writings of Frithjof Schuon
Series

WORLD WISDOM
THE LIBRARY OF PERENNIAL PHILOSOPHY

The Library of Perennial Philosophy is dedicated to the exposition of the timeless Truth underlying the diverse religions. This Truth, often referred to as the *Sophia Perennis*—or Perennial Wisdom—finds its expression in the revealed Scriptures as well as the writings of the great sages and the artistic creations of the traditional worlds.

The Perennial Philosophy—and its fundamental idea of the Religion of the Heart—provides the intellectual principles capable of explaining both the formal contradictions and the underlying unity of the great religions.

Ranging from the writings of the great sages who have expressed the *Sophia Perennis* in the past, to the perennialist authors of our time, each series of our Library has a different focus. As a whole, they express the inner unanimity, transforming radiance, and irreplaceable values of the great spiritual traditions. *Form and Substance in the Religions* appears in our series entitled The Writings of Frithjof Schuon.

The Writings of Frithjof Schuon

The writings of Frithjof Schuon form the foundation of our library because he is the pre-eminent exponent of the Perennial Philosophy. His work illuminates this perspective in both an essential and comprehensive manner like none other.

Form and Substance in the Religions

by
FRITHJOF SCHUON

World Wisdom

Form and Substance in the Religions
by Frithjof Schuon
© 2002 World Wisdom, Inc.

First English language version.

Mark Perry, Lead Translator
Jean-Pierre LaFouge, Translator

Originally published as
Forme et Substance dans les Religions
Dervy-Livres, Paris
June, 1975

Library of Congress Cataloging-in-Publication Data

Schuon, Frithjof, 1907-1998
    [Forme et substance dans les religions. English]
    Form and substance in the religions / by Frithjof Schuon.
        p. cm. — (Writings of Frithjof Schuon)
    ISBN 0-941532-25-9 (pbk. : alk. paper)
    1. Religions.   I. Title.
    BL85 .S3713 2002
    291.2—dc21

                                                        2002005224

Cover photo: Temples in Pagan, Myanmar (Burma).

Printed on acid-free paper in Canada

For information address World Wisdom, Inc.
P.O. Box 2682, Bloomington, Indiana 47402-2682

www.worldwisdom.com

Contents

Preface

When reading the essays contained in this collection, the reader will appreciate that we have in mind less traditional information as such than the exposition of intrinsic doctrine; in other words, our aim is to enunciate truths for which traditional dialectical expressions serve as vestments; we thus seek to expound various formulations that belong to all times and all places, not as a historian of ideas, but as a spokesman of the *philosophia perennis*. As in our book *Logic and Transcendence*, our intention is to offer in this present collection nothing less than a doctrine that is essential, integral, homogeneous, and sufficient unto itself; we would gladly say a "philosophy" or a "theosophy", were these terms not susceptible to being misinterpreted.

One point that always seems to elude *de facto* rationalists is that there is inevitably a separation between the thing to be expressed and its expression, that is to say, between reality and a doctrine. It is always possible to fault an adequate doctrine for being inadequate, since no doctrine can be identified with what it intends to express; no single formulation could take into account what the innumerable needs for causality might demand, whether rightly or wrongly. If the expression of a thing could be adequate or exhaustive in an absolute sense or from every point of view—as philosophical critique, clinging *a priori* to words, intends—there would no longer be any difference between the image and its prototype, and in that case it would be pointless to speak of thought or even simply of language. In reality, however, the role of doctrinal thought is to provide a set of points of reference which, by definition, are more or less elliptical while being sufficient to evoke a mental perception of specific aspects of the real. This is all that we are entitled to ask of a doctrine; the rest is a matter of intellectual capacity, good will, and grace.

Everything has already been said, and well said; but one must always recall it anew, and in recalling it one must do what has already been done: to actualize in thought certitudes contained, not in the thinking ego, but in the transpersonal substance of human intelligence. Being human, intelligence is total and thus essentially capable of grasping the Absolute, and in so doing of having the sense of the relative; to conceive of the Absolute is also to conceive of the relative as such, and then to perceive in the Absolute the roots of the relative and in the relative the reflections of the Absolute. All metaphysics and all cosmology transcribe, in the last analysis, this play of complementarity, which belongs to the universal *Mâyâ* and which as a result inheres in the very substance of intelligence.

To return to our book, we shall say that its dialectic is inevitably the result of its message; and this dialectic cannot take into account the exorbitant pretensions of a psychology—even a biology—that tends to substitute itself absurdly for philosophy, if not for thought itself. One cannot in fair logic reproach us for using a naïve and old-fashioned type of language when our dialectic finds its essential justification precisely in the content of the ideas expressed, a content that is commensurate with the Immutable.

There is no spiritual extraterritoriality: because he exists, man shares solidarity with everything Existence entails. Because we are capable of knowing, we are called upon to know all that is intelligible—to know, not what is intelligible according to our convenience, but what is so according to human capacity and the nature of things.

Frithjof Schuon

Truth and Presence

The saving manifestation of the Absolute is either Truth or Presence, but it is not one or the other in an exclusive fashion, for as Truth It comprises Presence, and as Presence It comprises Truth. Such is the twofold nature of all theophanies; thus Christ is essentially a manifestation of Divine Presence, but he is thereby also Truth: "I am the Way, the Truth, and the Life." No one enters into the saving proximity of the Absolute except through a manifestation of the Absolute, be it *a priori* Presence or Truth.

In Christianity, the element Presence takes precedence over the element Truth: the first element absorbs, as it were, the second, in the sense that Truth is identified with the phenomenon of Christ; Christian Truth is the idea that Christ is God. From this arises the doctrine of the Trinity, which would not make sense if the point of departure in Christianity were the element Truth, that is, a doctrine of the Absolute, as is the case in Islam where God presents Himself in paramount fashion as the One Real, or in the measure allowed by a Semitic exoterism.[1]

Islam is thus founded on the axiom that absolute Truth is what saves, together of course with the consequences this entails for the will; the exoteric limitation of this perspective is the axiom that Truth alone saves, not Presence. Christianity, on the contrary, is founded on the axiom that the Divine Presence saves; the exoteric limitation here is the axiom on the one hand that only this

---

1. This reservation means that the theological point of view, by the very fact of its devotional and voluntarist perspective, cannot avoid a certain dualism.

1

Presence, not another, saves, and on the other hand that only the element Presence can save, not the element Truth in Itself.[2]

To say with Islam that it is Truth that saves—since it is the Truth of the Absolute—means that all the consequences of Truth must be drawn and that It must be accepted totally, namely, with the will and the sentiments as well as with the intelligence. And to say with Christianity that it is Presence that saves—since it is the presence of Divine Love—means that one is to enter into the mold of this Presence, sacramentally and sacrificially—and let oneself be carried towards Divine Love. It is necessary first to love, then to will, and then in due course to know—to know in relation to the love of God; whereas in Islam first one must know, then will, and in due course one must love—to love in relation to this knowledge of God, if such a schematic way of presenting these matters is allowed.

A priori or exoterically, the element Truth in Christianity is, as we have said, the axiom that Christ is God, and that Christ alone is God; but *a posteriori* or esoterically, the Christic Truth means, on the one hand, that every manifestation of the Absolute is identical with the Absolute and, on the other, that this manifestation is at once transcendent and immanent. Transcendent, it is Christ above us; immanent, it is Christ within us; it is the Heart, which is both Intellect and Love. To enter the Heart is to enter into Christ, and conversely; Christ is the Heart of the macrocosm as the Intellect is the Christ of the microcosm. "God became man that man might become God": the Self became Heart that the Heart might become the Self; and this is why "the kingdom of God is within you".

It is in this gnosis that Islam and Christianity meet, for the Heart is the immanent Koran or the immanent Prophet, if the emphasis is placed on the active and inspiring function of the Intellect. This amounts to saying that in Islam the element Presence is represented by the Koran on the one hand and by the Prophet on the other; to give full value to this element Pres-

---

2. The saving Truth of Islam is "Truth"—not "such and such" a Truth—for it concerns the Absolute and not a phenomenon.

ence—with respect to the element Truth, which is the point of departure in Islam—is to become identified sacramentally and eucharistically with the Koran,[3] and it is also to be identified with the Prophet by entering the Muhammadan mold, which is none other than the "primordial norm", the *Fitrah*. One enters into this mold by enclosing oneself in the *Sunnah*, the body of rules of conduct prescribed by the Prophet, and personified by him; now these rules are "horizontal" as well as "vertical": they concern material and social as well as spiritual life.

The Koran itself, too, is both Truth and Presence: it is Truth by its doctrine, which teaches that there is but one Absolute, and it is Presence owing to its theophanic or sacramental quality, which is the origin of *Dhikr*, the quintessential prayer.

*

* *

If Christ is the Truth of Presence for Christians, that is, the real Presence or the only true Presence of God, the Prophet on the contrary is the presence of Truth for Muslims, which is to say that he alone makes present pure or total Truth, Truth as such; this explains why for Muslims, who are impervious to other arguments, Muhammad is the greatest of "Messengers". "This Truth, this Prophet", Muslims seem to argue, whereas for Christians Truth seems on the contrary to depend totally on the incomparability of the God-Man.

For Muslims, only the Truth of the Absolute saves: hence their tendency to diminish or depreciate, in all of its aspects, the element Presence in Christianity; whereas for Christians, Presence alone—or this Presence—carries saving efficacy, whence their tendency to underestimate or to reject any form of "Platonism", in other words, any perspective based on liberating Truth.

The pre-eminence of Muhammad in Islam—the logical motivation of which we have just indicated, at least in its most fundamental regard—carries by way of consequence or concomitance a curious tendency to belittle the Messengers who came before Muhammad, if only incidentally and notwithstanding the venera-

---

3. There are Muslims who spend their life reciting the Koran, and there are non-Arab Muslims who chant the Koran even if they do not understand it.

3

tion Islam accords them. We feel obliged to mention this feature because it appears in Sufi works[4] as well as in exegeses of the Koran, and traces of it are to be found even in some *ahâdîth*.[5] In order to forestall too hasty an indignation on the part of Western Arabists, one should recall that a religion is what Buddhists term an *upâya*,[6] and that it has for this reason a certain right to defensive reflexes which, while objectively inadequate, are nonetheless logically appropriate for the religious axiom they serve and are justified by their effectiveness *pro domo* as well as by their indirect and symbolic truth.

From another point of view, concerning some disappointing opinions on Christ and the Virgin, it is necessary to take into account, on the one hand, the need of every exoterism to protect itself from the appeal of another religious perspective—in which case the end justifies the means, since human collectivities are what they are—and, on the other, a certain resentment on the part of Islam with regard to Christian anthropotheism. One can make the argument that an expression like the title "Mother of God" granted to a creature of surpassing eminence is a defensible metaphysical ellipsis; but one cannot deny that on the exoteric plane, and in the absence of subtle commentaries that would compensate for its audacity or imprudence, this expression places all metaphysics of the Absolute in abeyance, and marks a weakening of our immediate, full, and operative awareness of God's absoluteness; for either a phenomenon is God—which is contradictory—in which case it has no mother, or else it has a mother, in which case it cannot be God, at least insofar it has a mother and leaving out the initial contradiction of the hypothesis.[7] If you belittle the Absolute in this manner—Muslims seem to say—do

---

4. The *Fusûs al-Hikam* of Ibn Arabi offers some patent examples of this.
5. Perhaps not authentic, but in any case widespread, and not disavowed as regards their content.
6. The *upâya* is a "skillful means" by which Heaven seeks to win souls; since souls are in illusion, the "means" necessarily takes on something of the illusory, hence the diversity of doctrines, methods, and religions, or rather the incomparability of their various aspects.
7. This contradiction, of course, involves the literal meaning only and not the underlying mystery; for exoterism, however, it is the literal meaning that counts.

not become indignant if we belittle what is relative, since we do so for the sake of the Absolute and Its glory alone.[8]

Muslims are reproached for drawing no adequate theological conclusion from the virgin birth of Christ; Muslims might retort, however, that the ascensions of Enoch, Moses, and Elijah mean nothing for Christians, who place them in the "hells" of the Patriarchs until the historical advent of the unique Savior. If one is of the opinion that Muslims take extreme theological license in the name of the element Truth—which in their case emphasizes Transcendence to the detriment of aspects deemed dangerous in the element Presence—one could with no less reason consider that Christians take just as many liberties in favor of the element Presence and at the expense of certain metaphysical consequences of Transcendence, hence to the detriment of the element Truth; whether one likes it or not, one is thus forced to concede in a general way that the *upâya* has rights which at first sight seem exorbitant, but which in the end can be explained and justified by certain facts of human nature.

In a word, the misunderstanding between Christians and Muslims[9] is basically this: for Christians the Sacrament serves as Truth, whereas for Muslims the Truth serves as Sacrament.

8. According to an Islamic tradition, the sun and moon will be cast into hell at the end of time for having been worshiped by men; such an opinion is at the antipodes of the Hindu perspective and all other mythological or "pagan" perspectives founded, for their part, on what we have called on various occasions the metaphysical transparency of phenomena. It must be acknowledged, however, that this principle gives rise subjectively to many an abusive application—we do not have idolatry in mind here, which is a deviation and not merely an abuse—on the plane, for instance, of the quasi-ritual deification of certain maharajas, where anthropotheism is combined with all the meticulous pedantry of which the sacerdotal mentality is capable. The iconoclastic reflex of Islam is directed at idolatry in all its guises while, by the same token, rising up in the name of Transcendence against Immanence whenever Immanence seems to compete with Transcendence; only esoterism can in principle avoid this limiting tendency.
9. Or between Christians and Platonists, with all the necessary reservations or nuances.

The Islamic accentuation on the element Truth can be described in the following way: Monotheism as such, which is that of Abraham and the Patriarchs, is derived from the element Truth, since it is the Truth of the One God that saves; this is to say that man is saved by faith and nothing else, his works depending on faith or sincerity. The Christian perspective, for its part, is determined essentially by Divine Manifestation—a theophany which redounds upon the very conception of God—and this manifestation gives rise to a spirituality of sacrifice and love; this anthropotheism, along with the resulting trinitarianism, is certainly one spiritual possibility among others, but it is not Monotheism as such.

Now Islam, which represents Monotheism as such and nothing else, is logical in reproaching Christianity for not emphasizing the message of Monotheism, and for replacing it with another, precisely that of the divine manifestation; Islam is equally logical in reproaching Judaism, first, for having nationalized Monotheism, and second for having monopolized prophecy. Certainly, Mosaism and Christianity are intrinsically orthodox, but this is not what is at issue when it comes to setting forth the essential, characteristic, and universal message of Monotheism, as Islam intends to do.

Truth and Presence: these two notions, quite apart from questions of emphasis, are obviously complementary; but they can likewise give rise *de facto* to conflicting positions, as is shown not only by the antagonism between Christianity and Islam, but also—within the very bosom of Islam—by the schism between Sunnism and Shiism. Owing to a particular calling, Shiism adheres in its fashion to the element Presence, whereas Sunnism, in conformity with Islam as such, manifests the element Truth. That each of these two branches of the faith carries within it, to a certain degree and in a certain sector, the complementary element is a fact which we have already noted and which need not be demonstrated in detail at this point; suffice it to recall that Shiism is still Islam, and that it is inseparable from the monotheistic idea,

6

whereas Sunnism presents the element Presence through the *Sunnah*, which in a way perpetuates the soul of the Prophet.

The elements Truth and Presence are personified respectively by Abu Bakr, "the Truthful" (*Siddîq*) and Ali, "the Lion of God" (*Asad Allâh*). Ali, the Prophet's nephew, adopted son, and son-in-law, is part of the "Family" (*Âl*) of Muhammad, together with Fatimah, Muhammad's daughter, and their two sons Hasan and Husayn; as for Abu Bakr, his surname "the Truthful" indicates his nature and his link with the element Truth. This partition of affinities explains the profound reasons for the conflict between Abu Bakr and Fatimah after the Prophet's death; Fatimah laid claim to inherit an oasis in the name of the Muhammadan "Presence" and Abu Bakr denied it to her in the name of Islamic "Truth". In Sufism, Ali and Abu Bakr are considered to be the two immediate and intimate disciples of the Prophet who stand at the very base of the "chain of initiation" (*silsilah*); in a certain respect, perfection demands the concurrence of complementaries, for the Divine Dimensions—pure Being and pure Consciousness—are independent; their union is Beatitude.[10]

The theophanic notions of "Truth" and "Presence" bring us to two analogous notions that are specific to Amidism, namely, the "power of Oneself" and the "power of the Other" (in Japanese *jiriki* and *tariki*).[11] The first power is that of intelligence and of will seen from the point of view of the salvific capacity which they possess in principle and which consequently can operate in fact once the required conditions are met; in the first case, man is freed thanks to his intelligence and by his own efforts, at least according to human appearances, for metaphysically the enlightening and liberating power lies outside the grasp of an individual, who is simply its instrument. The second power does not belong to us in

---

10. It is this hypostatic constellation that produces the ternary *madhkûr, dhâkir, dhikr* ("Invoked, Invoker, Invocation"), which in fact recapitulates in its own fashion the Vedantin ternary *Sat, Chit, Ânanda* ("Being, Consciousness, Bliss").

11. Or *Shôdô-mon*, "School of the Sacred Path", and *Jôdo-mon*, "School of the Pure Land".

any way; it belongs to the "Other" as its name indicates and as its reason for being demands; in this context, man is saved by Grace, which does not however mean that he need not collaborate with this salvation by his receptivity and according to the modes that human nature allows or imposes on him.

Intelligence, which refers to the element Truth, pertains essentially to the "power of Oneself", and this is what Zen, which is founded on the immanent and liberating Truth, intends to represent; faith, which refers to Grace and therefore to the element Presence, pertains for its part to the "power of the Other", and that is what *Jôdo*, founded on the transcendent and saving Presence, intends to represent. Inevitably—one must insist on this— the element Truth, or the immanent Intellect, when this element is envisaged subjectively, actualizes the element "Presence", which surpasses us and determines us, whereas conversely the element Presence, in order to save us, appeals to faith and consequently to our intelligence and the element "Truth".[12]

A digression concerning the practical interpretation of the two "powers" (*jiriki* and *tariki*) might be appropriate at this point: without wishing to formulate a reproach on a plane pertaining to intrinsic orthodoxy—though this plane belongs nonetheless to the relativity of the *upâya*—one cannot help feeling that there is something excessive in the totalitarianism of a Zen, on the one hand, that sets out to dispense with all trace of *tariki* and of a *Jôdo*, on the other, that aims to pass over *jiriki* entirely. It is certain that man can, in principle, save himself "by his own means", but it is necessary that such an effort be blessed by a celestial Power, hence a "power of the Other"; and it is likewise certain that man can, in principle, be saved by simply abandoning himself to Mercy, but such an abandonment must contain an element of initiative, for the absence of any "power of Oneself" is contrary to the nature of man. The followers of Shinran, a protagonist of extreme *tariki*, sometimes reproach Honen, who was Shinran's spiritual master, for maintaining that the act of invocation combined with faith is the cause of salvation, which appears to them

12. As is shown by the *Yin-Yang* in Taoism—on the one hand, two opposite regions are given a form representing a kind of entwining and, on the other, an element of each region is transferred to the other.

as lacking in faith; for them faith alone saves, and the activity of prayer is no more than a token of gratitude. Now the more Shinran seeks to make the path easier, the more he makes it difficult in fact for us to trust, because if everything depends on faith and not on deeds, the validity—or the psychological substance—of faith becomes all the more tenuous; formulated differently, it is humanly difficult to believe in a Mercy that requires absolutely nothing on our part. With Honen, on the contrary, deeds contain an objective guarantee of authenticity with respect to faith since they facilitate and strengthen it, thus favoring the essential condition for rebirth in the "Pure Land"; this way of seeing things, far from compromising our trust in Mercy, contains furthermore an active element of happiness. Besides, it is not so much Shinran's intrinsic thesis that we are criticizing here as the partisanship displayed by his followers in criticizing Honen's thesis, which is sufficient and irreproachable, though doubtless less striking from the point of view of a certain totalitarianism that is both logical and emotional.[13]

Buddhism presents itself *a priori*, that is, in its formal framework, as a way of the "power of Oneself", hence one based on the element Truth as an immanent power of enlightenment and liberation; but it gives rise *a posteriori*, with perfect logic and without straying from its initial design, to a path according to the "power of the Other", hence one based on the element Presence as a transcendent power of mercy and salvation. Buddhist revelation offers in fact two principles, one general and the other particular—the second being inset within the first: first the principle of salvation through one's own effort, of which the young Gautama seated under the *Bodhi* tree is the paradigm, and then a principle of salvation by virtue of the saving power inherent in the state of *Buddha* obtained by Gautama. First, Gautama shows us the path by

---

13. The question that matters here is less one of knowing who is right than of knowing to whom the messages are addressed. Be that as it may, Shinran did not bring any improvement; he simply shifted the doctrinal emphasis of Amidism—which in itself is acceptable, but not to the detriment of the previous position; to think otherwise is to fall into the illusion of "theological progress". All told, there are three possible paths: predominance of the "power of Oneself"; predominance of the "power of the Other"; and a balance between the two.

his example; and then, having become Buddha, he preaches this same path while at the same time giving himself—his Buddha-hood[14]—as a sacrament; and he does so in the form of the "Pure Land" Sutras or, to be more precise, in the form of the saving Name of Amitabha Buddha, of which he himself, Gautama Buddha, is in some way the present earthly personification. Amitabha Buddha thus appears as the Logos as such, whereas the historical Buddha is a given Prophet manifesting the Logos by right of identification. Gautama or Shakyamuni is the individual become Buddha and showing how to become one, and Amitabha is eternal and hence pre-existent Buddhahood, which attracts by its all-powerful Mercy.

In other words, the path according to the element Truth participates actively in the enlightening realization of the Buddha, and the path according to the element Presence participates receptively in the immeasurable merit of this same realization. On the one hand, the follower imitates the example of the Bodhisattva Shakyamuni, and this is the way of the Theravadins and also, within Mahayana itself, that of the adherents of Zen, the disciples of Bodhidharma; and, on the other hand, the follower avails himself of the avataric and sacramental power of the Buddha—or of the saving power of Buddhahood—and this is the way of Amidists, from Vasubandhu to Shinran.

The question of knowing why a man can, and sometimes must, follow the path of the "power of Oneself" when he could follow that of the "power of the Other" need not be asked, for human nature is diverse—as is also, before all else, the Divine Possibility that creates it; furthermore, the two paths are most often combined,[15] so that their opposition in the form of Zen and Amidism is merely a phenomenon of extreme polarization.

14. This Buddhahood is also presented as "Body of the Law", *Dharma-kâya*; the absolute Buddha is identified with the *Dharma*-Principle, whereas the personality of the earthly Buddha is the Law as theophanic Presence. Analogously, the soul of the Prophet—according to Aishah—is identified with the Koran, or more precisely with the "human substance" of the Koran, that is, with its Arab character.
15. The Tendai, Shingon, and Kegon schools accept in principle or in fact the combination of the two methods, namely, the cult of Amida and intellective meditation.

*

* *

In man's natural constitution, the element Truth is represented by Knowledge, the element Presence by virtue;[16] Knowledge is soundness of intelligence, and virtue soundness of will. Knowledge is perfect only when there is some participation by virtue, and conversely; it is evident that intelligence, when well applied, can produce or strengthen virtue since it informs us of its nature and necessity; it is equally evident that virtue, for its part, can favor Knowledge since it determines some of its modes. In other words, we know metaphysical Reality, not only because we understand or conceive, but also because we are able to will; therefore, we know by virtue of what we are, for our knowledge of God cannot be other than what God Himself is, and God is both Majesty and Beauty (in Arabic *Jalâl* and *Jamâl*);[17] now the Beauty of the Object can be understood fully only by the beauty of the subject. Universal Reality is at once geometric and musical, intellectual and existential, "abstract" or incomparable (*tanzîh*) and "concrete" or analogous (*tashbîh*),[18] transcendent and immanent. "Truth" is like a fire that burns away the world of accidents, leaving only the intangible Substance to subsist, whereas "Presence", on the contrary, renders this same Substance tangible through translucent accidents that reveal It according to varied and innumerable modes.[19]

16. In Islam, the terms *salâh* and *salâm*, "blessing" and "peace"—added to the name of the Prophet—refer respectively to these two elements, leaving aside their more immediate meanings.
17. This second term immediately evokes, for Islamic sensibility, the idea of *Ikrâm*, "overflowing generosity": Allah, who comprises essentially "Majesty" and "Beauty", is called "Possessor of Majesty and Overflowing Generosity" (*Dhû 'l-Jalâli wa 'l-Ikrâm*) in the *Surah Ar-Rahmân*.
18. It is to this polarity that the two Testimonies in Islam refer metaphysically, that of the one God, *Allâh*, which excludes, and that of His Prophet, *Muhammad*, which reintegrates.
19. Modes of "Mercy" (*Rahmah*), or of Beauty and Love, as Ibn Arabi would say.

Form and Substance
in the Religions

For a religion to be considered intrinsically orthodox—extrinsic orthodoxy depending on specific formal factors that cannot be applied literally outside of the perspective to which they belong—it must be founded on a doctrine of the Absolute which, taken as a whole, is adequate;[1] this religion must then advocate and achieve a spirituality that is proportioned to this doctrine, which is to say that it must comprise sanctity both in notion and in fact. Therefore, the religion must be of divine and not of philosophical origin, and consequently it must be the vessel for a sacramental or theurgic presence made manifest notably in miracles and also—though this may be surprising to some—in sacred art. Specific formal elements, such as apostolic personages and sacred events, are subordinated inasmuch as they are forms to the principial elements just mentioned; their meaning or value can therefore change from one religion to another—human diversity making such fluctuations inevitable—without this constituting any contradiction with regard to the essential criteriology that concerns both metaphysical truth and salvific efficacy, and secondarily—and on that basis—human stability; this stability can make demands that seem paradoxical at first sight given that it necessarily entails a certain compromise between earth and Heaven. Islam may appear markedly problematical from the Christian point of view, but it answers unquestionably to the

1. Whether it is conceived *a priori* in a mode that is personal or impersonal, theistic or nirvanic.

13

overall description given above; it is intrinsically orthodox while differing extrinsically from the other orthodox monotheistic forms, and it is bound to differ most particularly from Christianity owing to a kind of regression—in appearance—to an Abrahamic and as it were timeless equilibrium.

Every religion has a form and a substance; Islam spread like lightning by virtue of its substance; but its expansion was brought to a halt on account of its form. Substance possesses every right; it derives from the Absolute; form is relative; its rights are therefore limited.[2] One cannot, in full knowledge of these facts, close one's eyes to this: first, there can be no absolute credibility on the plane of mere phenomena; and then, the literalist and exclusivist interpretation of religious messages is contradicted by their relative ineffectiveness, not of course within their own area of providential expansion, but with regard to believers in other religions: "Had God truly wished to save the world," a Chinese emperor replied to some missionaries, "why did He leave China in darkness for endless centuries?" In no wise does the irrefutable logic of this argument prove that a given religious message is false, but it does prove that it is outwardly limited by its form, exactly in the same way that a particular geometric form cannot, by itself, take account of the possibilities of space. Quite evidently, such a principial argument has other aspects or other applications: for instance, had God truly wished to save the world by means of the Christian religion and by no other, how would one then explain that several centuries later, and when Christianity had not yet even established itself in Europe, He permitted another religion, both lightning-like and monolithic, to establish itself in those very regions where Christianity's influence was meant to penetrate, thus closing once and for all, as with an iron bolt, any spread of Christianity toward the East.[3] Inversely, if the advent of Islam

---

2. Heresy is a form severed from its substance, hence its illegitimacy, whereas wisdom on the contrary is substance considered independently of forms, hence its universality and its imprescriptible nature. The success of heresy is due, not to an inner worth which is in fact largely absent, but to external and more or less negative causes, unless the determining factor in a given setting is a specific traditional element that has remained intact.

3. When speaking of Muslims, St Bernard said that God "will scatter the princes of darkness" and that "the swords of the brave will soon complete

meant that the whole world was to embrace this religion, one could not explain why God would provide it with a human imagery that clashes with Christian sensibility and renders the West irremediably refractory to the Muhammadan message; if one objects that man is free—that consequently God grants him the freedom to create, in any place and at any time, a false religion—words then become meaningless: for an effective divine intervention had to take into consideration the freedom of man to oppose it; it had to do so at least in a measure that safeguards what is essential in this intervention and allows the message to be universally intelligible and heard by all men of good will. One might well respond that God's will is unfathomable; however, if it is so and to such an extent, then religious argumentation itself loses much of its force. It is true that the relative failure of religious expansion has never troubled the minds of the faithful, but the question clearly could not have arisen in times when man's outlook on the world was still limited and when, precisely, the halt to the expansion had not yet been experienced; and if the attitude of the faithful did not change later, once this halt became perceptible, this proves positively that religions offer intrinsic values that no terrestrial contingency can impair, and negatively that partisanship and lack of imagination are part of human nature and that in fact these two traits constitute a protective screen without which most men would be unable to live.

the extermination of the last of their satellites" (*Praise of the New Militia,* 5). He was compelled finally to admit that "the children of the Church and all those who bear the name Christian lie fallen in the desert, victims of battles and of famine," and that "the leaders of the expedition quarrel among themselves"; and that "the judgment God has just pronounced upon us is such an abyss of mystery that to find in it no occasion for scandal is, in our eyes, already sanctity and beatitude" (*Considerations* 2:1). Sufis recall that, beyond all oppositions, the diversity of Revelations are the rays of the same Divine Sun: "The man of God," Rumi sings in his *Dîwân,* "is beyond infidelity and religion. . . . I have looked into my own heart: it is there that I beheld Him (*Allâh*); He was not to be found elsewhere . . . I am neither Christian, nor Jew, nor Parsee, nor Muslim; I am neither of the East nor of the West, neither of the land nor of the sea. . . . I have put duality aside, I beheld that the two worlds are but one; One alone I seek, One alone I know, One alone I see, One alone I call."

15

To convert from one religion to another is not only to change concepts and means; it is also to replace one sentimentality with another. To speak of sentimentality is to speak of limitation: the margin of sentiment that envelops each one of the religions proves in its fashion the limit of all exoterism and, as a result, the limits of exoteric claims. Inwardly or substantially, the claims a religion makes are absolute, but outwardly or formally, namely on the plane of human contingency, they are necessarily relative; if metaphysics did not suffice to prove this, the facts themselves would prove it.

Let us place ourselves now, by way of example, in the position of exoteric—hence totalitarian—Islam: at the beginning of the Muslim expansion, circumstances were such that Islam's doctrinal claims compelled acceptance in an absolute manner; later, however, the relativity that is part of every formal expression was bound to appear. If Islam's exoteric—that is, non-esoteric—claims were absolute and not relative, no man of good will could resist such claims or such a "categorical imperative": any man who held out against it would be fundamentally bad, as was the case in the first days of Islam, when one could not without perversity prefer magical idols to the pure God of Abraham. St John Damascene held a high office in the court of the Caliph in Damascus;[4] he did not, however, convert to Islam, any more than did St Francis of Assisi in Tunisia, or St Louis in Egypt, or St Gregory Palamas in Turkey.[5] Now this leads to one of two inescapable conclusions: either these saints were fundamentally bad men—an absurd supposition since they were saints—or Islam's claims contain, as do those of any religion, an aspect of relativity; and this is metaphysically evident since every form has limits, and since each religion is outwardly a form, the quality of absoluteness belonging to it only in its intrinsic and supra-formal essence. Tradition relates that the Sufi Ibrahim bin Adam had as his occasional master a Christian hermit without either of them converting to the religion of the

---

4. This is where the saint wrote and published, with the caliph's consent, his famous treatise in defense of images, which had been prohibited by the iconoclast Emperor Leo III.
5. While a prisoner of the Turks for a year, St Gregory carried on friendly discussions with the Emir's son and yet did not convert, nor did the Turkish prince become a Christian.

other; likewise, tradition relates that Sayyid Ali Hamadani, who played a decisive role in the conversion of Kashmir to Islam, knew Lalla Yogishwari, the naked *yoginî* of the valley, and that, in spite of the differences in religion, the two saints held the deepest respect for each other, to such a degree that one speaks of there being reciprocal influences.[6] All of this shows that the absoluteness of each religion lies in its inner dimension, and that the relativity of the outer dimension becomes necessarily apparent on contact with other great religions or with their saints.

$$*$$
$$* \quad *$$

Christianity superimposes on man's post-Edenic misery the saving person of Christ; Islam takes its point of support in the incorruptible nature of man—by virtue of which he cannot cease to be what he is—and saves man, not in conferring upon him a new nature, but in restoring him to his original perfection by means of the normal contents of his immutable nature. In Islam, the Message—the pure and absolute Truth—reflects upon the Messenger: he is perfect in the measure the Message is so, or since the Message is perfect. Christians are very sensitive—in a negative sense—to the extra-divine and socially human character in which the Prophet of Islam manifests himself, and find this character unpardonable in a founder of a religion that came after Christ; Muslims, for their part, are likely to see a certain unilateral character in the doctrine of the Gospels, and in fact share this feeling with Hindus and Buddhists. This is, quite clearly, a mere matter of form since every religion is by definition a totality; but it is precisely such formal particularities that separate religions and not the limitlessness implicit in their content.

"Judge not that ye be not judged"; "All they that take the sword shall perish by the sword"; "Whichsoever of you is without sin, let him cast the first stone". These sayings become fully mean-

---

6. In our day, Kashmir Muslims still venerate Lalla, the dancing Shaivite, as they would a saint of Islam, and side by side with Sayyid Ali; Hindus share in this dual cult. The doctrine of this woman saint is condensed in one of her songs: "My guru gave me but a single precept. He told me: from without enter thou into thy most inward part. This for me became a rule: and this is why, naked, I dance" (*Lalla Vakyani*, 94).

17

ingful only when one takes into account their characteristic intent, namely that they address, not man as such, but passional man, or else the passional side in man: for it is only too obvious that it can and must happen that one man legitimately pass judgment on another— otherwise there would be no "discerning of spirits" and no justice; or that men may rightly draw their swords without thereby having to perish by the sword; or again, that men may cast stones with good reason and without having to ask themselves whether they are sinners or not, for it goes without saying that neither judges nor executioners are called upon to ask this question when exercising their function. To contrast the laws of Sinai or those of the Koran and the *Sunnah* with those of Christ is not to establish a contradiction, but simply to speak of things that are different.

The same remark applies to the divergences in sexual moralities or conceptions of sexuality: whereas Semites, like most other Orientals, define marriage in terms of physical union and its religious conditioning, Christian theologians define it in terms of what comes "before" and "after" this union or what comes "beside" it. "Before": by the pact which makes spouses of the betrothed; "after": by the children who make parents and religious educators of the spouses; "beside": by the fidelity of the spouses, which gives them the courage to face life while guaranteeing the social order. According to St Thomas Aquinas, marriage is made "holier *sine carnali commixtione*," which is true from a certain ascetico-mystical point of view, but not when meant in an absolute fashion. Be that as it may, this opinion leaves no doubt as to Christianity's fundamental tendency in these matters. And since this tendency rests on an aspect found in the nature of things, it goes without saying that it is to be encountered to one degree or another in every religious climate, including that of Islam, just as, conversely, sexual alchemy could not have been totally absent from the Christian esoterism of the Middle Ages, nor from Christianity as such.

Christianity makes a distinction between the carnal as such and the spiritual as such, and this is logical when maintaining this alternative in the hereafter: Paradise is by definition spiritual; therefore it excludes what is carnal. Islam, which makes a distinction between carnality in its crude state and a carnality that is sanctified, is equally logical in admitting in its Paradise the second possibility: to reproach the garden of the houris for being too sensual—according to this word's current and earthly acceptance[7]— is as unjust as to reproach the Christian Paradise for being too abstract. Christian symbolism takes account of the opposition between the cosmic degrees, whereas Islamic symbolism has in view their essential analogy; but the issue is the same.[8] It would be an error to think that authentic Christianity is hostile to the body as such; [9] the concept of the "Word made flesh" and the glory of Mary's virginal body forbid from the outset any possibility of Manichaeism.

A consideration that calls for mention here, since we are speaking of parallels and oppositions, is the following: the Koran has been reproached for bringing the Blessed Virgin into the Christian Trinity; we want to respond to this objection here, not only in order to explain what the Koranic intention is, but also by the same token to clarify the problem of the Trinity through a specific metaphysical accentuation. According to an interpretation which is not theological in fact but is so by right, and which

7. Traditional polygamy depersonalizes woman in view of Femininity as such, the Divine *Rahmah*. But this polygamy, possessing a contemplative foundation, can also, as in the case of David, be combined with the monogamous perspective: Bathsheba was the one and only Wife given that, precisely, she "personified" the "impersonal" Femininity.
8. There is opposition between the body and the soul, or between earth and heaven, but not in the case of Enoch, Elijah, Jesus, and Mary, who ascended bodily into the celestial world; in the same way, the resurrection of the body manifests or actualizes a reality that abolishes this opposition. Meister Eckhart rightly specifies that in ascending to heaven these holy bodies were reduced to their essence, which in no wise contradicts the idea of bodily ascension.
9. St John Climacus relates that St Nonos, when baptizing St Pelagia who had entered the pool naked, "having seen a person of great beauty began greatly to praise the Creator, and was so transported in the love of God through this contemplation that he wept"; and he adds: "Is it not extraordinary to see that what is the cause of a fall for others becomes, for this man, a reward beyond the bounds of nature? He who through his efforts attains to the same sentiments in similar circumstances is already resuscitated incorrupt before the general resurrection. The same may be said of melodies, either sacred or profane: those who love God are led by them to divine joy and love and are moved even to tears" (*The Ladder of Divine Ascent*, 15).

19

finds support in the Scriptures, the "Father" is God as such, that is as metacosm; the "Son" is God insofar as He manifests Himself in the world, hence in the macrocosm; and the "Holy Spirit" is God insofar as He manifests Himself in the soul, hence in the microcosm. From another point of view, the macrocosm itself is the "Son", and the microcosm itself—in its primordial perfection—is identified with the "Holy Spirit"; Jesus corresponds to the macrocosm, to the entire creation as divine manifestation, and Mary corresponds to the "pneumatic" microcosm; and let us recall in this respect the equation that has been made sometimes between the Holy Spirit and the Divine Virgin, an equation that is linked, in some ancient texts, to the feminization of the Divine *Pneuma.*[10]

*

* *

There is no bridge from Christian theology to Islam just as there is no bridge from Jewish theology to Christianity. In order to make itself legitimate, Christianity must change planes; and this, precisely, is an unprecedented possibility which enters into none of the ordinary categories of Judaism. The great novelty of Christ, within the framework of the Judaic world, was therefore the possibility of an inward and hence supra-formal dimension: to worship God "in spirit and in truth", and to do so even to the point of the possible abolishing of forms; as a result, the passage from Judaism to Christianity takes place, not on the plane of theology as Christian polemicists paradoxically imagine, but by a return to a mystery of inwardness, of holiness, of Divine Life, from which a new theology will spring forth. The weakness of Judaism, from the Christian point of view, lies in having to accept the assertion that one must descend from Jacob in order to belong to God, and that accomplishing prescribed actions is all that God asks of us; whether such an interpretation is exaggerated or not, Christ shattered the frontiers of ethnic Israel in order to replace it with a purely spiritual Israel; and he placed the love of

10. The Hebrew word *Ruach*, "Spirit", is feminine. And let us also point out that one finds in the Gospel of the Hebrews the expression "My Mother the Holy Spirit" (*Mater mou to Hagion Pneuma*)—*Homily* 15.

God before the prescribed act, and in a certain manner replaced the one with the other, even while introducing in turn, and of necessity, new forms. Now this extra-theological passage from the "ancient Law" to the "new Law" quite logically forbids Christians from applying to Islam the narrowly theological argumentation which they do not accept on the part of the Jews; and it obliges them in principle to admit at least the possibility—in favor of Islam—of a legitimacy based on a new dimension that cannot be grasped word-for-word in their own theology.

We have seen that, from the point of view of Islam, the limitation of Christianity is in having to accept the notion, first, that man is totally corrupted by sin and, second, that none but Christ can deliver him from it; and, as we have likewise mentioned, Islam bases itself upon the axiom of the unalterable deiformity of man: there is in him something which, participating as it does in the Absolute—otherwise man would not be man—permits salvation provided he possesses the necessary knowledge, and this is precisely what is provided by Revelation; what man stands in absolute need of is not therefore a specific Revealer, but Revelation as such, that is, Revelation considered from the point of view of its essential and invariable content. And this crucial point could also be brought up: what Islam blames Christianity for—but not the Gospels—is not that it should admit a trinity within God, but that it should place this trinity on the same level as the Divine Unity; not that it should attribute to God a ternary aspect, but that it should define God as triune, which amounts to saying either that the Absolute is triple or else that God is not the Absolute.[11]

A point which was mentioned above, and upon which we wish to insist further before proceeding, is the following: according to the usual Christian perspective,[12] nature in its entirety is corrupted and more or less accursed as a result of the fall of man and the resulting corruption. As a consequence, sensory pleasures are justified only in the measure required for the physical preserva-

---

11. It is true that God as creator, revealer, and savior is not to be identified with the Absolute as such; it is likewise true that God in Himself, in the full depth of His reality, is not to be reduced to the creative Function.
12. A traditional perspective can never be equated with a total limitation; this is *a priori* evident and is proven by numerous examples.

21

tion of the individual and of the human species. In the Islamic perspective, pleasure, if it remains within the limits allowed by nature and within the framework of religion, contains in addition a contemplative quality, a *barakah* or blessing, which is related to celestial archetypes[13] and which, therefore, is of benefit to virtue and contemplation;[14] the question that presents itself to Islam is that of knowing, not the worth or meaning of a given pleasure for a given individual, but the meaning of pleasures that are normal and noble within the measure of their possibilities, for man ennobled by faith and by the practices and virtues this faith requires. For Christians, the distinction between the "flesh" and the "spirit" presents itself readily as an irreducible alternative that is mitigated only on the aesthetic plane by the superficial and expeditious notion of "sensory consolations"; the Islamic perspective adds to this alternative, whose relative legitimacy it would never deny, two compensatory aspects: the spirit manifesting itself in the flesh, and the flesh manifesting itself in the spirit—an intertwined complementarity that recalls, once again, the *Yin-Yang* of Taoism. In summary, Christians insist on renunciation and sacrifice, Muslims on nobility and blessing; one might say also that Christians place the emphasis on the accidental container or on the level of manifestation, whereas Muslims place the emphasis on the essential content and the operative symbolism. Gnosis both embraces and transcends the two attitudes.[15]

Seen from the literal interpretation of Christian theology, Islam appears as a painful scandal;[16] and, from the perspective of

---

13. In Paradise: "As often as they are regaled with food of the fruit thereof, they say: This is what was given us aforetime [= on earth]. . . . There for them are pure companions [= free from earthly stains]" (*Surah Al-Baqarah* ["The Cow"], 25).
14. The hedonism of the Vishnuite school of Vallabha seems to be a deviation of this perspective. As for Greek hedonism, that of an Aristippus or an Epicurus, it rests on a philosophy of man and not on the metaphysical nature of sensations; nonetheless, at its origin, it was a measured and serene hedonism, not gross as is the case with the 18th century materialists.
15. In fact, both attitudes are encountered in all traditional spirituality.
16. Nonetheless, in favor of Islam, there is the following argument adduced by Massignon: "And I will make of thee a great nation, and I will bless thee, and make thy name great . . . and in thee shall all families of the earth be blessed" (Gen. 12:2-3). This divine promise encompasses all of

the most impeccable rabbinical logic, the case of Christianity is analogous.[17] Each of these Messages must be understood from its own standpoint and according to its profound intention; a reasoning that stems from axioms that are foreign to these Messages cannot grasp their intrinsic truth. And this brings us to the following point: the phenomena which are characteristic of a given religion are not criteria proving that it alone is legitimate; they result from a Divine intention meant to offer a spiritual perspective and a way of salvation. In the Christian "system of salvation"—in the sense of the Buddhist term *upâya*—Christ "has" to be born from a Virgin, barring which he cannot appear as God manifested; and being Divine Manifestation—this expression constituting the very definition of Christianity as a "divine means" or *upâya*—Christ "has" to be unique and there is thus no salvation except through him; the universal and hence timeless role of the *Logos* coincides here, for obvious reasons, with the historical person of Jesus. In the case of Islam, the *upâya* is founded on the idea that there is nothing save the Unique Real, whether understood exoterically and separatively or esoterically and unitively, whether through transcendence or through immanence; consequently there is no "need" for the Prophet to be more than a man, and there is no reason why he should be unique, other Prophets having preceded him. In the case of Judaism, the *upâya* testifies to the possibility of a Pact between God and a consecrated society, hence one that is collectively sacerdotal, similar examples of which are offered by Brahmanism and Shintoism; therefore Israel "has" to hold the role as the only "chosen people"—since it embodies this fundamental possibility of a Heavenly Pact—even

the descendants of Abraham, including the Arabs, thus including Islam as well, all the more so since it is Islam and Christianity—not Judaism—which reach out to "all the families of the earth"; in other words, a false religion could not be covered by the promises made by God to Abraham.

17. The Testimony that God bore on Sinai concerning His own nature was not a half-truth; it was an affirmation—of unsurpassable gravity—concerning the unicity and indivisibility of the Absolute. Admittedly, this Testimony does not mean that there is not a mystery in God such as the Trinity; but it means that on the level on which Unity affirms Itself, there is nothing other than It and that, therefore, there is nothing that can be added to It.

23

though the need of the monotheistic influence to spread could find a solution only through subsequent forms of Monotheism.[18]

Since it was not necessary for Muhammad to present himself—any more than Abraham and Moses—as the Manifestation of the Absolute, he could, like them, remain wholly Semitic in style, a style which attaches itself meticulously to human things, not scanting even the smallest; whereas in Christ—paradoxically and providentially—there is an element that brings him closer to the Aryan world, that is, a tendency in his nature toward the idealistic simplification of earthly contingencies.[19] The fact that Christ is Manifestation of the Absolute has suggested to Westerners—with the inducement of Greco-Roman cosmolatry—that the Absolute is of this world; and this is what is expressly denied by Islam, which clothes everything terrestrial with a maximum of relativity—fire does not burn, "God alone" makes it burn, and so on. This same fact has contributed through many a twist and turn, and by being combined much later with a Jewish messianism become irreligious, to the pursuit of a horde of earthly pseudo-absolutes that can never be realized and are of an increasingly explosive character. The fact that Islam is accused of naiveté, sterility, and inertia betrays an error in outlook, the reason for which is to be found in a faith in the absoluteness of earthly values and human enterprises; but when seen objectively and positively, the traits which provoke these reproaches indicate an intention of Biblical equilibrium before

18. For analogous reasons—or even, in a certain sense, for the same reason—Buddhism had to leave the closed world of Brahmanism.
19. We hope that our way of expressing things gives a sufficiently clear account of our intentions, for we are obliged to condense matters with a few key words that may strike some as "ill-sounding". Thus, on the basis of this caveat, we shall say that Christ, who was destined to be an "Aryan god", has himself, by way of anticipation, a certain Aryan quality, which shows itself in his independence—seemingly "Greek" or "Hindu"—toward forms; and likewise the Buddha, destined to be a "Mongol god", has something that is providentially Mongol apparent in the horizontal monotony and the static depth of his manifestation. As for the "independence" of the Aryan spirit, it must be specified that this can be a quality or a defect, depending on the case, exactly as Semitic formalism can be; all told the whole question is relative, and each thing must be put in its proper place.

the real and sole Absolute. For Muslims, time is a rotation round a motionless center, and it would even be reversible "if God so willed it"; history is of interest only insofar as it turns back toward the Origin or, on the other hand, sweeps on toward the "Last Day". For God is "the First and the Last".

Islam seeks to combine the sense of the Absolute with the quality of Equilibrium: the idea of the Absolute determining Equilibrium, and the realization of Equilibrium in view of the Absolute. This Equilibrium includes all that we are, thus collective man as well as individual man; with respect to the Absolute, we are entitled as men to all that is normal for humans, without this right excluding particular vocations of withdrawal. Christianity, for its part, has a dramatic quality about it: it has the sense of the Sublime rather than that of the Absolute, and the sense of Sacrifice rather than that of Equilibrium; on the basis of this second aspect, it extends a vocation that is specifically ascetic to a whole society— in the Latin Church more particularly—which is certainly its right according to its particular *upâya*, but which has nonetheless provoked historical disruptions of equilibrium which have been both fatal and providential.[20]

From the point of view of Muslims, Christians have "Christified" God: since the advent of Christ, God can no longer be conceived of or worshiped apart from the God-man, so that whoever conceives of God in a pre-Christian way is accused of not knowing God; to worship God apart from Jesus—or not to admit that Jesus is God—is to be the enemy of Jesus, and so the enemy of God, even if one combines the worship of the One God with love of Jesus and of Mary, as indeed Muslims do. In short, Muslims see Christians as having, so to speak, "confiscated" the worship of God for the sake of the exclusive and absolute worship of a specific

20. European humanity has something promethean and tragic about it; as a consequence, it needed a religion that could surpass and sublimate the dramatic nature of the Greek and Germanic gods and heroes. Moreover, the creative genius of Europeans implies a need to "burn what one has worshiped", and from this comes a prodigious propensity for repudiation and change; the Renaissance offers the plainest proof and the most astonishing example of this, not to mention what is taking place in our own times and on a level that is incomparably graver. What is at stake is always "Man", but with totally different accentuations.

Divine Manifestation, to the point of disowning all preceding religions, whereas Islam, on the contrary, recognizes the validity of pre-Christian monotheistic cults, while adopting in its turn an exclusive attitude as far as the last cycle of humanity is concerned, to which it corresponds. And this is important: the dazzling evidence of the "rights" of the Absolute—thus of God-as-Unity—seems to necessitate a distinctly human character in the Muhammadan manifestation, in the sense that this evidence is sufficient unto itself and must be understood as being sufficient, so that a super-human messenger would not add anything to it.

By starting from the idea that each religion is founded on a Revelation emanating from the sole and same Infinite Consciousness, or from the same Celestial Will of attraction and equilibrium, one can specify—as we have done more than once—that Christianity is founded on the Saving Marvel of God, and Islam, on the saving Truth: that is to say, from the Christian point of view—very summarily speaking—the virgin birth of Jesus proves that the Christian religion alone is true,[21] whereas from the Muslim point of view, this same miracle simply proves that the Divine Power had a sufficient reason for producing it, but not that it is—or ever could be—the sole criterion of Divine Authority or the sole guarantor of Absolute Truth and could thus take precedence over a given aspect of metaphysical Evidence. In short, Islam seeks to avoid the impression that this Truth or this Evidence results from the superhuman nature of its bearer:[22] it is as though God were "jealous"—in the Biblical and metaphorical meaning of the word—of His earthly vicars, and mindful of manifesting, or

21. The reasoning implicit in this affirmation is really the following: the Vedantin doctrine is false since Christ, who is born of a virgin, did not teach it, and since Badarayana, who taught it, is not born of a virgin. It must in any case be added, on the one hand, that Vedantin postulates are sporadically encountered in Christian metaphysics and mysticism and, on the other, that the truth of such and such an Aristotelian or Platonic thesis has brought Christians who understand it to Christianize it, which amounts to saying that all truth derives from the Eternal Word.

22. It goes without saying that it is not a question here of challenging the soundness of the Christian *upâya* as such, but of taking account of an aspect, or underlying argument, of the Islamic phenomenon, which taken as a whole appears as a corrective that re-establishes a certain equilibrium with respect to voluntaristic Christocentrism.

recalling, His absolute pre-eminence and His indivisible essentiality. This "jealousy" is strictly logical or ontological, for it is based on the nature of things—from which nothing can escape in the end—as well as on Mercy, since Divine Truth possesses essentially a saving quality that compensates in a certain sense for its lofty or majestic character. This saving quality of Pure Truth is the great thesis of Islam, along with that of the Unity of God.

Muslims *a priori* raise the question of knowing, not whether Jesus is God, but whether God can make Himself man in the sense in which Christians understand this; if one envisages God as Muslims do, that is to say from the point of view of absoluteness, God as such cannot become man because the Absolute as such cannot become contingent. In the Trinitarian doctrine, God can become man because Manifestation is already anticipated in the Principle, which is considered in terms that are already relative; the same applies to the Hindu doctrine of the *Avatâras*, but not to that of *Âtmâ* insofar as It transcends and excludes *Mâyâ*. When Manifestation is found to be prefigured in the Principle, then it is precisely because the Principle is not considered with regard to its absoluteness; now the reason for the existence of Islam is that it should place dogmatic stress on this aspect of absoluteness and thus be the message of the essence and the timeless. This truth had to take form in the monotheistic cycle, whatever might be the legitimacy and merits of other equally possible perspectives.

Dogmatically speaking, the divergence between Christianity and Islam is irreducible; but metaphysically and mystically, it is no more than relative, just as two points that are opposite each other become complementary in virtue of the circle upon which they are situated and which coordinates and unifies them once it is perceived. One should never lose sight of the fact that dogmas are key-coagulations of supra-formal light; to acknowledge a coagulation is to acknowledge a form and hence a limitation and exclusion. The Spirit can be manifested, but It cannot be enclosed; *Spiritus autem ubi vult spirat.*

Certain clarifications about Sufism would seem opportune at this point. It has been claimed, with rather surprising assurance,

27

that original Sufism knew only fear; that the Sufism of love came later, and that of gnosis later still; and this succession has inevitably been described as an evolution whose phases have been attributed to foreign influences. But this unfolding in three phases corresponds in fact to a normal cyclical projection of the spiritual virtualities contained in Islam; what in principle is of the highest order must manifest itself—from the point of view of the general accentuation—in the last instance, and this obviously can give the illusion of progress if one does not understand the deeper reasons for the phenomenon, and also if one ignores that the three elements—fear, love, knowledge—necessarily existed from the beginning and above all in the very person of the Prophet, as is attested in the Koran and the *Sunnah*; otherwise they could not have flowered later in specific forms of doctrine and method.

One finds here two parallel and compensatory movements: on the one hand, the collectivity declines as it moves further away from the origin; but on the other hand, there are successive flowerings in the ascending order just described, though clearly without an overall increase in spirituality, in the sense that values implicit at the origin deploy themselves in the doctrinal domain and become explicit so that one could say that there is a sort of compensatory progressive unfolding that occurs within the very framework of the general decay. This is a phenomenon that can be observed in all religious cycles, notably also in that of Buddhism;[23] and this is why, in the heart of each religion, "renewers" (*mujaddid*) appear, who are "prophets" in a derivative and secondary sense.[24] In Islam, Rabiah Adawiyah, Dhun-Nun al-Misri,

---

23. Five hundred years after the Buddha, the tradition was in danger, if not of extinction, at least of becoming increasingly reduced to a monastic community with no possibility of world-wide diffusion; all efforts converged upon the *Pratyeka-buddha*, the silent and solitary contemplative. It was then that the *Mahâyâna* intervened with its ideal of the *Bodhisattva*, the personification not only of heroic detachment but also of active compassion. Mention can be made in this context that Buddhist "pity" means that total Knowledge essentially implies, not a specific outward activity, of course, but participatory consciousness in a dimension of Being, namely, Beauty or Benevolence; and this is precisely an aspect of the Divine Essence, according to Ibn Arabi.
24. It would be a rather poor joke to identify them with "reformers", whose function is exactly the reverse. We have heard it said that if St Francis had

Niffari, Ghazzali, Abd al-Qadir al-Jilani, Ibn Arabi, the Imam Shadhili, and Rumi are among their number.

A paradoxical reason for this phenomenon is that the blossoming forth of the perspective of love presupposes a human milieu molded by the perspective of fear,[25] and the emergence of the perspective of gnosis presupposes a milieu steeped in that of love. This is to say that a religion must have the time to form its humanity so that it can project, with the benefit of this ambiance, different types of spiritual accentuations; the case is altogether the same for sacred art or for liturgy in general.

The Sufi ternary of "fear" (*makhâfah*), "love" (*mahabbah*), and "knowledge" (*ma'rifah*) is manifested, on the scale of integral Monotheism, in the forms of the three Semitic religions respectively, each one comprising in its turn and in its way, with either greater or less emphasis, the three modes under discussion. Christianity begins with the rough Desert Fathers; it flowers again more gently in the Middle Ages under the sign of the Virgin-Mother, and gives rise afterwards, though in a rather precarious way since the whole emphasis is placed on charity, to manifestations of gnosis, which are discernible, in varying degrees, particularly among the Rhineland mystics and in scholasticism, not omitting the German theosophists—in a kind of traditional exile—and other more or less isolated groups.

Nor, in Judaism, could the period of the Psalms and of the Song of Songs be that of the Pentateuch, and the Cabalists could not manifest or flower before the Middle Ages.[26] And it should be remembered in this context that Judaism, which emphasizes the

not come, Christ would have had to return, a symbolic formulation that suggests very clearly what kind of function is at issue here.

25. For reasons already alluded to, one would have no grounds to object here that many of the *ahâdîth* treat of Love and that it could not have been absent at the beginning of Islam. Love does not enter explicitly at the origin into the postulates of Sufism, which is based—as mentioned earlier—upon active "conversion" (*tawbah*) and upon journeying through the "stations" (*maqâmât*). "Islam is the religion of Love", said Ibn Arabi: as to the results yes, but not as regards the general premises; yes with respect to the essence but not with respect to the methodical postulates. The "Wine" (*khamr*) and the "Night" (*Laylah*), or contemplative drunkenness and quasi-divine inward femininity, enter into play only in esoterism.

26. Philo of Alexandria was a Platonist, not a Cabalist.

relationship between God and Israel, is on the whole a perspective of faith and fear; the fear of God is the framework for the perspectives of love and knowledge, neither of which could be absent,[27] love being closely bound here to hope.

For its part, Christianity places the emphasis not *a priori* on the Divine Nature, but on the Divine and redemptive Manifestation; it is a perspective of love which, in its own fashion, provides the framework for the perspective of fear and that of gnosis. Finally, Islam places emphasis on the Divine Unity and on the human consequences it entails; it represents a perspective of faith and knowledge, with fear and love depending in this case on faith.[28] We mention these things here, not in order to define once again what the religious perspectives are, but to underline the fact that they contain each other.

27. Such near-definitions are both exact and approximate, for it is hardly possible to do justice to all necessary shades of meaning in so few words.
28. Indeed, many *ahâdîth* see in the love of God and in the fear of sin or of the world criteria of a sincere faith which as such is always stressed. One may note this saying of Hassan al-Basri, an eminent spokesman for nascent Sufism: "He who knows God, loves Him, and he who knows the world, turns away from it."

30

Âtmâ-Mâyâ

The substance of knowledge is Knowledge of the Substance: that is, the substance of human intelligence, or its most profoundly real function, is the perception of the Divine Substance. The fundamental nature of our intelligence, quite evidently, is discernment between what is substantial and what is accidental, and not the exclusive perception of the accidental; when intelligence perceives the accident it does so, as it were, in relation to the substance that corresponds to it—he who sees the drop sees also the water—and, with all the more reason, intelligence must do this in relation to Substance as such.[1]

To speak of the Divine Substance is necessarily to speak of its ontological prolongation, since we, who speak, derive from this prolongation which is Existence—Relativity in its manifested mode, the cosmic *Mâyâ*. Absolute Substance extends Itself, through relativization, under the aspects of Radiance and Reverberation; that is to say, It is accompanied—at a lesser degree of reality—by two forms of emanation, one that is dynamic, continuous, and radiating, and the other static, discontinuous, and formative. If there were not, apart from Substance, the Radiance

---

1. The terms substance and essence, which—rightly or wrongly—are taken in practice to be more or less synonymous, differ in that substance refers to the underlying, immanent, permanent nature of a basic reality, whereas essence refers to reality as such, that is as "being" and, in a secondary sense, as the absolutely fundamental nature of a thing. The notion of essence denotes an excellence which is, so to say, discontinuous with respect to accidents, whereas the notion of substance implies on the contrary a kind of continuity, and this is why we employ it when speaking of *Âtmâ* in connection with *Mâyâ*.

31

and Reverberation to extend It by means of relativization, the world would not be.

But this projection of God—if one may put it thus—requires an element that makes it possible, an element that helps to explain why the Substance does not remain an exclusively "hidden treasure". This diversifying, exteriorizing, or relativizing element is none other than *Mâyâ*: its nature could be defined with the help of various terms, such as Relativity, Contingency, Separativity, Objectification, Differentiation, Exteriorization, and others still; even the term Revelation could be appropriately applied here in an altogether fundamental and general sense.

In everything that exists, there is the Substance, without which what has come into existence would be pure nothingness; now the fact that things "exist" means that they are actualized by virtue of "Existence" in the highest sense this term may convey;[2] and this "Existence" or this Relativity ensues from the Substance by virtue of Its Infinitude; that is to say, Divine Reality would not be what It is if It did not comprise the paradoxical dimension of a kind of tendency towards a nothingness which obviously is never attained, for nothingness has no other reality than that of providing, wholly indirectly, a point of reference which in itself can never be grasped or realized.

There is a primary duality, which is the Substance, and—principially within It but in fact outside its absolute Reality—there is Relativity or *Mâyâ*; now *Mâyâ* comprises the two aspects just mentioned, Radiance and Reverberation: the "Holy Spirit" and the "Son"[3] are actualized in and through *Mâyâ*. Expressed in geo-

---

2. It is in this sense that one can speak of the "Existence of God". In this question of terminology, what matters is to know with respect to what a reality "exists": if it is with respect to the Absolute, this reality is relative; if it is with respect to nothingness, it is merely real, and can be principial as well as manifested. In the subconscious of current language, "existence" stands out more directly from the negative or abstract void that inexistence represents than it does from this positive or concrete Void that is God.

3. The opinion that the trinitarian relationships—or the hypostatic Persons—"constitute" the Absolute is not inherent in Christianity; this opinion has come down to us from an Orthodox not a Catholic source, but it may be a "sublimation" rather than a strict definition. According to the scholastics, Divine Reality is neither purely absolute nor purely rela-

metric terms, the Substance is the center, Radiance is the cluster of the radii, and Reverberation, or the Image, is the circle; Existence, or the "Virgin", is the surface which enables this unfolding.

*

* *

Divine *Mâyâ*, which is both metacosmic and cosmic, comprises essentially the following powers or functions: first, the function of separation or partibility—beginning with the scission into subject and object—the aim of which is the production of a plane of manifestation for the two consecutive functions, Radiance and Reverberation, to which motion and form correspond. Just as, in God, Relativity constitutes—though outside of absolute Substance—a plane for the actualization of Radiance and Reverberation as principles, so too it projects forth from this divine order—by projecting itself—another plane that is distinctly more relative, namely the entire Cosmos. The same process of segmentation is then repeated within this Cosmos, down to that terminal point marked by the material world; and on each one of the planes thus projected in its descent—the angelic world, the animic world, the material world—it will manifest an appropriate mode of Radiance and Reverberation; there is no order of Relativity that does not comprise these two functions or dimensions. The element Substance is represented at each ontological or cosmic level according to an appropriate mode; and with all the more reason, pure Substance, or Substance as such, underlies each one of its secondary manifestations.

In the material world, *Mâyâ* will be the plane of space and time; Substance will be ether; Reverberation or the Image will be matter; and Radiance will be the energy. But needless to say, there are still far more restricted applications of the same symbolism,

tive, but it contains *formaliter eminenter* both absoluteness and relativity; nonetheless, theologians seem disinclined to grasp the full import of the two terms, since they scarcely draw the conclusions entailed. We shall seize this opportunity to make the following remark: the fact that the hypostases possess a personal character—or are "Persons"—since Substance imparts to them its own Personality, in no wise prevents them from being, from another point of view or relationship, Modes of the One Substance, as Sabellius maintained.

and inevitably so, given that all matter, all form, and all motion or change refer respectively to the three principles involved. The complementarity of "space-time"—or, in concrete terms, "extension-duration"—indicates moreover that there are, in Relativity or Ex-sistence as such,[4] two dimensions, the one expansive and conserving and the other transforming and destructive; whence the complementarities between the worlds and cycles at all levels of the Universe. Within God Himself, the element "Space" is *Mâyâ* inasmuch as it contains or conserves the possibilities, and the element "Time" is *Mâyâ* inasmuch as it transmits these to the world; the first aspect is intrinsic and contemplative, and the second aspect is extrinsic and creative; in other words, the first aspect of *Mâyâ* contemplates the undifferentiated groundedness of the possibilities in the Substance, whereas the second aspect enables the realization of these possibilities in view of their cosmic manifestation.

The role of Relativity is essentially to produce a succession of planes, hence the hierarchy of the universal orders; now it is important to understand that these planes or degrees are incommensurable, and the more so as they are closer to the Substance. There is no common measure, or almost none, between the material world and the animic world, which envelops and penetrates it in some fashion, the possibilities of which vastly exceed those of space and matter; and this disproportion becomes nearly absolute when creation is compared to the Creator; we say "nearly" because metaphysically, but not theologically, these two planes can be equated by virtue of their common Relativity, that is to say, by being both determined by *Mâyâ*. Now *Mâyâ*, in its turn, becomes extinct before the absolute Substance, namely, before the Absolute as such; but this way of seeing things necessarily falls outside the perspective of theology,[5] which by definition must consider the

---

4. We allow ourselves this orthographic neologism in order to indicate clearly that what is at issue here is not existence in the current sense of the term, which belongs to cosmic manifestation.
5. Nonetheless, a Meister Eckhart is perfectly aware of this mystery, and he is doubtless not alone in this in a scholastic and mystical setting.

Âtmâ-Mâyâ

Divine Principle in relation to the world and, even more specifically, in relation to man. It is this very perspective, and the reality to which it refers, that has led us to have recourse, more than once, to the paradoxical notion of a "relative absolute"—an unavoidably ill-sounding but metaphysically useful expression.

The error—which appeared in a monotheistic climate—of a Divine Freedom capable, by virtue of Its absoluteness, of not creating the world or of creating it free from any inner necessity, is repeated—on a lesser scale and in a more excessive way—in the Asharite error of a Divine Power capable, also by virtue of Its absolute character, of punishing the righteous and of rewarding evil-doers, "if God so willed". What is forgotten in the first case is that Necessity—not constraint—is a complementary quality of Freedom;[6] and what is forgotten in the second case is that Goodness, hence Justice too—not impotence, nor subordination—is a complementary quality of All-Mightiness.[7] The necessity, for the virtuous man, to practice virtues is not a constraint; with all the more reason, if God "must" do what His Perfection entails and "cannot" do what is contrary to it—namely, abstain from creating or from punishing the innocent—it is neither from lack of freedom nor from lack of power. The Goodness of God implies that He can be above His Justice, but not beneath it; His Freedom implies that He can create everything, but not that He cannot create at all. His transcendence with respect to creation is to be found in His undifferentiated Substance, with respect to which there is no creation nor any qualities belonging to it.

*
* *

In the celestial world, there is no place for those privative manifestations—or those "existentiations of the naught"—which one is entitled to call "evil". Evil as such originates only at the level of the animic world and extends all the way to the material world;[8] thus evil belongs to the domain of form and change. As we have

---

6. Freedom refers to the Infinite, and Necessity to the Absolute.
7. God is just, not because He *a priori* owes man some justifications, but because, being good, He could never be unjust.
8. According to the Koran, Satan is a jinn, not an angel; he is made of "fire", not of "light".

had occasion to say several times, evil occurs as a result of the distance separating the formal world from the formless Principle: in other words, form contains by its very nature the danger of separation and of opposition with respect to the Principle or the Substance; when this danger is actualized—and it is prefigured in the separation and opposition entailed by existence—the element Radiance, having become illusorily autonomous, draws away from God, and the element Image, by making itself divine, becomes idol. Form is nothing other than individuation: now, the individual tends to seek his end in himself, in his own accidental nature and not in his principle, not in his Self.[9] The countershock is the presence among normal or perfect forms, or forms that are good in some capacity, of privative, false, and hence ugly or vicious forms, both on the psychic plane as well as on the physical plane; ugliness is the ransom so to speak of the ontological revolt. The tendency towards evil is Radiance deviated and inverted; the form of evil is the Image falsified and inverted in its turn; it is Satan, and consequently it is vice or sin on all planes, not just on the moral plane.

Formal *Mâyâ*—which is not angelic and much less divine—exerts a coagulating, separative, and individualizing magic that, as a result, can be subversive in due course; the cause for this is that it has become too remote from the Principle or the Substance, that it has advanced too far in encountering nothingness, even though nothingness is no more than a signpost or a direction and not a concrete reality. In a certain fashion, nothingness is the only metaphysical enigma, precisely because it is nothing and yet can be the object of thought and even something towards which one can tend; nothingness is like the "sin of *Mâyâ*", and this sin confers upon *Mâyâ* an ambiguity that evokes the mystery of "Eve and Mary", or the "Eternal Feminine" which is at once seducing and saving.

This ambiguity, which is quite relative and far from symmetrical, in no wise tarnishes *Mâyâ*; "I am black, but beautiful," says the Song of Songs, and also: "Thou art all fair, my love; there is no spot in thee"; the glory of Mary wholly effaces the sin of Eve, which is to say that with regard to the total breadth of Existence

---

9. The devil was the first to say "I", according to some Sufis.

36

and, above all, with regard to its Divine Summit, there is no more ambiguity, and evil does not exist. Universal Existence, whose function is a play of innumerable veilings and unveilings, is eternally virgin and pure, while being the mother of all the reverberations issuing from the one Substance.

*

* *

In the Catholic sign of the cross a ternary is superimposed on a quaternary: while the content of this sign is indeed the Trinity, the sign itself comprises four stations—the fourth station coinciding with the word *Amen*. One could propose that this asymmetry or this inconsistency is compensated by the fact that the word *Amen* represents the prayer of the Church, and thus the mystical body of Christ considered as a prolongation of God; but one can also maintain that this fourth station of the sign belongs to the Blessed Virgin as Bride of the Holy Spirit and Co-Redemptress, that is, ultimately, as *Mâyâ* both human and Divine. This is in fact the meaning of the *Amen* itself, given that it expresses the *Fiat* of Mary.

The color black of the beloved in the Song of Songs, and found in many images of the Blessed Virgin, represents less the ambiguity of Existence, which is altogether very relative, than its "self-effacement":[10] in the Trinity, Relativity cannot be personified since it is the space, as it were, in which personification takes place; and likewise, in the Universe, *Mâyâ* is neither the Radiance nor the Image: it is the principle of projection or the container. On earth, we perceive things and changes; we do not perceive space and time directly. Even so, were Mary not a kind of hypostasis,[11] she

---

10. In the famous tale of Laylah and Majnun—he who sublimized the beloved inwardly to the point of forgetting the earthly Laylah—it is said that people reproached Majnun for loving a woman of so black a complexion; this is certainly not without meaning in the doctrinal context that holds our attention here.
11. Theology is scarcely suited to take account of this mystery of Mary, for it can operate only with simple notions, clearly defined and concretely useful; in its philosophical dimension, it can refine but not surpass this structuring, though it can happen that, in spite of everything, it will incidentally step outside of this framework.

could be neither the "Spouse" of the God-Radiance nor the "Mother" of the God-Image.[12]

"In the name of the Father, and of the Son, and of the Holy Spirit, Amen"; this final word becomes a hypostasis by the very symmetry of the formula and the gesture indicating it. Cosmic *Mâyâ* is identified metaphysically with the Word of creation "Be!", and thus with the creative Act, of which it is the effectuation and thereby the hypostatic prolongation. Now "God is Love", and He "has created the world out of Love": He is Love in Its bipolarization as Radiance and Image—by virtue of *Mâyâ*—and He has created the world out of Love, thus through *Mâyâ*—which is Love projecting Itself into the night-tide of the naught, or projecting Itself illusorily "outside God" so that even the naught might somehow be enfolded within Divine Reality.

Love, whether within God or the Universe, comprises the poles of Goodness and Beauty: Beauty pertains to Form, Image, and Reverberation, and Goodness to Energy, Act, and Radiance; all cosmic phenomena are derived from this polarity, whether directly or indirectly, positively or negatively, whether imparting or depriving. It is not the Divine *Mâyâ* that produces privative phenomena directly, for She bewails these from behind Her veil; She bewails these fissures which the diverse modes of evil or the absurd represent while being unable to avoid them since creative radiance implies finally, at its outermost limits, the possibility of subversive and corrupting remoteness. Evil is the ransom of Relativity or Existence; however, Existence compensates in advance for evil by its victorious Divinity; Eve is infinitely forgiven and made victorious in Mary.

According to a Muslim tradition, Eve lost her beauty after the expulsion from Paradise, whereas Mary is the very personification of beauty itself: "And her Lord . . . vouchsafed to her a beauteous

---

12. According to the revelations of Sister Mechthild of Magdeburg (13th century), the Blessed Virgin attests to her quality as Logos in these terms: "There I was the single betrothed of the Holy Trinity and mother of the sages, and I carried them before the eyes of God lest they fall, as so many others did. And as I was thus mother to many noble children, my breasts filled with the pure and unmingled milk of true, sweet Mercy in such wise that I nurtured the Prophets, and they prophesied before God (Christ) was born" (*Das fliessende Licht der Gottheit*, 1: 22).

growth", says the Koran. But even if we do not have recourse to the Eve-Mary complementarity, by applying to Eve alone the symbolism of the ambiguity of *Mâyâ*, we can discern in Eve on the one hand two defects, which are sin and loss of beauty, and on the other two glories, which are reintegration into Perfection and the incorruptible beauty this glory confers on the elect.[13]

*

* *

The whole cosmological problem unfolds according to the following sequence: the infinitude of the Divine Substance requires and produces Relativity or Existence; and Existence requires or produces—or by definition implies—Cosmic Manifestation; in so doing, however, it implies or carries in its wake the mystery of remoteness from God and thereby, incidentally, evil, for God alone is the Absolute Good. In other words, the apparent negation of this Good is bound to take place on a certain plane given that Divine Possibility has no limits. Evil, if it is real within limits that are nonetheless metaphysically illusory, is no more than a fragment of a greater good which, so to speak, compensates and absorbs it; in the very center of its existential possibility, a center that surpasses its accidentality, evil ceases to be; it is reabsorbed into an ever pure substance: within it, evil has never been.

God is the Absolute Good who wants the relative Good, that is, the relativity which is the concomitant possibility of His own Good; however, the price of this relative Good is evil. The argument that the "good" is simply a moral notion and a mere matter of human appreciation fails to take into account two factors: first, that the Good is a universal reality of which moral good is but one application among others and, second, that to say something is a matter of human evaluation makes sense only on condition of not overlooking that man as such is by definition predisposed for making an adequate evaluation of things. Notions inherent in

13. As Dante said: "The wound which Mary closed and anointed, she who is so beauteous (*quella ch'è tanto bella* = Eve) at her feet opened and thrust" (*Paradiso* 32:4-6); Eve recovered in Eternity her primordial beauty. One might mention, too, that if Mary is *Mâyâ* in its immutable and inviolable reality, Eve then represents *Mâyâ* not only under its aspect of ambiguity but also of final victory, hence of fundamental goodness.

39

man's substance are necessarily real; it is only the individual who, by applying them wrongly, can be mistaken. The fact that sentiment derives satisfaction from the notion of the good in no wise proves the inadequacy of this notion or that it is meaningless, or that it is the product of desire alone; the Good is not a value because man loves It; rather man loves the Good because It is a value. Or again: a value is not considered "good" because it is loved by man, but it is considered "good" inasmuch as it is objectively lovable by virtue of its qualities, whether direct or indirect, of truth and happiness. Now neither Truth nor Beatitude has been invented by man: the fact that man tends towards them intellectually, volitively, or sentimentally does nothing to lessen their objective reality.

The price of the relative Good, as we have said, is evil. Now it is absurd for man to accept or to desire the relative Good without by the same token accepting, not evil in such and such a form, but the inevitability of evil; every man, by definition, accepts and desires the relative Good in some form, and he must therefore accept the phenomenon of evil as the basis for finally rising above it. To be fully human is, on the one hand, to note and accept the ineluctability of the absurd and, on the other, to free oneself from the absurd by distinguishing between the accident and the Substance—a victorious discernment which is precisely the whole vocation of the human being. The earthly *Mâyâ* frees itself through man, for each separate liberation is something absolute which, from a certain point of view, achieves Liberation as such.

The Substance is not only the Supreme Reality, but as such It is also the Supreme Good, as we have said; now "it is in the nature of the Good to communicate Itself",[14] and this ontological tendency provides an explanation, not only for Relativity—or "Ex-sistence"—as a *hypostasis*, which is therefore radiant and reverberant in God Himself, but also for cosmic existence, which by definition is also radiant and reverberant, though "outside of God". Thus

---

14. *Bonum est essentialiter diffusivum sui,* according to the Augustinian principle, which proves moreover that creation is not an "absolutely gratuitous act" and that Platonic emanationism is in no way opposed to the intrinsic Freedom of God. And likewise, this *hadîth qudsî:* "I was a hidden treasure and wished to be known; thus I created the world."

Âtmâ-Mâyâ

Mâyâ is not only "illusion" as the Advaitins propose, but also the necessary concomitance of the Goodness inherent in the Absolute Real; in other words, if the Substance is good, It must project *Mâyâ*; and if God is good, He must create the world. What follows from this causality is that *Mâyâ* is good; were it not so, it would have no place in God and could not proceed from Him. And if *Mâyâ* is good it is because, in a mysterious though not inconceivable fashion, it is "not other than God".

Mâyâ is the breath of *Âtmâ*: *Âtmâ* "breathes" through *Mâyâ*.[15] This respiration—aside from its inward or substantial prefigurations—is outward, in the manner of our earthly breathing where the connection is made between the inside, the living body, and the outside, the surrounding air. The Universe proceeds from God and returns to Him: these are the cosmic cycles belonging to the microcosm as well as to the macrocosm. *Mâyâ* is the air *Âtmâ* breathes, and this air is a quality of *Âtmâ*'s own Infinitude.[16]

---

15. In medieval German, *âtem* still meant "spirit", whereas modern German retains only the meaning of "respiration". In old German, the "Holy Spirit" was called: *der heilige âtem*.
16. In the language of Sufism, the world proceeds from Goodness-Beauty, or from Beauty-Love, *Rahmah*; this is what is called the "Breathing out of the infinitely Good" (*nafas Ar-Rahmân*) or the "Compassionate Breathing out" (*nafas rahmânî*). Allah "breathes", and this breathing is Goodness, Beauty, Love, Mercy; *Rahmah* is almost synonymous with *Mâyâ*.

41

Substance: Subject and Object

Once the Divine Substance—by virtue of one of Its dimensions—"desired" and "had to" bring the world and its multiplicity into being, by the same stroke It "desired" and "had to" bring into being witnesses of this world and of this multiplicity; otherwise the Universe would be an unknown space filled with blind stones and not a world perceived under a multitude of aspects. Where there are objects, there must also be subjects: creatures that are witnesses of things form an indissoluble part of creation. In its unfurling, the veil of *Mâyâ* strewed the void, not only with knowable things, but also with beings endowed with knowledge in varying degrees; the summit-degree is man, at least for our world, and the sufficient reason for his existence is to see things as only an intelligence endowed with a sense of objectivity, synthesis, and transcendence can.

We say that the Substance "desired" and "had to" produce the world; now to "desire" and to "have to" coincide in God, if by these terms are respectively understood Freedom and Necessity—the first perfection referring to Infinitude and the second to Absoluteness—for in God there is neither constraint nor arbitrariness. For most theologians, however, God does not appear as perfect unless His desires are gratuitous; the subjective fact that man cannot grasp all the motives of Divine Activity seems to amount, in their minds, to an objective divine character; what this means for them, in other words, is that there is in practice a divine right to arbitrariness and tyranny, though this is clearly contrary to God's Perfection, which entails fundamental Goodness, as well as Beauty and Beatitude.

43

The Koranic saying "My Mercy hath precedence over my Wrath" lends itself to a very important and even fundamental cosmological application, from the point of view of the microcosm as well as of the macrocosm. "Wrath", or "Rigor", does not pertain to the absolute Substance; it pertains to the degree of the "Energies" and intervenes only in the formal world, whether outside or within us; if man can pierce this layer and advance all the way into the superior layer—"the Kingdom of God is within you"—he will then escape the reign of Rigor. The ice must be broken, which cannot be done without God's help; once the soul has reached the underlying waters, no further breach is possible; the noisiness of the outward is followed by the silence of the inward. This silence "follows", but in reality it is there before us; the soul enters it as into a stream without origin or end—a stream of silence, but also of music and light.

Let us return, though, to the veil of *Mâyâ* strewing the void with both knowable things and beings capable of knowing them. Where there is an object, there is a subject: for this reason there is in Being an objective and passive pole, principial *Materia* or *Prakriti*, and a subjective and active pole, the manifesting, determining, diversifying *Spiritus*, namely, *Purusha*; and the same holds true *mutatis mutandis* at each rung of the Universe. However, if one starts with the idea that the Substance is the Self, the absolute and infinite Subject[1] whose Object is, on the one hand, Its own Infinitude and, on the other, Its universal unfolding, there is no scission into a subject and an object on any ontological plane whatsoever: there will always be only one single and selfsame Subject at mul-

---

1. The Absolute and the Infinite are complementary, the first being exclusive and the second inclusive: the Absolute excludes everything that is contingent; the Infinite includes everything that is. Within contingency, the Absolute gives rise to perfection and the Infinite to indefiniteness: the sphere is perfect, space is indefinite. Descartes reserved the term "infinite" for God alone, whereas Pascal speaks of several infinites; one must agree with Descartes, yet without taking Pascal to task, for the absolute meaning of the word does not result from its literal meaning; images are physical before they are metaphysical, even though the causal relationship is the converse. Theology teaches that God is infinitely good and infinitely just since He is infinite; but this would be a contradiction if one were too fastidious, for an infinite quality in the absolute sense would exclude any other quality.

tiple degrees of objectification and exteriorization; for in this case the Subject is not a complementary pole: It is simply That which is. If It is nonetheless designated as "Subject", this is to express the fact that *Âtmâ* is the absolute Witness—at once transcendent and immanent—of all things and that It is in no wise, as pantheists and deists imagine, an unconscious Substance, though animated with energy. Furthermore, when the perception of the Object is so intense that the subject's consciousness vanishes, the Object becomes Subject, as takes place in the union of love; but then the word "subject" no longer has the meaning of a complement which, by definition, is fragmentary; on the contrary, it has the meaning of a totality that we conceive as subjective since it is conscious.

When the emphasis is placed on objective Reality—that is, when the pole object takes precedence in the relationship between subject and object—the subject becomes object in the sense that, being entirely determined by the object, it forgets the element consciousness; in this case, the subject as fragment is reabsorbed by the Object as totality, just as the accident is reintegrated into the Substance. However, the other perspective, which sees everything as resolvable into the Subject, takes precedence over the point of view granting preeminence to the Object: if we worship God it is not for the simple reason that He presents Himself to us as an objective reality of dizzying and crushing immensity—otherwise we would also worship the stars and the nebulae—but it is above all because this reality, *a priori* objective, is the greatest of subjects; because He is the absolute Subject of our contingent subjectivity; because He is Consciousness at once almighty, all-knowing, and essentially benefic. The subject as such takes precedence over the object as such: the consciousness of a creature able to conceive of the star-filled heavens is greater than space and the heavenly bodies; the argument that the senses can perceive a subject superior to our own is without merit, for the senses never perceive more than the objective appearance, not subjectivity as such. In the world, the objective element, *a priori* virtual, came before the subjective element that is able to actualize it through perception—the Book of Genesis testifies to this—since, in the principial order, the subjective comes before the objective; the world retraces this in reverse fashion, precisely, since it is as it were a reflective surface.

According to the Advaitin perspective, the element "object" is always internal with respect to the element "subject", so that things—including subjects inasmuch as they are considered objects by virtue of their contingency—are the imaginings and dreams of a subject who obviously surpasses them; the formal world, for instance, is the dream of a particularized divine Consciousness that envelops and penetrates it. Hindus are all too ready to affirm—if only by way of ellipsis—that the world is only in our mind, and this suggests the solipsist error, which holds that it is we who create the world by imagining it; now it is evidently not the creature—itself a content of the cosmic dream—that is the imagining subject, but He who dreams the world: it is *Buddhi*, the projection of *Âtmâ*, or the "Archangelic Consciousness", if one will. The individual can imagine only his own thoughts; he is powerless before those of the Gods.[2]

Having created the material world, God projected subjects into it capable of perceiving it, and last of all He delegated man, who alone is capable of perceiving it totally, that is, in connection with the Cause or Substance; this means that man is the measure of things, as is attested in all traditional doctrines. Man is situated, spatially speaking, between the "infinitely big" and the "infinitely small"—to follow Pascalian terminology—so that it is his subjectivity and not a quality of the objective world that creates the line of demarcation. If we have the impression of being tiny in stellar space, it is solely because what is big is far more accessible to us than what is small, which quickly eludes the grasp of our senses; and this is so, too, because it is the big and not the small that, for man, reflects the Infinitude and Transcendence of God. All of this, however, is still only a symbol, because in a far more real way man is a point of junction between two infinitely more important dimensions, namely, the outward and the inward: it is precisely by virtue of the dimension of inwardness, which opens onto the Absolute and so onto the Infinite, that man is quasi-divine.[3] Man

2. We use the plural form to specify that the direct Subject of the world is a projection—differentiated while remaining one—of the Self, and not the Self directly as such.
3. "The Kingdom of Heaven", which objectively speaking is "above us", as is the visible sky which reflects It, is nonetheless in a more real and concrete

is at once subject and object: he is subject in relation to the world that he perceives and the Invisible that he conceives of, but he is object in relation to his "own Self"; the empirical ego is really a content, hence an object, of the pure subject or of the ego-principle, and all the more so in relation to the immanent Divine Subject, which in the final analysis is our true "One-Self". This brings us to the Advaitin inquiry "Who am I?" made famous by Shri Ramana Maharshi; I am neither this body, nor this soul, nor this intelligence; what alone remains is *Âtmâ*.

Man is thus called—by definition, in fact—to choose between the inward and the outward: the outward is compressive dispersion and death; the inward is dilating concentration and life. Our relationship with space furnishes a symbol for the hostile character of outwardness: in launching himself out into planetary space—whether in fact or in principle—man plunges into a cold, despairing, mortal night, with neither up nor down and no terminal point; the same applies to any scientific investigation that goes beyond what is normal for man, as determined by the law of equilibrium that rules him ontologically.[4] By contrast, when man advances towards the inward, he enters a welcoming and appeasing boundlessness, which is fundamentally blissful though not easy in fact to achieve; for it is only through deifying inwardness, whatever its price, that man is perfectly in conformity with

way "within us", to paraphrase the Gospels. Elevation implies, requires, and engenders depth.

4. There is cause to reproach the protagonists of experimental science, allegedly "exact", not for having discovered or understood such and such a situation in the physical world, but for having locked themselves into a scientific curiosity that is disproportionate with respect to what is essentially knowable, hence for having forgotten what man's total vocation is. For this very reason, pioneers of scientism have never understood that average humanity is intellectually and morally incapable of confronting facts contrary to collective and immemorial human experience; and above all they do not understand that the science of the relative, by definition partial, cannot detach itself with impunity from the science of the Absolute, by definition whole. Galileo, and through him Copernicus, was accused of heresy, just as Aristarchus was accused well before them—for the same motive—of "disturbing the peace of the Gods"—which is plausible when one takes into account all of the factors in question, for man is not made for astronomy alone.

his nature. The paradox of the human condition is that nothing could be more contrary to us than the requirement to transcend ourselves, and yet nothing could be more essentially ourselves than the core of this requirement or the fruit of this self-overcoming; the contradiction of all egoism is to want to be oneself without wanting to be so completely, that is, without also wanting to go beyond the empirical ego and its desires; or the contradiction is to refer everything back to oneself, but without becoming interiorized, that is, without learning to refer everything back to the Self.[5] The whole absurdity of the human condition lies in this contradiction.

Liberating inwardness, or the obligation of interiorization, ensues from the very notion of Substance, or more precisely from our understanding of this notion, which is to say that the idea of Unity frees when it is accepted with all the consequences entailed by the sincerity of faith.[6] To grasp the nature of the One—hence unique and total—Substance is first of all a thought, and thus the complementary opposition between a subject and an object. Now this duality is contrary to the content itself of the thought of Unity: by objectifying the One Reality, we grasp it poorly; such an error is comparable, not to a square meant to represent a circle, but to a circle meant to be identified with a sphere. The error is dimensional, not essential; in a domain where the sphere alone is effective, the circle is virtually inoperative, even though it is the shadow of the sphere and even

---

5. With respect to "egoism", we want to specify that we are not contrasting it with an "altruism" that is sentimental and devoid of sufficient reason, but with a self-love that occurs simply from the right of existence and the duty to fulfill its meaning. "Love thy neighbor as thyself" means that we are to love ourselves, but in accordance with God.

6. The inestimable value of the idea of the Absolute enables one to understand the Islamic axiom—excessive at first sight—of salvation through the notion of Divine Unity; every sin can be forgiven except the rejection of Unity, for It is none other than the Substance.

though, in planar geometry, it is identified with the sphere as truth is identified with reality.

It is certainly possible to conceive of Substance on the plane of thought, but one cannot attain It. Thought is consequently an imperfect and provisional adequation, at least in a certain respect; on this plane the awareness of Unity stops as if at midpoint. The truth of the One Substance can be realized only in the Heart, where the opposition between a knowing subject and an object to be known is transcended; or in other words where any objectification—by definition limitative—is reduced to its limitless source within infinite Subjectivity itself. Objective manifestations of transcendent Substance are discontinuous in relation to It; only in the Heart is there continuity between consciousness and immanent Substance, either virtually or effectively.

In other words, and at the risk of repeating ourselves, we shall say: though the Divine Substance is beyond the subject-object polarity—even though, being absolute Subject, It is Itself Its own Object—we necessarily conceive of It as an objective reality, be it transcendent or abstract; now this conception, whatever its metaphysical cogency may be, is imperfect and in some respect inadequate precisely because, by implying a separation between a subject and an object, it is not truly proportioned to its content, which is absolutely simple and non-polarized. The passage from distinctive or mental knowledge to unitive or cardiac knowledge follows from the very content of thought: either we understand imperfectly what the notions of Absolute, Infinite, Essence, Substance, Unity mean, in which case we content ourselves with concepts—and this is what is done by philosophers in the conventional sense of the word; or else we understand these notions perfectly, in which case they oblige us, by virtue of their very content, to transcend conceptual separativity in order to find the Real in the depths of the Heart, not as adventurers, but by availing ourselves of the traditional means without which we can do nothing and are entitled to nothing; for "he that gathereth not with me scattereth abroad". Transcendent and exclusive Substance reveals Itself then as immanent and inclusive.

It could also be said that since God is All that is, it behooves us to know Him with all that we are; and to know What is infinitely lovable—since but for Him nothing would be lovable—is to love Him infinitely.[7]

7. "Lo, verily, not for love of the husband is a husband dear, but for love of the Self in him. Lo, verily, not for love of the wife is a wife dear, but for love of the Self in her" (*Brihadaranyaka Upanishad*, 4:5-6). "It is *Âtmâ* alone who must be loved. For him that loveth *Âtmâ* alone, that which he holdeth dear is not perishable" (*ibid.* 1:4-8). "Thou shalt love the Lord thy God with all thy heart, and with all thy soul, and with all thy mind" (Matt. 22:37).

The Five Divine Presences

From the point of view of the world, the Divine Principle is hidden behind a number of envelopes, the first of which is matter. Matter presents itself as the outermost sheath, the shell or crust, of that invisible Universe whose main features are made known to us both by the Intellect and Revelation. In reality, however, it is the Principle that envelops everything; the material world is only an infinitesimal and eminently contingent content of this invisible Universe. In the first instance, God is—to speak in Koranic terms—"the Inward" or "the Hidden" (*Al-Bâtîn*) and, in the second, He is "the Vast" or "the One Who Contains" (*Al-Wâsî*), or "the One Who Encompasses" (*Al-Muhît*).

The various degrees of reality contained within the Divine Principle, enunciated now in Vedantin terms—though adding other equally possible designations—are in ascending order the following: first, the gross or material state, which can be designated also as corporeal or sensorial; secondly, the subtle or animic state; thirdly, formless or supra-formal manifestation, namely, the celestial or angelic world; fourthly, Being, which is the "qualified", "self-determined", and ontological Principle and which for this reason we may call, paradoxically but adequately, the "relative" or "extrinsic Absolute"; and fifthly, Non-Being or Beyond-Being, which is the "non-qualified" or "non-determined" Principle, and which thus represents the "intrinsic" or "Pure Absolute". The material and animic states constitute the whole of formal manifestation; the latter, together with supra-formal or angelic manifestation, constitutes Manifestation as such; finally, the whole of Manifestation and of Being is the domain of Relativity, of *Mâyâ*. Formulated differently, if Being and Beyond-Being belong to the

51

principial or non-manifested degree, to which in a certain sense Manifestation is opposed while prolonging it in its relative and "illusory" mode, Relativity for its part begins already on the plane of the Principle, for it is Relativity that detaches Being from Beyond-Being; this is also what allows us to use, provisionally, such a paradoxical expression as "relative Absolute". The ontological Principle plays the part of the Absolute with regard to what it creates and governs; It is relative, however, with regard to the supra-ontological Principle, as it is with regard to the Intellect, which perceives this relativity and which, in its profoundest nature, transcends *Mâyâ*, not existentially, but by virtue of its essence. It is nevertheless impossible to transcend intellectually the degree of Being without the very grace of Being; there can be no effective metaphysics without Heaven's help, and certainly it is not enough to immerse oneself in mental abstractions in order to free oneself from Relativity. If someone asserts that the Intellect is strictly separate from God, he is not mistaken, though this is only part of the truth; if on the other hand someone asserts that the Intellect is not separate from the Divine, he would likewise be right and even more so, but he would not be completely right unless he also admitted the validity of the first point of view. Here, as in other similar cases, one reaches the truth only to the extent that one accepts seemingly opposite points of reference that are in fact situated on the same circumference, hidden at first sight.

If it can be said that Relativity "infringes" on the Principle, by conceptually detaching Being from Beyond-Being, or the personal Creator from the impersonal Self, it can be equally affirmed that the Principle "annexes for Itself" part of Manifestation, namely Heaven, that cosmic center or summit which is the domain of the Paradises, the angels, and "reintegrated" souls. In other words, if Relativity encompasses an aspect of the Principle, the Principle in turn will encompass outwardly—by virtue of its incorruptibility and beatitude, not its exclusive reality—supra-formal manifestation, thus all that enters into the celestial domain. For him who is "in Heaven" and "close to God", there is no more privative separation, though the metaphysical distance be infinite, nor any risk of a fall. Relativity is thus "reintegrated", so to say, by that participation in the Absolute or the Infinite which is sanctity: in and through Being, God "makes Himself world a little" so that, in and through Heaven, the world may "become God a little". If this is possible, it is by virtue of the metaphysical identity between the Principle and Manifestation—an identity that is certainly difficult to express, but attested to in all esoterisms. *Mâyâ* "is"—or "is not other than"—*Âtma*; *Samsâra* "is" *Nirvâna* or *Shûnya*; *al-khalq*, "creation", "is" *Al-Haqq*, the "Truth", barring which there would be a reality other than Allah and alongside Him.

*

* *

In Sufism, these universal degrees are called the "Five Divine Presences" (*khams al-Hadharât al-ilâhiyah*). In Sufi terminology they are: the "human realm" (*nâsût*), that is, the domain of the corporeal, since man is created out of "earth"; then the "realm of royalty" (*malakût*), so called because it immediately dominates the corporeal world;[1] next comes the "realm of power" (*jabarût*), which, macrocosmically, is Heaven[2] and, microcosmically, the created or human intellect, that "supernaturally natural" Paradise which we carry within us. The fourth degree is the "Realm of the Divine" (*Lâhût*), which is Being and which coincides with the uncreated Intellect, the *Logos*; the final degree—if provisional use can be made of such a term—is none other than "Quiddity" or "Aseity" or "Ipseity" (*Hâhût*, from *Hua*, "He"), in other words, the Infinite Self.[3]

---

1. *Malakût* is derived from *malik*, "king", and not from *malak* (originally *mal'ak*), "angel"; the translation "angelic realm", which one encounters sometimes, is not literal. Be that as it may, the word *malak* includes also the jinn, all the more so as angels necessarily manifest themselves in the subtle state when they wish to reach earthly men or act on the material plane, to such a degree that experience cannot always at first sight distinguish between them and the creatures of the subtle realm.
2. "Power" indeed comes from the angels in the sense that it is they who rule over all physical laws, both in the subtle as well as in the gross domains. For our purposes, "physical" is synonymous with "natural" and not with "material".
3. In Buddhist terms, *Jabarût, Lâhût,* and *Hâhût* would respectively be *Bodhisattva, Buddha,* and *Nirvâna*. Instead of *Buddha*, one could also say *Dharmakâya* or *Adi-Buddha*, just as the term *Nirvâna* could be replaced with *Shûnya*. The realities under consideration are the same whether the con-

In taking our point of departure in the Manifestation that surrounds us, and in which we are as it were woven as threads in a piece of cloth, it is possible to establish—always on the basis of the "Five Presences"—the following boundaries or syntheses: the totality of the corporeal and animic states forms the "natural" domain, that of "nature"; the totality of those two states and of supra-formal manifestation constitutes the cosmic realm; the totality of the cosmic realm and of Being is, as we have seen, the realm of Relativity, of *Mâyâ*; and all of the realms considered together with the Supreme Self constitute the total Universe in the highest sense.

Inversely, if one starts from the perspective of the Principle and ends up at the extreme limit of the process of manifestation, one will say first of all that by "Principle" is meant both Beyond-Being and Being; as for "Heaven", this is the totality of the Principle and of supra-formal manifestation, if such a formulation is permissible; finally, the totality of Heaven and of formal animic manifestation constitutes the supra-sensible, or the domain of the Invisible understood in the higher sense of the term. Here again—when adding one last degree to our syntheses, that of matter—one reaches a concept of the total Universe considered now starting from the Principle and not from manifestation.

Let us recapitulate the foregoing as follows: if one starts with the distinction "Manifestation-Principle", the first concept includes the "body", the "soul", and the "Intellect", and the second concept includes the "Logos" and the "Self"; if one starts with the distinction "individual-universal" or, what amounts to the same, the distinction "formal-essential", the element "formal" contains the "body" and the "soul", whereas what pertains to the "essential" is at once the "Intellect", the "Logos", and the "Self", notwithstanding measureless metaphysical distances. Or to take the distinction "Relativity-Absoluteness": all is relative save the "Self"; if, on the other hand, one makes a distinction—from the most contingent point of view possible—between the "mortal"

cepts are "theist" or "non-theist"; whoever admits, first, the possibility of an Absolute and, secondly, the transcendence of this Absolute—without which the notion would be entirely relative and therefore false—can never be an atheist in the conventional sense of the word.

and the "immortal", one will say that everything is immortal, except the body.[4]

To understand correctly the Arabic terminology mentioned above (*nâsût, malakût, jabarût, Lâhût, Hâhût*), it must be appreciated that the Universe is considered as a hierarchy of divine "dominions", which is to say that God is "most present" in the supreme degree and "least present"—or the "most absent"—on the corporeal plane; it is here that He apparently "dominates" the least or the least directly; but the word "apparently" is almost a pleonasm, for to admit Relativity and Manifestation is to admit illusion or appearance.

*

* *

The Koranic premises for the doctrine of the "Five Presences" are the following: the first Presence is the absolute Unity—or non-duality—of God (*Allâhu ahad*); the second is God as Creator, Revealer, and Savior; this is the degree of the Divine Qualities. The third Presence is the "Throne" (*'Arsh*), which can be interpreted in many different ways on different planes, but which from a cosmological perspective represents most directly the supra-formal manifestation which penetrates all the remainder of the created Universe and which is thus identified with the world in its entirety; the fourth Presence is the "Footstool" (*Kursî*) on which rest the "two Feet of God", which means here that animic manifestation—for this is what the Footstool symbolizes—comprises both Rigor and Mercy, whereas the Throne— Heaven—is solely beatific; but the duality of the "Feet" also means, in this context, that the world of forms—for we find ourselves here in formal manifestation—is that of dualities and oppositions. Below the

4. The theory of the Five Presences could be represented by two diagrams each containing five concentric regions, one showing the Principle in the center and the other situating It on the periphery; these would correspond respectively to the microcosmic and macrocosmic or to the human and divine "ways of seeing". This is necessarily one of the meanings of the *Yin-Yang*: the black part, containing a white dot, represents the night of the microcosm with the luminous divine center, whereas the white part, with the black dot, can symbolize the Infinite insofar as It "contains" the finite.

Footstool is situated the most indirect or farthest of the Presences, namely earth (*ardh*), which corresponds to the "human realm" (*nâsût*)[5] because this is the plane of existence of man, who has been created as "vicar on earth" (*khalîfatun fi'l-ardh*).

The relationship between the Throne as angelic world in the macrocosm and the Throne as Intellect in the microcosm is enunciated in the following Muhammadan teaching: "the heart of man is the Throne of God". Accordingly, our soul reflects the Footstool and our body the earth; and our intellect is quite evidently the passage leading to the mysteries of the uncreated and the Self, without which there could be no possible metaphysical intellection.

The two fundamental formulas of Islam—the two Testimonies (*Shahâdatân*), one concerning Allah and the other His Prophet—likewise symbolize the degrees of reality. In the formula *lâ ilâha illa'Llâh* ("there is no divinity save the one Divinity"), each of the four words denotes a degree, the final *hâ* of the Name *Allâh* symbolizing the Self (*Huwa*). This formula contains two parts: the first two words, which constitute the *nafy* (the "negation"), and the last two words, which constitute the *ithbât* (the "affirmation"); in the present instance the *nafy* stands for formal manifestation or the individual order, and the *ithbât* stands for the whole of supraformal manifestation and the Principle, which corresponds to the universal order. Owing to this, the Sufi sees in each material form, including his own, the *lâ* of the *Shahâdah*, and so forth; the microcosm that we are is none other than a concrete manifestation of the *Shahâdah*, and the same is true for the macrocosm surrounding us and of which we are part.

The second Testimony, that of the Prophet, establishes an analogy between Muhammad and formal manifestation when this manifestation is seen in a positive sense, that is to say, as "Divine Presence" and not as absence or opposition; in this same formula

---

5. It is impossible to mention here some of the other meanings that can be given to the word *nâsût* and other analogous terms or, in general, to point out all the variations of perspective linked to these expressions. For instance, a relationship has been proposed between *nâsût* and *sharî'ah* on the one hand and between *malakût* and *tarîqah* on the other, and so on and so forth; but this is an altogether different way of looking at things from the one that concerns us at present.

Muhammadun Rasûlu'Llâh ("Muhammad is the Messenger of Allah"), the word *Rasûl* refers by analogy to supra-formal manifestation insofar as it is a prolongation of the Principle. The Sufi, who sees God everywhere, thus discerns in every physico-psychic form the perfection of existence and symbolism, and in the Intellect and in the angelical realities he discerns the quality of *Risâlah*, of "Divine Message".

In this manner each word of the two Testimonies denotes a "way of being" of God, a "divine station" in the microcosm as well as in the macrocosm.

*

* *

It may be worthwhile in this context to recall Plotinian emanationism: the primordial One, which is the absolute Good, and which rational knowledge cannot reach, produces through emanation an image of Itself, which contemplates It; this image—the Universal Spirit (*Nous*)—contains the ideas or archetypes. The Spirit produces the soul (*psyche*), or more precisely the animic or subtle state, which in turn produces matter (*soma*), the "non-existent" or evil; the latter is the negation of the sole Good, at least in its way or according to a certain point of view; as a result, the Spirit, the soul, and matter correspond by analogy to the Vedantin ternary *sattva, rajas, tamas*. Iamblichus adds Beyond-Being to Plotinian Unity since it is the Principle that is involved here in both cases, whereas Plotinus did not mention—though without denying it—the distinction between Being and the supra-ontological Absolute; and if Plotinus appears to consider archetypes only on the level of supra-formal manifestation and not on the level of Being—a valid point of view since ontological causality is less direct, while being more essential, than cosmic causality—Iamblichus' "intelligible universe" seems to coincide with diversified Being, that is to say, inasmuch as Being contains the Divine Qualities from which the angelic essences and the existential archetypes are derived.

But let us return to the Sufis. Mention has been made of five degrees, some cosmic and the others metacosmic; now a greater number can be obtained when subdivisions or intermediary possibilities are considered, or when different perspectives are included, some centered, for example, either on the pole "knowledge" (*shuhûd*) or on the pole "being" (*wujûd*). It is possible to conceive of an intermediary possibility between the body and the soul—or, in the macrocosm, between the material universe and the animic universe—namely, a living and animate body, which is clearly different from the purely material and in some fashion corpse-like body; this intermediary possibility could be termed the "vital" or "sensorial state"; according to certain cosmological doctrines, which make use of astronomical symbolism, this state or body corresponds to the "world of the spheres". Similarly, between the soul and the Intellect—in the macrocosm, between formal manifestation and supra-formal manifestation—a degree of intuition has been conceived which, all told, corresponds to reasoning in that it is no longer imagination and not yet intellection; in the macrocosm, this is the degree of the ordinary angels, who are situated above the jinn and below the four archangels or the "Spirit" (*Rûh*). In perspectives of this kind, the symbolism of the degrees represented by "body" and "soul" borrows its imagery, where the macrocosm is concerned, from astronomy: one speaks of "spheres" and of the "sublunary world", that of matter (*hyle*) and the body.

In this same range of ideas, let us specify that the ontological Principle consists of the "Calamus" (*Qalam* or "Pen") and the "Tablet" (*Lawh*); supra-formal or celestial manifestation, as we have seen, is identified with the Throne (*'Arsh*), which in astronomical symbolism corresponds to the Empyrean; the subtle order of formal manifestation corresponds to the Footstool (*Kursî*) or the sphere of the fixed stars; and finally, the gross order of formal manifestation contains two degrees, namely, the sensorial and the material: the first corresponds to the seven planetary spheres, and the second to the four sensible elements.

The five Divine Presences have been enumerated above under the designations respectively of *nâsût, malakût, jabarût, Lâhût,* and *Hâhût*. According to a slightly different terminology, one may distinguish, in the same ascending order, the following degrees: the "world of the kingdom" (*'âlam al-mulk*), the "world of royalty" (*'âlam al-malakût*), the "world of power" (*'âlam al-jabarût*), the "world of Glory" (*'âlam al-'izzah*). Ibn Arabi defines *al-mulk* in his *Istalahât as-Sûfiyah* as the "world of the manifested" (*'âlam ash-*

shahâdah), and *al-malakût* as the "world of the hidden" (*'âlam al-Ghayb*); according to him, *al-Ghayb* is "everything which God ("the Truth," *Al-Haqq*) hides from thee, but not from Himself". The terms *malakût* and *jabarût* are interchangeable; thus, according to Abu Talib Al-Makki, quoted by Ibn Arabi, *al-jabarût* is the "world of the Infinite" (*'âlam al-'Azhamah*), which according to Jurjani means the "world of the Names and Qualities of God" (*'âlam al-asmâ wa' s-sifât al-ilâhîyah*),[6] whereas for most authors *al-jabarût* is the "intermediary world" (*'âlam al-wasat*). According to Ghazzali, *al-jabarût* is situated between *al-mulk* and *al-malakût*: compared to the pure stability of *al-mulk*, he says, and with the pure movement of *al-malakût*, the intermediary nature of *al-jabarût* can be compared to the motion one senses on a boat, which is clearly a reference to the subtle or animic domain; but it is finally the terminology of Makki that prevailed. We shall also mention Jili, who teaches that "everything in existence is divided into three parts, an outward one called *al-mulk*, an inward one called *al-malakût*, and a third part that transcends the two and is called *al qism al-jabarûtî al-ilâhî*"; and he adds that by "outward part" he means the "form" (*surah*) and by "inward part" the "soul" (*nafs*); the third part is the "secret" or "essential truth" (*haqîqah*) of the thing under consideration, that is, its link on the one hand with Being as such, and on the other hand with a certain aspect of Being, or with a certain aspect of the Divine Intellect or the Creative Will.

The doctrine of the five Divine Presences is sometimes presented—notably in the case of certain commentators on Ibn Arabi—in the following terminology: the first Presence is the world of the "body" (*jism*); the second, that of the "imagination" (*khayâl*), namely, the psychic domain; the third, that of the "Intellect" (*'aql*), that is to say, the angelic world; the fourth, "Unicity" (*Wâhidîyah*), namely Being, the world of ontological possibilities; and the fifth, "Unity" (*Ahadîyah*), Beyond-Being. Others yet will

---

6. The "Qualities" (*sifât*) are distinguished from the "Names" (*asmâ*)—insofar as they can be distinguished—by the fact that they are situated already on the plane of relativity, whereas the Names can represent aspects of the Absolute as such; thus one distinguishes between the "Names of the Essence" (*asmâ dhâtîyah*) and the "Names of Quality" (*asmâ sifâtîyah*).

add the "Essence" (*Dhât*) as a sixth Presence: the Essence is seen then as being situated above the other Presences while at the same time being immanent within them; in this case, *Wâhidîyah* and *Ahadîyah* are interpreted as two aspects of Being, the first corresponding to outward Unity or "inassociability" and the second corresponding to intrinsic Unity or "indivisibility". In this order of ideas, one might further mention that even though *Hâhût* ("Ipseity") corresponds to *Huwa* ("Him") and to *Huwîyah* (the quality of being "He"), *Lâhût* ("Divinity", Being) does not correspond in a strict sense to Allah, nor to *Ulûhîyah* (the quality of being Allah), for the simple reason that these two latter terms carry no exclusive or limitative meaning, whereas *Lâhût* designates only the ontological aspect of the Principle.

On the other hand, the doctrine of the Divine Presences is confined sometimes to a four-fold division: *nâsût, malakût, jabarût, Lâhût*; in this case, the first term designates formal manifestation—without any internal distinction—and the second term, supra-formal manifestation; here *jabarût* corresponds, not to the world of the angelic powers, but to that of the Divine Powers or Qualities, hence that of the Ontological Principle, whereas *Lâhût* is the Absolute Principle or the Supreme Self. Another variant of the doctrine of the Presences is the following: *Hadrat al-ghayb al-mutlaq*, the "Presence of the Absolute Hidden", is the Principle; *Hadrat al-ghayb al-mudâfî*, the "Presence of the relative Hidden", is the intermediary region between God and matter; and this region can be subdivided into two degrees, namely, *al-jabarût*, supra-formal manifestation, and *'âlam al-mithâl*, the "world of the symbol", which is none other than subtle or animic formal manifestation; after this comes *Hadrat ash-shahâdat al-mutlaqah*,[7] the "Presence of the totally manifest", that is to say, the material universe; finally, the whole of all of these domains forms *Hadrat al-jâmi' ah*, the "Presence-Synthesis".

---

7. The terms *ghayb* and *shahâdah* appear together several times in the Koran, notably in the verse: "He is Allah, than whom there is no other God, the Knower of the Invisible and the Visible" (*'âlim al-ghayb wa' sh-shahâdati*) (59:22). The word *shahâdah* does not mean "testimony" here but "that of which one can be a witness," namely, the visible.

*

* *

The Doctrine of the Five Presences explains the relationships between the Principle and Manifestation, which can be conceived of in various ways. First of all—borrowing from geometric symbolism—there is the relationship of "point and circumference": there is no contact between center and periphery, or between the center and the concentric circles; Manifestation is strictly separate from the Principle just as, within Manifestation itself, the natural order is strictly separate from the supernatural. But there is also the relationship between "center and radii": no matter how far the radii extend from the center, they will always be nothing other than a prolongation of the center; water "symbolizes" Universal Substance, and thus, in some fashion, it "is" not other than that Substance; the existential segmentation is only illusory, and this brings us to the "sacrifice of *Purusha*". The difference between the relationships "point and circumference" and "center and radii" is the same as that between existential analogy and essential identity.

If the concentric circles are replaced with a spiral, one obtains an image of the cosmogonic "unfolding"—or "emanation"—and at the same time that of the initiatic "coiling up"; there is both analogy and identity. And if the central point is surrounded, not with radii to form a star, but simply with other points meant to indicate the directions of space, one obtains an image of creative multiplication: the Principle repeats Itself through a multitude of reflections, each of which is a unity symbolizing the One, but none of which is the One; there is "repercussion" rather than "emanation".

The degrees of Reality, however, have not only a static aspect or an aspect of simultaneity, but also a dynamic aspect or an aspect of succession, and this evokes the doctrine of the universal cycles: each of the degrees of the Universe contains a different cyclical rhythm, which means that this rhythm of apparition or manifestation—or of "crystallization", whether principial or existential, depending on the case—becomes more and more "rapid" or "multiple" as one moves farther from the immutable Center; and this is expressed geometrically by the increase of surface towards the periphery. Therein lies the whole doctrine of the "days", "years", and "lives" of *Brahmâ*.

Nonetheless, a reservation needs to be made concerning Being, or pure *Mâyâ*,[8] for it is clearly impossible to attribute a "rhythm" to the Ontological Principle since It is outside of time. To the question whether there can be *in divinis* something that bears a resemblance to what we know as "motion", the answer is both yes and no, and for the following reason: since there is nothing in God that is a privation, there is in Him neither "inertia" nor "modification"; God cannot be deprived of either necessity or freedom—nor of immutability or life. Thus, in this sense, one can say that if God possesses on the one hand the perfection of immutability, since He is absolute, He possesses on the other hand the perfection of "mobility", since He is infinite; but this is not a contingent mobility determined by change, and it is therefore in no sense contradictory. Insofar as motion corresponds to a quality—and in this respect only—it cannot have its prototype and source other than in the divine order; it is thus quite permissible to conceive of a "respiration" going from Being to Beyond-Being that is the model and cause of all the movements and cycles.[9]

*
* *

In presenting here—or in recalling—conceptions pertaining to cosmogonic emanations, we start with the idea that all of the philosophical and scientific errors of the modern world proceed essentially from the negation of the doctrine under discussion; in other words, what falsifies modern interpretations of the world and of man at their very base, thus depriving them of whatever validity they might have, is their monotonous and obsessive ignorance of the supra-sensible degrees of Reality, or of the "Five Divine Presences". This is an observation that cannot escape anyone who is more than a simple logician of sensory experience.

---

8. Vedantists make a distinction between a *Mâyâ* that is "pure"—Being or *Îshvara*—and a *Mâyâ* that is "impure", souls or manifestations in general.
9. There is in this a relationship with the Christian Trinity, or with "Trinitarian Life", understood in its deepest sense, which is supra-ontological.

For example, evolutionism, that most typical offspring of the modern spirit, is no more than a kind of substitute: it is a compensation on a "flat surface" for the missing dimensions; given that one no longer conceives, and no longer wishes to admit, supra-sensible dimensions proceeding from the outward towards the inward through "fiery" and "luminous" states[10] all the way to the Divine Center, one seeks the solution to the cosmogonic problem on the sensible plane and replaces real causes with imaginary causes that conform, in appearance at least, to the possibilities of the material world. In place of the hierarchy of the invisible worlds, and in place of creative emanationism—which, it may be said, is in no way opposed to the theological idea of *creatio ex nihilo*, but on the contrary explains its meaning—one puts evolution and the transformation of the species and at the same stroke human progress, the sole possible response to the materialists' need for causality; in so doing, one forgets what man is, and likewise one forgets that a purely physical science, when it reaches vast proportions, can lead only to catastrophe, either through violent destruction or through degeneration, which in practice amounts to the same thing.[11]

The negation of the animic world, in which we are immersed like crystals floating in a liquid—though appearances lead us to believe that this world is found within our bodies or behind the material husk of things—carries in its wake a reduction of psychic realities to material causes, and consequently leads to a false evaluation of all that pertains to the mental order; it is the death of all spirituality. Not only is nothing known of the vast domain that is the purview of magic, but the higher is explained by means of the lower, and this brings us to a complete dehumanization of the human.

10. Heat and light symbolize respectively the animic and angelic states.
11. One of the most pernicious abuses of language is to call erudite physicists "sages": their intelligence—notwithstanding their genius, if they have any—is usually very ordinary and ignores all that transcends the physical world, in other words everything that constitutes wisdom. Never has there been more talk of "intelligence" and "genius" than in our epoch of intellectual night, and never has it been more difficult to agree on the meaning of these words; what is certain is that men have probably never been so cunning and ingenious as in our day. There is plenty of "intelligence" to spare, but truth is something altogether different.

But even when the existence of the animic plane is accepted, while the higher planes are denied, the dehumanization is scarcely less significant since there is a rejection of supernatural causes, that is to say, of causes that pertain to supra-formal manifestation and that cannot therefore be confined within the limits of natural and "horizontal" causality; this is the origin of psychologism, that is, the prejudice of wishing to bring everything back to psychological causes, which can only be individual and profane. Everything then becomes the fruit of a contingent elaboration: Revelation becomes poetry, religions are inventions, sages are "thinkers" and "researchers", that is, mere logicians, if indeed they are still such; infallibility and inspiration no longer exist; error becomes an "interesting" and quantitative "contribution" to "culture", and so on; if every mental phenomenon is not reduced to material causes, there is at least the denial of any supernatural or even simply supra-sensory cause and, by the same token, the negation of any principial truth. According to this way of seeing things, man is doubtless more than just his body, but he is nonetheless reduced to being a human animal, which means that he is no longer anything; for man limited to himself is no longer truly human.

Psychoanalysis, for those who believe in it, has thus the same compensatory function as evolutionism: since one cannot—nor will—conceive of true causes, one invents false ones; in other words: since one has no grasp of causality "in depth", one projects it "on the surface", as if instead of explaining an act by the thought that precedes it, one sought its cause in the blood or in the bones; but this would still not be so serious were one not seeking to replace the highest causes with the basest of hypotheses.

The denial of the five degrees of reality precludes an understanding, not simply of magic, but notably also of miracles; now it is not for nothing that the Church declares anathema whosoever rejects the one and the other. The first argument that one must set against this double rejection is the following: since the subtle or animic state exists, it cannot but erupt—assuming certain more or less exceptional conditions are met—onto the plane of material or sensible phenomena; and since the supra-formal world, the world of essences and of incorruptibility, also exists, and does so even before the formal world, it cannot but intervene "vertically"—and contrarily to the so-called "natural" laws—in the world of forms and matter. In order to parry any misunderstanding, it is first of all necessary to agree on the meaning of the word "natural"; what is beyond "nature" is in no wise the irrational or the absurd, but that whose causality eludes the measures and laws of the world of matter and sensations. If the "natural" coincided with all that is "logical" or all that is "possible", one would then be compelled to say that God too is "natural", and a miracle likewise; but this would be an abuse of language that would deprive us of all means of distinguishing verbally between a causality operating horizontally and another operating vertically. Be that as it may, when scientists hear the "supernatural" being spoken of, they basically imagine that what is involved is a belief in phenomena that lack causes or, more precisely, that lack real and possible causes.[12]

In view of the fact that modern science is unaware of the degrees of reality, it is consequently null and inoperative as regards everything that can be explained only through these degrees, whether it be magic or spirituality, or any belief or practices of any peoples; and it is in particular incapable of accounting for human or other phenomena situated in a historical or pre-historical past whose nature, or key, eludes it totally or as a matter of principle. Thus there can be no more desperately vain an illusion—far more naive than is Aristotelian astronomy—than to believe that modern science will end up reaching, through its dizzying course towards the "infinitely small" and the "infinitely great", the truths of religious and metaphysical doctrines.

*

* *

It is necessary to specify at this point what is meant by "form" and "essence": a form is a coagulated essence, which is to say that the relationship resembles that between ice and water; the formal world—the material and animic states—thus possesses the prop-

---

12. "The essence of criticism," said Renan, "is the denial of the supernatural," which amounts to saying that the essence of knowledge is the ignorance of all that is essential.

erty of "congealing" spiritual substances, of individualizing them, and hence of separating them more or less fundamentally from each other. This does not mean that in the higher spheres of Existence there is no longer any ego, but the ego of the blessed is supra-formal or essential, in the sense that it does not constitute a limit that excludes or an opaque screen with regard to other spiritual substances; thus the blessed can assume diverse forms without thereby ceasing to be a transparent mirror of God and of the angelic realms. Earthly form—both "gross" and "subtle"—finds itself reabsorbed into its essential substance; the "immortal person", far from being dissolved thereby, is on the contrary freed from a limitative condition, while remaining limited by virtue of being a manifestation; what form is with regard to essence, manifestation—whether essential or not—is with regard to the Principle. In the celestial hereafter, the "person" remains and, owing to this fact, can always reassume its individual and earthly form; "re-absorption" is not "annihilation", but "transfiguration". The same is true *a priori* for angels, who for their part have never possessed an earthly individuality, but who can nonetheless assume a form and an ego, as Sacred Scriptures offer us numerous examples of. In a word, the fact that celestial beings have transcended the formal condition carries no privative meaning—quite the contrary—for whosoever possesses the "greater" also possesses the "less".

There is still a question of proportions that must be considered. The material state extends around us and vanishes in the abysses of space; and yet this space, with its galaxies and metagalaxies, or with its billions of light-years, is nothing but a grain of dust in comparison with the animic state that surrounds and contains it, though not of course spatially. The animic state, in its turn, is nothing but an infinitesimal particle next to supra-formal or heavenly manifestation; and the latter is nothing in comparison with the Principle.

This "mathematical regression" from the higher to the lower is compensated—but this is only a manner of speaking—by a "progression" in the same descending direction: regions shrink as they move farther away from the Principle, while at the same time they multiply; the analogical antipode of the Infinite is quantity.

The most outward region, the material or gross state, is not only the sensible world that we know, for the outer limit of Universal Manifestation can only be contingent and approximate, and there is nothing absolute about it. There are, "enveloped" by the animic or subtle state, myriads of crystallizations or materializations comparable to our own sensible world, but having no relationship with it, and totally inaccessible to our faculties of sensation. Similarly, with respect to the supra-formal or angelic cosmos, there are many worlds whose nature is subtle or "fiery"; and likewise with respect to the Principle, those worlds of light which are the Paradises extend in an unimaginable profusion, like the drops of a fountain as if enraptured by a ray of sunlight. This law of mathematical progression towards the outer is prefigured *in divinis* by the aspects of Being—the Names of Quality (*asmâ sîfâtiyah*)—and also by the richness of the possibilities of manifestation which, "pouring" into the womb of the *Natura naturans* or of the *Materia prima*, are crystallized in a vertiginous multitude of creations and creatures; the Supra-ontological Self is the Absolute One, but Its "inner reflection" contains the first diversification which, on manifesting Itself, gives rise to ever more diversified series of projections, while being unable ever to rejoin the plenitude of the indivisible Infinite.

Of all this, experimental and pragmatic science knows nothing; the unanimous and millenary intuition of human intelligence means nothing to it, and scientists are obviously not prepared to admit that, if myths and dogmas are so diverse, in spite of their agreement with regard to the essential—namely, a transcendent and absolute Reality and, for man, a hereafter conforming to his terrestrial attitudes—this is because the supra-sensory is unimaginable and indescribable and allows for indefinitely varied ways of seeing adapted to different spiritual needs. The Truth is one, but Mercy is diverse.

Not only is scientistic philosophy ignorant of the Divine Presences; it ignores their rhythms and their "life": it ignores, not only the degrees of reality and the fact of our imprisonment in the sensory world, but also cycles, the universal *solve et coagula*; this means that it ignores the gushing forth of our world from an invisible and fulgurant Reality, and its re-absorption into the dark light of this same Reality. All of the Real lies in the Invisible; it is this above all that must be felt or understood before one can speak of knowledge and effectiveness. But this will not be understood, and the human world will continue inexorably on its course.

The Cross of Space and Time
in Koranic Onomatology

"He is the First (*Al-Awwal*) and the Last (*Al-Âkhir*) and the Outward (*Az-Zâhir*) and the Inward (*Al-Bâtin*) and He knows infinitely all things" (Koran 57:3). This verse of the *sûrah* "Iron"[1] is among those that contain—like the *Shahâdah*—a doctrine that is at once metaphysical and cosmological, and by the same token a spiritual alchemy as well; in it a temporal symbolism is "crossed" by a spatial symbolism; the result is a synthesis that embraces all fundamental aspects of the Universe.

"The First" is the Principle inasmuch as It precedes Manifestation; "the Last" is the Principle inasmuch as It follows it. The Principle "externalizes" itself through Manifestation or Existence, but It is also "the Inward" or "the Hidden" insofar as It is veiled thereby like an invisible center, although in reality It contains Manifestation. Universal Manifestation is the wave that "issues forth" from the Principle and "re-enters" It, if such a manner of speaking may be permitted despite its apparent emanationism.[2] At the same time, Universal Manifestation "is" the Principle in its aspect of "outwardness", while in another relationship, this same Principle remains transcendent and "inward" with respect to its illusory crystallization.[3] "Anteriority", "Posteri-

---

1. Thus named because it mentions iron as a gift from Heaven "in which there is immense calamity but also utility for men".
2. It would only amount to emanationism or pantheism if Manifestation were conceived as a part of the Principle, and if the Principle were deemed to be modified by Manifestation.
3. It must not be forgotten that the illusory is also the "relatively real".

ority", "Exteriority", "Interiority": these four aspects of the Principle express the Principle-Manifestation relationship in terms of succession and of simultaneity, or in other words, from the point of view of "becoming" as well as "being"; in the first case the perspective is that of the cycle or cycles, and then that of Existence as such.[4]

There is an evident analogy between "the "First" and "He who is without beginning" (*Al-Azal*) on the one hand, and between "the Last" and "He who is without end" (*Al-Abad*) on the other. It is the same in the case of the following Names: "the Primordial" (*Al-Qadîm*) and "the Perpetual" (*Ad-Dâ'im*); "the Initiator of all things" (*Al-Mubdi'*) and "He who brings all things back to Himself (*Al-Mu'îd*);[5] "He who brings forward" (*Al-Muqaddim*) and "He who retards" (*Al-Mu'akhkhir*); "He who creates out of naught" (*Al-Badî'*) and "He who subsists" (*Al-Bâqî*). The Names *Al-Azal* and *Al-Abad* denote, not the position or the function of the Principle in relation to Manifestation considered as a cycle, but two aspects of the very nature of the Principle, aspects that are themselves considered also in relation to Existence: the Divine Principle is not only "the First" because It "existentiates" or creates and "the Last" because It judges and finally reabsorbs, but It is also in itself without origin and without end. It is itself eternally its own origin and also its own goal, its own cause and its own effect, its own absoluteness and its own infinitude. God is "the First" and "the Last" in relation to the things He has created;[6] but He is "the Primordial" (*Al-Qadîm*) in relation to the world taken in its entirety,

---

4. "Before this universe was, I alone was . . . After manifestation I continued to be, in Myself as well as in the form of the world of phenomena; and when the universe has ceased to exist I will be. . . . Just as one may say of the sensible elements that they have entered into all living beings (since these beings live by them) . . . or that they have not entered into them (since they constitute them *a priori*), so also one can say that I entered into these living beings (as such) or that I did not enter into them (since there is no reality other than I)" (*Srimad Bhâgavata Mahâpurâna*, 2, 9:32, 34).
5. It is in this connection that God is "the Inheritor" (*Al-Wârith*) as well as "King of the Day of Last Judgment" (*Maliku yawmi'd-Dîn*).
6. "Verily we belong to *Allâh*, and verily to Him we shall return" (Koran 2:156). "What Thou hast created returns to Thee", says a prayer of the Iroquois in reference to the smoke of the Calumet, which symbolically carries all creatures back to Heaven, these creatures being represented by the portions of tobacco that have been consecrated to them.

and "the Perpetual" or "He who endures" (*Ad-Dâ'im*) in the sense that He "survives" the world. All these Names denote in various ways the transcendence of the Divine Principle; each one presupposes the others: thus, God is named "the First" because He is without beginning and because He is eternally anterior to every consequence of His Infinitude, and He is named "the Last" because He is without end and eternally beyond all duration. Universal Manifestation is a path that leads from God to God, a "moving away" (*bu'd*) that contributes to the "revelation" (*tajallî*) of "proximity" (*qurb*).[7]

We have seen that the Principle is, not only "the First" in relation to the world, but that It is so also in itself; this is equivalent to saying that the Essence (*Dhât*) is first in relation to the Qualities (*Sifât*), which for their part pertain to Being, and thus to the inward determination effected by the Principle in view of Manifestation. In Vedantin language, the Qualities, without emerging from *Âtmâ*, belong already to the domain of *Mâyâ*; in other words, relativity is already affirmed in the principial order, and this order accordingly contains the divine prefiguration both of Creation and—at the heart of Creation—of Revelation. In metaphysics one may either put the accent on the Self alone and envisage Being solely with reference to Mâyâ,[8] or conversely one may envisage Being solely in its character of pure Principle, and thus with reference to its Divinity; or one may even envisage Relativity exclusively as an internal dimension of the Absolute and thus reduce Manifestation to the Principle, with all the precautions and reservations such a formulation calls for depending on certain mental

---

7. It is opportune to point out here that ninety-nine, the number of the Divine Names, is symbolical and by no means fixes or exhausts the multitude of the Qualities of *Allâh*. These qualities can always be reduced to a limited group of fundamental differentiations—for example, to the triad "Wisdom-Clemency-Rigor"—but these polarizations are susceptible of indefinitely diverse reverberations, All-Possibility having no limits.
8. In Islamic language what the Hindus call *Mâyâ* is the "veil" (*hijâb*) or the indefinite series of veils that envelop the Essence. The multitude of Qualities, while revealing the Divine nature, veils the non-dual Unity of *Allâh*. *Mâyâ*, as the Divine Power of externalization or of illusion, is "still not manifested" (*avyakta*) and pertains in this connection to the supreme Self, of whom in its unfolding it is as it were the "art", the "play", or the "trace".

contingencies. Relativity, while it brings about a first polarization *in divinis*, does not encroach upon the intrinsic Divine nature; one may even extend this affirmation to cover the whole domain of *Mâyâ* and therefore of universal Manifestation as such; this is exactly what is signified by the Divine Name "the Outward": *Az-Zâhir* is the world inasmuch as it is necessarily divine and on pain of not being at all; the world is "the Outward" or "the Visible" inasmuch as we see Being through our five senses;[9] but since we cannot see Being—nor with all the more reason Beyond-Being— in itself, God is from this point of view "the Inward".

No creature is identifiable with "God-the-Outward",[10] who in Himself is Existence, Life, and Consciousness; He is also space, time, form, number, matter, and their positive contents, the perceptible reflections of the Divine Qualities. *Az-Zâhir* assumes forms, life, and other contingencies without becoming confused with this or that. One can thus say that He is all that exists, but not any one thing in particular; we see Him because He is "the Outward", while yet not seeing Him because He is God.

Universal Manifestation is a mystery of "emanation", but the use of this term must not be allowed to obscure the fact that philosophico-scientific and deistic emanationism takes no account of transcendence and in practice sees in the cosmos a "fragment" of God—*quod absit*—and not an extrinsic aspect; which is to say that in practice it reduces the Principle to Manifestation, irrespective of the terminology employed; the Principle, in manifesting Itself, would thereby be modified, as if It gave up something of its Substance, thus impoverishing Itself for the ben-

---

9. The senses are a prison which it is absurd to try to elevate into the position of criterion and basis of total knowledge, as modern science would have it. What is the good of providing exact information about galaxies and molecules if it is at the expense of a knowledge—infinitely more real and more important—of the total Universe and of our absolute destiny?
10. Except the Prophets—whence the testimony "He who has seen me has seen God" (*Al-Haqq*, "the Truth" or "the Reality")—and the sacred symbols such as the letters and sounds of the Divine Names, or the great phenomena of nature, or some of them, depending on the Revelation or traditional perspective involved.

efit of its creation. If one nevertheless holds to the assertion that Manifestation "emanates" from the Principle and is finally "reabsorbed" into It—and this is a proposition that can be maintained when rightly understood—one will have to add that, for the Principle Itself, there is neither manifestation nor emanation of any kind, but only the permanent possibility—sufficing in itself—of what appears from our point of view as creatures as an "emergence" from the Principle or, in another and more partial perspective, as *creatio ex nihilo*.

Between "the First" and "the Last" there is the world, but there is also God, for Manifestation is a "message from Him, by Him, to Himself", as the Sufis would say; and God, insofar as He "situates" or "projects" Himself—one might almost say "incarnates" Himself—between "God-the-First" and "God-the-Last" is none other than "the Outward". In this case, Manifestation is envisaged, not as a separate substance, but as a "deployment" or "revelation" illusorily "outward"—because projected into "nothingness", or rather in the direction of a nothingness in itself non-existent—of the Divine Principle, which is always changeless and virgin; in this revelation or this theophany, the Real differentiates Itself more and more: It "hardens" Itself by waves or by stages, segments Itself like foam and finally consumes Itself on reaching the providential limit of its outflowing, so that It may flow back—as "God become naught"[11]—by stages and by waves ever more inwardly directed into its source, that is to say, into its true nature which has never in reality ceased to be what it has been from all eternity.

This true nature, which has never "emerged" from Itself, but which, from the standpoint of contingency, may appear as "the Outward"—or in another respect as "the First" or "the Last"—is none other than "the Inward". Seen from this Center, if one may put it thus, there is no "Outward", or there is an "Outward" only in the form of an essential possibility included in the Principle; and the Principle Itself is inward only from a standpoint that is still contingent, and which is conditioned precisely by this illusory outwardness.

One might perhaps say that "the Last" corresponds analogically, and in certain manner, to "the Inward", in the sense that the

11. This is the metaphysical foundation of the Christic mystery.

action of drawing all things back into Itself is more directly in conformity with the Essence than the creative act, which entails a "moving away". In other words, in the process of manifestation, it is manifestation that is the goal, whereas in the process of reintegration or *apocatastasis,* the goal is the Principle;[12] the return to God is thus a reality analogous to the inwardness of God. As "the First", God projects Himself towards existential nothingness because "He desired to be known" distinctively, and thus to be known in what is "other than Himself"; whereas insofar as He is "the Last", God has in view only His own essential and undifferentiated reality or, from a more relative point of view, His victory over disequilibrium. *Al-Awwal* desired to see Himself in "the other"; He consequently desired "the other", whereas *Al-Âkhir* desires to see this vision "in Himself"; He desires therefore to see "Himself". The relationship is analogous—but in no sense identical—to that which exists between the terrestrial Paradise and the Heavenly Jerusalem, or between creation and redemption.[13] "The First" and "the Last" are as it were two divine phases, just as in another dimension—this time belonging to spatial symbolism— "the Outward" and "the Inward" are two divine aspects , two poles that appear as such only by virtue of the veil that separates us from the unalterable Unity of Allah.

In order to make this account as clear as possible, it may be summarized and completed in the following manner. "The First" is manifested for us by our existence, and thus by our birth; He is also manifested around us by the existence of the world, and thus by creation; in a completely universal sense, God as "the First" is affirmed by the unfolding of *Mâyâ,* of which He is the principal and transcendent origin.

Similarly, "the Last" is in our consciousness, in the first place through the certainty of death, then by the evidence of the Last

---

12. This is also true for the secondary and still relative modes of the "reflux" in question, and therefore for every cyclical ending; the analogy is in any case sufficient to justify the use of a synthetic language.
13. The Names *Ar-Rahmân* and *Ar-Rahîm,* which are commonly translated as "the Clement" and "the Merciful"—although the first comprises also the meaning of intrinsic Beatitude—are respectively referable, according to a particular interpretation, to creation and salvation, or to Manifestation and Deliverance.

Judgment, and thirdly through the metaphysical notion of the *apocatastasis*; death is the antithesis of birth, Judgment is that of Creation, and the *apocatastasis* that of *Mâyâ*.

"The Outward" is manifested by our existence as such and in its actuality, then by the existence of the world—envisaged likewise in itself and independently of origin and of end—and *a fortiori* by *Mâyâ*, envisaged, not as the creative power "preceding" its content, but in its aspect of universal exteriorization: in this connection *Mâyâ* is itself all that it contains; it is the veil into which all phenomena are woven.[14]

Again, "the Inward" is manifested in the microcosm by the Intellect; on the macrocosmic scale and without here taking account of that existential—and therefore not essential—intermediary which is the Divine Spirit (*Ar-Rûh*) at the center of the cosmos, "the Inward" is affirmed by pure Being; and in relation to total Reality, It is the Self. The Intellect is veiled by the ego, Being by the world, Beyond-Being or the Self by *Mâyâ*, which includes *Îshvara* or Being. In other words, for the manifested Universe it is Being—since It is the Principle of the Universe—that is "the Inward"; but this same Being—with all that it comprises in its creative dimension—is "the Outward" whenever It is envisaged in relation to the Self; the Self is the "Principle of the Principle" and the "Inwardness of the Inward".[15]

14. It is the Divine "Outwardness" that makes it permissible to affirm that all things are *Âtmâ*, to speak in Vedantin terms. Normally "the Outward" corresponds to what the Hindu doctrine understands by *Vaishvânara*; it is only from a viewpoint that looks beyond mere ontology that "Outwardness" can be assimilated to *Mâyâ* envisaged in its total unfolding and not simply in its sensible manifestation; and it should be remembered that ordinary theologies are ontologies and consequently fall short of the idea of the Self or of Beyond-Being. In Hindu terms "the Inward" would be either *Prajnâ* or *Turiya* depending on the level of reality envisaged.
15. In fact, Being is only the Principle of Manifestation; It is only with respect to Manifestation that It is "the Inward", and not with respect to Divinity "in Itself".

The Sufi lives under the gaze of *Al-Awwal, Al-Akhir, Az-Zâhir,* and *Al-Bâtin;* he lives concretely in these metaphysical dimensions as ordinary creatures move in space and time, and as he himself moves in them insofar as he is a mortal creature; he is consciously the point of intersection where the divine dimensions meet; strictly "engaged" in the universal drama, he suffers no illusions about impossible avenues of escape, and he never situates himself in the fallacious "extra-territoriality" of the profane, who imagine that they can live outside spiritual reality, the sole reality there is.

The world, whatever it may contain of things permanent or transitory, is never detached from God; it is always the same celestial substance fallen into a void and hardened in the cold of remoteness; the limits of things, and the calamities that result from these limits, bear witness to that remoteness. The sage sees in things and through things the divine origin now distant, and also—as he considers limitations and miseries—the terminal point of the fall which is inevitable and into which the world will finally be dashed; he discerns in phenomena the flux and reflux, the expansion and the return, the existential miracle and the ontological limit.

But above all the Sufi perceives through the "eye of the heart" that "all things are He"; the world, while not God from the standpoint of its particular existence, is nonetheless "the Outward" from the standpoint of its fundamental possibility or the permanent miracle on which it is suspended at every moment, and without which it would collapse into nothingness. In one sense the world is not God, but in another sense it is "none other than He" by virtue of its divine causation. It may be that words will never be able to describe this mystery in a satisfactory manner; but at a certain point the world "is God", or else it is nothing. God is not the world, and that is why it is impossible to speak of "the Outward" without also speaking of "the Inward"; the former is true only through the latter.

Every man is as it were suspended between "the First" and "the Last": every man has fallen from the primordial state and is threatened with death; behind him is the Divine Law, which was before him, and in front of him is the Judgment consequential on this Law; God is "the First" not only as Creator but also as Legislator. In the same way man extends from his bodily form—"made

76

in the image of God"[16]—through the soul and the spirit as far as Being and as far as the Self; he is thus as it were woven into "the Outward" and opens onto "the Inward", thanks to that Divine spark within him to which no limit can be assigned.

From the point of view of succession, we are a flux emanating from "the First"; from the point of view of simultaneity, we are a coagulation supported by "the Outward". Now the flux that is ourselves must carry within itself the sense of its own relativity and the desire for the reflux—for the movement towards "the Last"—on pain of being animal and not human; and the coagulation that is ourselves—or our individuation—must carry within itself a consciousness of "the Inward", the sufficient reason of man being the "manifestation of the Non-manifested" and not manifestation as such.[17]

"The Outward" is situated between "the First" and "the Last", whereas "the Inward" is both at once and is neither the one nor the other, for It is as much the Principle turned toward Manifestation as It is the Principle in Itself.

That which comes from "the First" must return to "the Last": this is the foundation of the eschatological drama of man. We are "a message from God to God" as the Sufis would say, but we must make the journey freely since, being men and not animals, the reason for being of our nature is the plenary manifestation of freedom. Now freedom is a two-edged sword; but since it is a possibility it cannot but be realized; man is therefore necessary. Freedom carries with it the possibility of the absurd; that is, the absurdity of the wish to be oneself "the First" from whence one comes and "the Last" whither one goes, as if Existence proceeded from ourselves, whereas in reality we exist by another's will and are incapable of creating *ex nihilo* or even of annihilating.

*

* *

It might also be said that man, who has obtained nothing from himself and has received everything, is made for obedience; it is

16. Hence the sacred character of nudity in Hinduism and elsewhere. Man was naked at his creation, he is so at his birth, and he will be so at the resurrection.
17. As the materialists and the vitalists would have it.

only in view of—and in the framework of—obedience that his freedom finds its meaning. There is no contradiction in this, for this framework is wide enough for human freedom to find fulfillment within it; we mean positive freedom, that is to say: the freedom that chooses the truth and the good and, having chosen them, decides vocationally in favor of a certain truth and a certain good;[18] to be positively free is to choose submission, spiritually speaking.[19] Before receiving our faculties of sensation and of action we received existence; having received it, with all its essential content, it belongs to us only conditionally; it is obviously absurd to claim total possession of something that is outside our control. The curse of modern man is that he believes himself wholly free *de jure*, when in fact no contingent consciousness could possibly be so; it could only be so on a higher plane than its own and beyond obedience, in the supernatural where the creature, in surpassing itself—by way of a gnosis that is but one with the grace of God—rejoins Freedom as such, the only freedom there is. But it is not then man who possesses Freedom; it is Freedom that has taken possession of man.

The "mystique" of modern man is one of revolt. Between the spirit of revolt and the spirit of submission there is no transition point: like oil and water they neither mix nor understand one another; they speak different languages or lead incompatible lives; there is between them a fundamental divergence of imagination and sensibility, to say the least. This spirit of revolt has nothing to do with holy wrath, which is by definition directed against error and vice, but is a case of pride posing as victim; it marks both a hardening and a freezing of the soul; it is a spiritually deadly petrification—for it harbors an element of hatred—and an aimless agitation, which only intelligence and grace can conquer. And since in the case of most men intelligence is unable to resist the passion of bitterness,[20] nothing but an explosion can break this carapace and appease this turmoil, whence the neces-

---

18. Not a fragmentary good that is opposed, in principle or in fact, to truth or to the total good.

19. The word *Islâm* means nothing else. According to Confucius, "filial piety and obedience are the foundation of humanity".

20. Bitterness shares close kinship with haughtiness; the zeal of bitterness leads to hell, according to St Benedict.

sity of miracles.[21] A miracle is an irruption of *Al-Bâtin* "the Hidden" into the domain of *Az-Zâhir* "the Visible" or "the Outward".

The celestial Paradise with its company of the blessed has an opposite significance, that of an entry of "the Outward" into the domain of "the Hidden" or "the Inward", making all necessary allowance for relativities since there can be no question here of an absolute polarity. In an analogous manner the great Revelations—which recapitulate, each in its own way, the "golden age"—are "belated" manifestations of "the First",[22] while cataclysms manifest "by anticipation" "the Last".

To be conscious of the permanent miracle of Existence is to abide in a devotional recollectedness that is as it were the complement of intellectual concentration: the latter is related to truth and the former to beauty and the virtues. To see Existence is to be no longer dispersed in the multitude of things; it is to perceive "accidents" as if they were in ourselves and without losing sight of "Substance". The sap of the human condition is devotion.

*
* *

What is Paradise? It is the inward nature of pure Existence; to be in conformity with that nature is to be carried by the wave of becoming toward Beatitude. To be in conformity with Existence is to submit; to submit ourselves to the celestial law is to conform to our own essence, the essence by which we exist and which is the innermost nature of things. Without Existence we would not be; how can we reasonably revolt against it and set ourselves against that by which we are, that which makes us to be ourselves? The essence of Existence is blissful; opposition to that essence—the idolatry of contents or of accidents—leads us away from Beatitude and encloses us in the blind alley of our own contingency and in the measureless hell of our own absurdity. The absence of Beatitude can be nothing else but hell, for where there is no pleasure

---

21. There is, besides, in every man a latent revolt which most commonly manifests itself in indifference towards God and towards the constraints of truth.
22. This is equally true—on a much reduced scale—of certain natural facts, such as springtime, youth, morning.

there is its opposite; now Existence, from which as human beings we cannot detach ourselves, is made of felicity, despite its knots and its fissures. What is true of Existence is with all the more reason true of Being, and thereby of Beyond-Being, which is the source of all.[23] The Sufis do not hesitate to speak of a "Paradise of the Essence" (*Jannat Adh-Dhât*), which is none other than the *Paranirvâna* of the *Tathâgata*, that supreme *Nirvâna* in which the very extinguishment of the lamp is consumed.

The question: "What is the Self" can be answered, while preserving a symmetry with the answer just given about Paradise, by saying that it is the inward or absolute nature of pure Intelligence; but then one must speak, not of obedience or submission as in the case of existential perfection, but of discernment and contemplative concentration; this is the station of "ipseity" and of "infinite consciousness". The universal pole that can be designated, synthetically and in a provisional way, by the term "Existence" is characterized by the qualities of Purity, Inviolability, and Mercy; and the pole—or the center—that may be called "Consciousness" or the "Self" enters into Existence like a luminous axis, irresistible and liberating.

The way that corresponds to *Az-Zâhir* is that of action and also that of love of the neighbor; it is the way of obedience and of charity, of works, of an active love of God. The way that corresponds to *Al-Bâtin* is that of the contemplative love of God and, at the summit, that of gnosis, of knowledge of the Self. But humanly speaking, what unites every intention or perspective is the warmth and freshness of devotion; without it there is no happiness; living without devotion is a pretense of living; it is living in death.

To the question of whether Reality is "good" or "bad" there are logically two answers: the first is that Reality is neither good nor bad; the second is that it is good. If good exists, it is because the ground of Existence is beneficent; if the good can be absent— to a minute degree when the world and the cycle are envisaged in

---

23. At least from the human point of view, which is that of separativity and illusion.

their totality—it is because the ground of Existence, or absolute Reality, is neither good nor bad, because it cannot be enclosed in an alternative or an opposition. What is important to understand is that this indifferentiation or this transcendence is essentially of such a nature as to reveal itself as the good; that is to say, the good essentially reveals the nature of the higher indifferentiation. The part can be relatively an evil, but the whole is good, whatever may be its degree of reality; in this sense the world is a positive manifestation, despite the negations it shelters provisionally. Or again, if a thing is bad, it can only be so as a fragment and not as a totality; evil fragments just as the good makes whole; the good dilates whereas evil contracts. God manifests Himself only in perfections, not in their absence; where there is a lack there cannot be either totality or center. A bad man is no more than a fragment of himself.

Three attitudes are possible with respect to the world: the first, which is properly speaking sub-human yet in fact only too human, is to accept sensorial phenomena as being "reality", and to indulge in them without restraint and with a dense will; this amounts to denying that God is not only "the Outward" but also "the Inward", and that His "outwardness" has no meaning save by virtue of His "inwardness". It amounts as well to denying that God is not only "the First" who has created us, but also "the Last", who awaits us at the end of our journey, the one having as before no meaning save in connection with the other.

The second possible attitude, considered as a pure attitude and overlooking combinations with other points of view, is the rejection of the world, of seduction, of sin. It is to see, in place of beauty, nothing but skeletons and ashes, and in place of pleasure, nothing but impermanence, trickery, impurity, suffering; from this point of view there is no "God-the-Outward"; the world is only something that is not God.[24]

The third possible attitude is based on what we have termed, on several occasions, the metaphysical transparency of phenomena; it is to see the world in its aspect of "divine outwardness"

---

24. Bodily asceticism is not dependent upon this point of view alone; it may have the purpose of eliminating dependence on matter and the senses, however they may be envisaged.

and to be aware that this "outwardness" is a function of a corresponding "inwardness". This attitude attains to essences by way of forms, but without in any way losing sight of the truth of the preceding attitude, namely, that no appearance "is" God and that every appearance has a reverse side which is derived precisely from "outwardness" insofar as the latter is separated from "inwardness". The sage "sees God everywhere", but not to the detriment of the Divine Law to which he is humanly subject.

Since most of our contemporaries seem to rebel against the idea that sin according to the flesh—which in their eyes cannot anyhow be a sin—can entail what theology calls "damnation", let us examine that question in the light of the doctrine now under consideration. Sexuality belongs to the domain of *Az-Zâhir*: carnal ecstasy in fact belongs only to "God-the-Outward" and not directly to man, who possesses no creative power nor beatific rapture; in this connection man is the instrument of the Divine Will concerning terrestrial expansion. The purpose of sexuality is consequently the preservation of the species and the multiplication of individuals; but it has also a contemplative function by virtue of its prototypes *in divinis* or, what amounts to the same, by virtue of the metaphysical transparency of symbols; from another point of view, one may say that nothing human is purely animal, for we are "made in the image of God". Carnal ecstasy, inasmuch as it betokens an irruption of the divine into the human, transmits something of the divine nature; the consequence is that outside the two conditions mentioned—procreation and contemplation—sexual enjoyment is a profanation which cannot but entail a downfall into the infernal states, considering its ontological gravity; it might almost be said that "one does not become God for nothing". To understand man is to understand the ontological gravity of his condition; it is to understand that we can, essentially, deserve hell or Paradise.

As for the contemplative element, it must find its place in the framework of what a particular sacred legislation prescribes or allows; it cannot therefore compromise *de jure* a traditional social equilibrium. Morals can vary of course, but the Divine Will remains on the whole the same, and furthermore It is in accordance with the best interest of human societies.

*

* *

If one wanted, not to form an image of *Al-Awwal*—for "the eye cannot reach Him"—but at least to approach His domain, one would have to be able to go back to the origins of the earthly Paradise and witness the dawning, in a luminous substance as yet scarcely material, of the innumerable states of existence and of consciousness that are creatures. Likewise, if one wanted under present conditions to form some idea of the coming of *Al-Âkhir*, one would have to be able to witness by anticipation that sort of explosion of matter, that sort of revulsion or existential reflux, which will mark the advent of God; one would have to be able to hear in advance the sound of the Trumpet—that rending irruption of primordial Sound—and to witness the breaking up and transmutation of our sensible universe.

In contrast, *Az-Zâhir* is always within our immediate reach; we see His grandeur in that of the virgin nature which surrounds us and in which we live; in the depths of the sky, in the majesty of mountains, in the boundlessness of seas and in their rhythms of eternity; we also see "God-the-Outward" in the splendors and symbols of sacred art. As for *Al-Bâtin*, He is at once near at hand and infinitely remote: He is "within us", but needless to say eludes the resources of an imagination made for contingencies and for this lower world. We sense "God-the-Inward" in the experience of truth, in the "supernaturally natural" miracle of pure intellection as well as, in varying degrees, in virtue and in grace; it may indeed be infinitely more than a presentiment, since, in penetrating by its Omnipresence the center and the secret of our heart, the Divine Self can consume at will the "veils" of separation.

For the animal, *Az-Zâhir* alone is God; for the ordinary believer, *Al-Bâtin* alone is God; but for one who "knows through Allâh" (*al-'ârif bi'Llâh*) both aspects are God, and at the same time neither of them is; that is to say, these two Names, insofar as they represent a necessary polarity—or result from such a polarity—must necessarily be resolved in a superior synthesis, namely, in the intrinsic unity of the Principle. To speak of "inwardness" is still to envisage God relative to "outwardness", and as being separate from the latter insofar as He is "the Inward". But God is what He is by Himself (*bi-Hi*) and "in Himself" (*fî-Hi*) and not in relation

83

to anything whatever that is foreign to His nature. He is either in every aspect or in none, according to the degree of reality envisaged by the Intellect "with the permission of God" (*bi-idhni'Llâh*).[25]

Finally, since the verse of the Koran containing the four Divine Names in question ends with the affirmation that "He knows infinitely all things", any misinterpretation tending to reduce the Principle to "states" or "substances" deprived of consciousness is thereby excluded in advance: *Allâh*—whether we envisage Him in the context of immanence or of transcendence or in any other equally possible context—cannot be "something less" when compared with His manifestations or creation; being the infinite Cause of all, He possesses every conceivable perfection, including therefore that of consciousness and that of activity, but without any possibility of conflict between these perfections and His perfection of unity and simplicity; all possibilities are prefigured in the infinitude of His very Substance. This is also the meaning of another verse, immediately preceding that of the four Divine Names: "His is the Sovereignty of the heavens and the earth"—these two worlds representing respectively and in a relative sense *Al-Bâtin* and *Az-Zâhir* and also *Al-Âkhir* and *Al-Awwal*—"and He is Able to do all things".

Allah is One; and since the polarity "Outwardness-Inwardness" is neither absolute nor eternal—any more than any other conceivable polarity—the "inward" sun will inevitably rise in the "outward" field. "God will come"; that is as certain as our birth and our death. It may also be said that "the Outward" will return to "the Inward";[26] according to this perspective or this mystery "the Inward" coincides with "the Last"; so that, beyond all distinctions of aspects and points of view, "nothing remains save the Countenance of Allah".[27]

---

25. For the Intellect, even though it attain to "the depths of God"—to the supreme Self and not to Being alone—can do nothing without Being, which is the "personal God".
26. This second way of looking at things is in a certain sense more "real" than the first, but the first corresponds nonetheless to a concrete aspect of the end of the world.
27. *Wajhu'Llâh*, which is to say *Adh-Dhât*, "the Essence". At this degree, which in fact is no longer a "degree", there has never been an "Outward".

Insights into the Muhammadan Phenomenon

Like Christianity, Islam teaches that Jesus had no human father, that he is the "Word of God", that he was born of a Virgin, and that he and this Virgin-Mother have the unique privilege of not having been "touched by the devil" at the moment of their birth, which is an indication of the Immaculate Conception; now as it is impossible, even from the Muslim point of view, that all of these incomparable privileges carry only a secondary meaning, or should have occurred only "in passing" without leaving any decisive traces, Christians will ask how it is that Muslims can without contradiction reconcile these sublime facts with faith in a later Prophet. To understand this—all metaphysical arguments notwithstanding—one needs to take into account the following: integral Monotheism comprises two distinct lineages, one Israelite and the other Ishmaelite; now whereas in the Israelite lineage Abraham is renewed or replaced, as it were, by Moses— the Sinaitic Revelation being like a second beginning of Monotheism—for the sons of Ishmael Abraham continues to remain the primordial and unique Revealer. The Sinaitic miracle called for the Messianic or Christic miracle: it is Christ who, from a certain point of view, closes the Mosaic lineage and completes the Bible, gloriously and irrevocably so. But this cycle, proceeding from Moses to Jesus, or from the Sinai to the Ascension, does not in fact encompass all of Monotheism: the Ishmaelite lineage, which is still Abrahamic, was situated outside of this cycle and remained in a certain fashion open; it called in its turn for a glorious completion, the character of which would not be Sinaitic

85

and Christian, but Abrahamic and Muhammadan and, in a certain sense, "of the desert" and "nomadic".

Abraham came before Moses; hence Muhammad had to appear after Jesus; the "miraculous cycle" extending from Sinai to Christ finds itself as if encompassed—in temporal terms—by another parallel cycle of a distinctly different character, one marked more by the one monotheistic Truth, with all the absoluteness and saving power inherent in its nature, and deeply attracted to primordial simplicity and "Platonic" transcendence; Islam and Abrahamism are fundamentally the religions of ahistoric nomads, burned by an ever-present and eternal Divine Sun. Man is nothing before this Sun: that the Caliph Omar should conquer a portion of the ancient world or that the Prophet should milk his goat amounts practically to the same thing; in other words, there is no "human greatness" in the profane and titanic sense; there is thus no humanism to incite man in the pursuit of vain glories; the one lasting grandeur allowed is sanctity, and this belongs to God.

Islam has perpetuated up until our times the Biblical world which Christianity, once it had been Europeanized, could no longer represent; without Islam, Catholicism would have soon invaded all of the Middle East and this would have involved the destruction of Orthodoxy and the other Eastern Churches, and the Romanization—thus the Europeanization—of our world up to the borders of India; the Biblical world would have been dead. One can say that Islam had the providential role of arresting time—thus of excluding Europe—in the Biblical part of the globe and of stabilizing, while universalizing, the world of Abraham, which was also that of Jesus; Judaism having emigrated and been dispersed, and Christianity having been Romanized, Hellenized, and Germanized, God "repented"—to borrow from Genesis—of this unilateral development, and out of the desert, the ambiance or background of original Monotheism, He brought forth Islam. One encounters here a play of equilibrium and compensations that the different exoterisms are not capable of situating, and it would be absurd to require them to.[1]

---

1. After reading these lines, Titus Burckhardt communicated to us the following thoughts concerning the Abraham-Muhammad cycle: "It is significant that the Arabic language is the most archaic of all of the living

It is said in Islam, not only that the Muslim religion is the completion of the preceding religions and that, owing to this,
Muhammad is the "Seal of Prophecy" (*Khâtam an-nubuwwah*), but
also that earlier prophetic missions—those of Abraham, Moses,
and Jesus—were carried out under a "Muhammadan mandate";
now this means not only that in Islam Muhammad is identified
with the Logos as such—no religion does less with its founder—
but also that earlier Prophets exercise a type of function within
the framework of Islam itself, a function of example and, sometimes, of esoteric inspiration.

In order to show in what way the Muslim religion considers
itself to be the completion and synthesis of earlier monotheisms,
we must first of all recall that its constitutive elements are *al-îmân*,
al-islâm, and *al-ihsân*, terms that can be rendered, not literally but
nonetheless adequately, as "Faith", "Law", and "Way". "Faith" corresponds to the first of the three monotheisms, that of Abraham;
"Law" to the second, that of Moses; and the "Way" to the third,
that of Jesus and Mary. In Abrahamism, the elements "Law" and
"Way" are as it were absorbed by the element "Faith"; in Mosaism,
it is the element "Law" that predominates and that, as a result,
absorbs the elements "Faith" and "Way"; and in Christianity, it is
the element "Way" that absorbs the two other elements. Islam, for
its part, intends to contain these three elements side by side, thus

Semitic languages: its phonetics preserve, with the exception of one, all
the sounds indicated by the most ancient Semitic alphabets, and its mor-
phology can be found in the famous code of Hammurabi which is more
or less contemporaneous with Abraham." – "Indeed, Mecca, along with
the Kaaba built by Abraham and Ishmael, is the forgotten sacred city—
forgotten both by Judaism, which disregards Ishmael's prophetic role,
and by Christianity, which inherited the same point of view. The sanctuary at Mecca, which is to the Prophet what the Temple of Jerusalem is
to Christ—in a certain sense, at least—is like the 'stone rejected by the
builders' which becomes the cornerstone. This forgetting of the Ishmaelite sanctuary, as well as the line of succession constituted by
Abraham-Ishmael-Muhammad—the Arab Prophet being of Ishmaelite
descent—this double factor shows us how the divine economy of things
likes to combine the geometric with the unforeseen. One can assign no
importance whatsoever here to the opinion of those who see in the
Abrahamic origins of the Kaaba a retrospective Muslim myth and who, in
so doing, completely lose sight of the fact that the Arabs of old possessed
a genealogical memory that was both extraordinary and meticulous, as is
in fact the case with most nomads or semi-nomads."

in perfect equilibrium, whence precisely its doctrine of the three elements *îmân, islâm,* and *ihsân.*

Al-îmân, "Faith", comprises basically the two Testimonies, that of the Unity of God and that of the prophetic quality of Muhammad; *al-islâm,* the "Law", comprises the five ritual obligations: the two Testimonies just mentioned, canonical Prayer, Fasting, Almsgiving, Pilgrimage. As for *al-ihsân,* the "Way", its central or quintessential support is the "Remembrance of God" (*dhikru'Llâh*), the modalities of which pertain finally to the "science of the inward" (*'ilm al-bâtin*); this means that one cannot define the content of the "Way" in exoteric terms. *Al-ihsân* is the domain of the Sufis, not of the "doctors of the outward" (*'ulamâ az-zâhir*).

Of necessity, all the Prophets possess all the virtues; however, according to a way of seeing things specific to Islam, one can, without implying any refutation of the foregoing, attribute to Abraham the virtues belonging to Faith, to Moses those of the Law, and to Jesus those of the Way; and if Islam, on the basis of this schematism, sees in Muhammad the synthesis of all these qualities, it does so in the same way as in the case of the synthesis of *îmân-islâm-ihsân* and with the intent of emphasizing the distinct manifestation of these qualities. One can even say that a specific virtue, and indeed every virtue, belongs by attribution to such and such a Prophet under a given aspect: thus when a given quality is attributed to Jesus, it is considered in relationship to *ihsân,* the Way, and not, it goes without saying, in any exclusive manner. In other words, each fundamental virtue can be considered on the basis of either Faith or certitude, of either the Law or obedience, either the Way or love, or sanctity; the fact that virtues refer more particularly to one or the other of these three elements does not invalidate this principle.

That the Arab Prophet can be considered as the "best of created beings" and as the Logos without any qualification, a being in whom other "Messengers" must in some fashion be incorporated, is a way of seeing things that is admissible in virtue of the fact that there is a cosmic sector extending from earth up to the loftiest of the celestial spheres, or up to the "Divine Throne" where Muhammad alone may truly be identified with the Logos; and this is so by virtue of a particular Divine Will, the same that decreed the advent of Islam, and thus also the existence of the cosmic sector under consideration here: every *Avatâra* is "the Logos" in the cosmic sector allocated to him.[2] Thus to see in a given Founder of religion the sole personification of the Word is a question, not only of perspective, but also of objective reality for those who find themselves enclosed in the corresponding spiritual sector; and this is independent from the question of knowing whether the Prophet concerned possesses—or should possess in function of the nature of his mission or the structure of his message—the same avataric breadth as another Founder of religion; for what matters to God is not the personality of the spokesman alone; it is the totality of his personality and mission taken together. This totality, whatever the forms involved, is always fully the Word of God; it thus constitutes an element of absoluteness and infinitude, of integral and saving Truth.

What we have just said may serve as an illustration of the principle that God alone is unique, a metaphysical principle that Buddhism, for instance, expresses through the doctrine of the countless Buddhas. If we have insisted here on this matter of the cosmic sectors, it is because those who grant the validity of all intrinsically orthodox religions generally limit themselves to emphasizing the oneness of Truth, which is not by itself sufficient in that exoteric claims are left unexplained, or are even considered to be errors pure and simple; such an assumption is inadmissible given the essential and salvific content of the great Revelations.

The religions can be likened to so many sectors of the "universal circumference", the center being the Divine Principle or the nirvanic Reality. God is unique; the personification of the Logos could never be so, except for a given sector.

*

* *

What appears in Islam as an irritating disproportion, when seen from the outside, is the contrast between the obviously human style of the Prophet and the claim of his pre-eminence in the hierarchy of religious messengers or simply of creatures. The totalitarianism specific to each religion obliges Islam to identify

---

2. It is to the "projection" or "establishment" of this sector that, for Islam, the "Night Journey" (*Laylat al-Mi'râj*, "Night of the Ascension") of the Prophet corresponds.

Muhammad alone with the total Logos, the other Prophets being able, in this case, to represent only particular functions of this same Logos; but since the Prophet of Islam does not have the right to be avatarically superhuman, for Islam intends in its own way to avoid the pitfalls of anthropolatry and titanism, no spokesman of Heaven is allowed to be so; on the one hand, Muhammad can be only a "man", and this condemns him in the Islamic perspective to present himself in the mold of the small-ness and complexity characteristic of the human species, while on the other hand, he must be situated at its summit, for the evident reasons just indicated above.[3] What in Islam compensates for the necessary smallness of the spokesman—since to be a creature is to be small—is the sublimation of the Prophet by virtue of his inward identification with the total Logos; whence the occurrence of a kind of void between the human smallness and the meta-physical greatness, a void which, in the avataric perspectives, is filled by the Man-God who is at once divine man and human God.

This simplicity, or this voluntary smallness of the Prophet, is in fact an unmistakable proof of his sincerity; an impostor coming after Christ would not have failed in declaring himself "Son of God" in his turn: The sincerity is here all the more striking since the Prophet admitted the virginal birth of Christ, which was hardly in his interest to do, either humanly or logically; at no time did the Prophet endeavor to appear as a superman.[4] Be that as it may, Muhammad was unquestionably an ascetic; it is well known that he had several wives, though incomparably fewer than David and Solomon who possessed hundreds; but, apart from that situ-ation, which was sacramental from his point of view, he never ate to satiety, spent his nights in prayer, and gave away as alms all that he did not strictly need. As for his political comportment, it is

---

3. Carried away by his zeal to refute the doctrine of incarnation, Ghazzali did not hesitate to affirm that the transformation of a staff into a snake by Moses was a miracle greater than the raising of the bodies by Christ. A manifest error, because to throw one's staff by divine order and then to flee before the snake is not to produce a miracle; the marvel is great of course, but Moses had nothing to do with it.
4. When in intimate surroundings and on the margin of his mission, the Prophet had a somewhat playful simplicity which recalls Krishna and, closer to us and at a more modest level, the Paramahamsa of Dak-shineswar, Ramakrishna.

worth recalling that the outward morality of Islam is identical to that of the Old Testament: it is *a priori* practical and not ascetical or mystical; thus it is first of all social. Intrinsic morality, that of the virtues, takes precedence over social morality while belonging to another sector which, though being no doubt parallel, is nonetheless independent; it acts towards the outward in the same manner that substance determines accidents *ab intra* and not *ab extra*; it is meant to inhere in all of our actions.

Before proceeding further, it is necessary to insert the following comments. Westerners feel compelled to reproach Muhammad for certain direct or indirect acts of cruelty, and in doing so they start either from the prejudice that the victims were necessarily innocent or from the error that there can be no culprits deserving of such a harsh treatment; one would retort, from the Muslim side, that the treatment in question was an adequate reaction to a moral and physical culpability, which is irrefutable if one assumes the fact of effective guilt; it is in any case impossible to prove that it was not so, and the tendency some historians have of attributing the basest motives in spite of psychological information proving the contrary, does nothing to help clarify matters nor to solve the problem in itself. It is incontrovertible that the satirical poet Kab was treacherously assassinated, but Judith did not act differently towards Holofernes, nor as a matter of fact Jahel with Sisera, in the times of the prophetess Deborah; in all three cases one finds an amoral relationship of cause and effect based on the deceitful nature of treachery, whether political or spiritual or both at the same time. If it is true that in some cases the means debase the end, it is equally true that in other cases the end sanctifies the means; all told, everything is here a question of circumstance and proportions.[5]

This said, let us return to our main subject. "Ye have in the Messenger of God a beautiful example," the Koran says, and not for nothing. The virtues one can observe among pious Muslims,

---

5. There remains one more very particular point to clarify, namely that the case of Kab presents an aspect of magic analogous to that occurring in the case of Shimei: the latter had implicitly cursed David—and thereby the Prophet-King's posterity; David accepted the outrage as a chastisement from God; and later, having become powerful again, he likewise accepted Shimei's excuses and swore to spare his life. Before dying, how-

including the heroic modalities that these give rise to among the Sufis, are attributed by the *Sunnah* to the Prophet: now it is inconceivable that these virtues could have been practiced throughout the centuries all the way to our day without the founder of Islam having personified them in the highest degree; likewise it is inconceivable that the virtues would have been borrowed from elsewhere—one would have to wonder from where—since their conditioning and style are specifically Islamic. For Muslims, the moral and spiritual worth of the Prophet is not an abstraction nor a conjectural matter: it is a living reality, and this is precisely what proves, retrospectively, its authenticity; to deny this amounts to claiming that there can be effects without a cause. The Muhammadan character of the virtues explains, moreover, the more or less impersonal bearing of saints: there are no other virtues than those of Muhammad; thus they can only be repeated by those who imitate his example; it is through them that the Prophet lives on in his community.

That a Muslim sees nothing outside of this particular phenomenon of greatness is the ransom of the subjectivism specific to any religious mentality; and it is almost a tautology to add that, in spite of all the painful and irritating misunderstandings concerning other possible modes of greatness, the Muslim compensates—or has to compensate—for his "lack of imagination" by an attitude that enables him to realize inwardly and qualitatively what he ignores outwardly. One finds here the whole system of the "love of the Prophet", or the love of the Logos as a terrestrial Divine Manifestation: man must love the human Logos so as to be loved by God. To love the Prophet is, in practical terms, to become integrated in the mold of the *Sunnah*; it is thus to take on before God the primordial human norm (*fitrah*), the sole one approved by Him.

ever, he enjoined Solomon to slay the insulter—his oath having engaged none but David himself—in order to avert from Solomon the curse which Shimei had uttered and which was still effective: its magic could be extinguished only by being turned back on its author. The rest of the Biblical story obliges us to add that Solomon combined the apparently contradictory wishes of his father in a kind of ordeal subject to divine judgment in which the ultimate verdict rested upon the particular behavior of the incriminated; in this manner, Shimei assumed the responsibility of his fate while making the verdict of God plain to see.

*

* *

The *Avatâra* is Divine Man and human God; *grosso modo*, Islam opts for the first of these aspects and Christianity for the second. "Divine Man" means here: perfect man, primordial and normative—undeformed image of the Creator, but image nevertheless, not Divinity. "Human God" means: Divine Spirit animating a human form, to the point of absorbing the soul so as to make one substance of both the soul and the Spirit.

We have seen that one of the stumbling blocks for a Westerner in his approach to Islam is the question of the sanctity of the Prophet; the difficulty resides mainly in the fact that the Christian perspective addresses this question from another angle than does Islam. The difference at issue here could perhaps best be illustrated with the following images: there is a type of sanctity that pertains *a priori* to formal perfection, at least as regards its usual manifestation: the saint is perfect as the sphere is the most perfect of forms, or as regular geometric figures are perfect when compared with asymmetrical or even chaotic and thus arbitrary figures. There is, however, another mode in which sanctity manifests itself that corresponds, not to the perfection of the form, but to the nobility of the substance; just as we could say that the sphere or the cube are perfect forms, whatever be their substance, in the same way we could now say that gold or a diamond are noble substances, whatever be their form.

In the case of a Christ or a Buddha, it may be said that their sanctity is proven outwardly by the perfection of their form; whosoever fails to realize a perfect form, as they possess, is not a saint. On the other hand, in the case of a Krishna, an Abraham, or a Muhammad, it may be said that everything they did was precious or infused with holiness, not owing to the form, but owing to the substance; it is the substance which makes the act legitimate and ennobles it, and which makes of it a positive sign and an element of benediction.

Whereas the Christian will say: he who possesses a celestial nature will prove it by his way of acting, the Muslim will say rather: the actions of one who has a celestial nature cannot but possess a celestial quality. Certainly, sanctity as substance excludes intrinsically imperfect acts, but it does not exclude acts that are ambiguous in their appearance; and sanctity as form is impossible without sanctity as substance; but a near perfect form without sanctity—hence hypocrisy—is something quite possible, though its prestige could not be more tenuous. If Krishna plays with the milkmaids, he still remains Krishna, and his play conveys something of the liberating Infinite; conversely, no matter how meticulously the Pharisees condemned by Christ may try to conform to the formal law, this is not enough to make of them saints; quite the contrary.

In Christianity, the majority of saints are monks or nuns, if not hermits, but there are also kings and warriors; in Islam, the majority of saints—those at the origin—are warriors or at least men of action; however, starting at a certain epoch, the majority of the Sufis kept apart from the world except, if the case arose, when preaching. With regard to the Prophet himself, one has the impression—keeping in mind the characteristic perspective of Islam—that God introduced into his life some seemingly fortuitous elements in order to show that the Messenger is but a man and that the fate of man is the contingent and the unforeseeable, in order to prevent the Messenger from being deified after his sojourn on earth. It is precisely this aspect of things that induces Islam to insist on sanctity as substance and to see beyond a "doing" that is engaged in the accidents and vicissitudes of the world—and lacking in itself the value of a decisive criterion—a "being" that is independent of this activity; this "being" or this holiness is revealed, for those who are its witnesses, through its tendencies and through the spiritual perfume it projects onto its manifestations.[6] On the one hand, the Muslim deduces from the absolute truth of the Message the total holiness of the Messenger, while the Christian proceeds the other way round; on the other hand, the Muslim bases himself on the accounts of those who, having known the Prophet, bear witness to his incomparability.

---

6. The famous "tea ceremony" in Japanese Buddhism is an example that has become liturgical of this interiorizing manifestation—or of this "manifestation of the Void"—of what even ordinary actions of men penetrated of God can be. The "tea ceremony" is great, not because of a moral sublimity, but by virtue of a "being" or a gnosis made manifest in an otherwise unimportant activity, thus highlighting the contrast between the profundity of "being" and the humbleness of the action. An example, of

*

* *

It is now indispensable to say something about the metaphysical basis of prophecy. Man cannot know, in any degree, the "Self" without the assistance—and "blessing"—of the "Divine Person"; likewise, he cannot approach the Divine Person without the assistance and the blessing of "God made manifest", that is to say, the divine reflection in the cosmic substance: "No man cometh unto the Father but by Me," said Christ, and a *hadîth* tells us that "no man shall meet Allah who hath not first met the Prophet."

There are indeed three great theophanies, or three hypostases, which in descending order are: firstly, Beyond-Being or the Self, Absolute Reality, *Âtmâ*; secondly, Being or the Lord, who creates, reveals, and judges; and thirdly, the manifested Divine Spirit, which Itself possesses three modes: the Universal or Archangelic Intellect, the Man-Logos, who reveals in a human language, and the Intellect in ourselves, which is "neither created or uncreated", and which confers upon the human species its central, axial, and "pontifical" rank, one which is virtually divine with regard to other creatures.

In a perspective as rigorously unitarian and transcendentalist—not immanentist—as Islam, it is this mystery of the "God made manifest" that accounts for the immense importance of the "prayers on the Prophet", a practice that would remain unintelligible were it not for the in some sense "Divine" character of the Messenger: traditional accounts of the person of the Prophet enable us to become aware of both the incontestably human and, equally, the incontestably superhuman nature of the manifested Logos.

To understand this doctrine more clearly—a doctrine which, from the Muslim point of view, is esoteric—the following image could be proposed: when the sun is reflected in a lake, one can distinguish first of all the sun, secondly the ray, and thirdly the reflection itself; now one could discuss without end the question

a different order, is provided in the life of Abd al-Qadir al-Jilani: the saint relates a little story about cats, and the whole audience begins to weep from spiritual emotion, after having listened with boredom to the brilliant sermon of a great theologian.

of knowing whether a creature who saw the reflection alone—the sun being hidden from sight by some obstacle—saw only the water, or whether, on the contrary, it really saw something of the sun itself. What is incontestable is that without the sun, the water would not even be visible—and it would in any case carry no reflection; therefore it cannot be denied that he who sees the reflected image of the sun sees thereby "in a certain fashion" the sun itself, as this Muhammadan saying enunciates: "He who hath seen me hath seen the Truth (God)."

Certainly, avatarism is altogether foreign to Islam; nonetheless, Islam cannot but attribute a unique virtue to the prophetic quality of its Revealer, since the sufficient reason for every manifestation of the Logos is to reveal Itself as the sole manifestation, or as the most ample, or as the first or the last, or as that of the essence of the Logos, and so on. No Divine Name is another Name, and yet each one is God; and each becomes central the moment It reveals Itself or the moment It is invoked, for it is God who reveals Himself in It, and it is God whom one invokes in It; and this applies also *mutatis mutandis*—to speak now in Buddhist terms—to the *Âdi-Buddha* who, though diversely projected in time and in space, both heavenly and earthly,[7] remains always the same Logos.

When discussing the great theophanies—Beyond Being, Being, and the Divine Center of Existence, or the Self, Lord, and Logos-Intellect—mention was also made, while relating it to the Logos, of the human Intellect, which is neither "created nor uncreated": this allows one to distinguish, if so desired, a fourth theophany, that of the Logos reflected in the microcosm; this is the same Divine Logos, but manifesting Itself "inwardly" instead of "outwardly". If "no man cometh unto the Father but by Me", this truth or this principle applies also to the pure Intellect within us: in the sapiential order—and it is only in this order that one can speak of Intellect and of intellectuality without adjoining

---

7. The Paradises are beyond extension and duration in the physical or terrestrial meaning of the terms; nonetheless, they comprise strictly analogous conditions for the simple reason that each cosmos requires, on the one hand, a condition of stability and simultaneity while requiring, on the other hand, a condition of change or succession. There is no cosmos without expansion and without rhythm.

implacable restrictions—what matters is to submit all the powers of the soul to the pure Spirit, which is identified, though in a formless and ontological manner, with the fundamental dogma of Revelation and thereby with the *Sophia Perennis*.[8]

*

* *

Islam readily insists on the Prophet's poverty, which sometimes appears as the quintessence of the virtues insofar as it is freely consented to and piously practiced. It can be said without exaggeration that one of the fundamental traits of Islam is its cult of poverty, a cult that extends from the *Sunnah* all the way to art: the splendor of the mosques is a richness imprinted with poverty; their glittering quality is neutralized by a calm monotony, even in Persian and Turkish art where the richness is more marked than in the art of the Arabs.[9] The Koran is the paradigm of this equilibrium: to recite the Koran is to drink holy poverty; the element of drunken rapture is not missing, but it is a sober rapture comparable to the poetry of the desert.[10] The dryness of the Koranic

8. When the Ancients considered that wisdom and felicity consisted in submitting to "reason", both human and cosmic, they were referring whether directly or indirectly, consciously or unconsciously, to the One Intellect. The proof of this lies precisely in the fact that they linked reason to universal Nature; the error occurred when many of them reduced in practice this Nature to human reason, after having first reduced God to Nature. This double reduction is the very definition of Greco-Roman paganism, or of the Greco-Roman spirit insofar as it was pagan and not Platonic; and one could add that it is only the Man-Logos or Revelation that gives full value to or "resuscitates" reason, just as it is the notion of the absolute Real alone and of its transcendence that gives meaning to Nature.
9. That Muslim art has an Arab character and a powerful originality of its own is denied by some on the pretext that it is composed of elements borrowed from other styles; this however, in the very relative measure in which it can be conceded, is wholly beside the point. For one thing, Muslim art—even Persian, Turkish, or Indian—is deeply Arab in virtue of the Islam which determines it; for another, this art is perfectly original and could not fail to be so owing to the fact that, whatever its models may be, it springs from an intrinsic orthodoxy and thus from a celestial inspiration.
10. According to an Islamic tradition, Adam at first refused to enter into a body made of clay and only resolved to do so once swayed by a celestial

style—with the exception of a few *sûrahs* and of some passages—has often been remarked upon, whereas the virile power of this style has been overlooked; to speak of God in Arabic, is to speak of Him with force. The truth is that the general dryness of the Koranic style prevents the engendering of a titanic and dangerously creative individualism; it creates a human type that is rooted in pious poverty and in holy childlikeness.

The Arab soul is made of poverty; it is from this background that the qualities of ardor, courage, tenacity, and generosity stand out. Everything is derived from poverty, deploys itself in it, and is resorbed in it; the originality of Arab eloquence, be it chivalrous or moralizing, is that it is poor; its prolixity is that of the desert.

There is in Islamic pauperism a universal message, found no less in the Gospels, but with less obsessive monotony; it is a matter of reminding man that the norm of well-being is not a maximum but a minimum of comfort and that the cardinal virtues are, in this respect, contentment and gratitude. But this message would not amount to much were it not the expression of a truth which encompasses our whole being, and which the Gospels express in these terms: "Blessed are the poor in spirit, for theirs is the kingdom of heaven." The Koranic basis for spiritual poverty according to Islam is the following verse: "O mankind! Ye are the poor in your relation to Allah. And Allah is the rich! He is the Absolute, the Owner of Praise." The "poor" are those who know that they have nothing by their own means and that they need everything from someone else; the "Rich" is He who suffices unto Himself and who lives from His own substance.[11] *Islâm*, inasmuch as it is "resignation" to the Divine Will, is poverty; but poverty is not an end in itself: its whole purpose for being rests in its positive complement, which means that perfect poverty opens onto richness, a richness that we carry within ourselves since the Transcendent is also the Immanent. To die for Transcendence is to be born in Immanence.

music; now this music is reproduced in the Koran under the form of the *sûrah* "Ya Sîn".

11. *Sûrah* of "The Angels", 15. The "Rich" is literally the "Independent" (*Ghanî*), who is in need of nothing and of no one since He is the source of everything and since He contains everything within Himself; and it is for this reason that He is also the "Praised" (*Hamîd*).

The Koranic Message of Sayyidna Isa

For Islam, Christ is: without a human father, "like Adam"; indissolubly bound to the Virgin; not understood (*et tenebrae eum non comprehenderunt*), whence the necessity of a final synthesis, that of Islam; perpetually journeying (*Filius autem hominis non habet ubi caput reclinet*), healing the sick, and resurrecting the dead; Seal of Sanctity (*Spiritus ubi vult spirat . . . sed nescis unde veniat aut quo vadat*), and thereby the pre-eminent exemplar—or the direct and miraculous manifestation—of esoterism under its twofold aspect of wisdom and love.[1] And yet for a Christian nothing appears more outlandish and less convincing than the reference in the Sacred Book of the Muslims to a Christ who is limited to confirming the Torah and to announcing the advent of another Prophet; as is often the case in the Koran, and in the Semitic Scriptures in general, the simplicity and strangeness of the literal meaning expresses—or conceals—a spiritual geometry whose principle must be understood and its content deciphered.[2]

---

1. *Hadîth*: "He who attesteth that there is no other divinity save God, who hath no associate; that Muhammad is His servant and His Messenger; that Jesus is His servant and His Messenger, His Word cast into Mary, and the Breath emanated from Him; that Paradise is a truth, as also is hell; God will have him brought into Paradise, whatever his deeds may have been."

2. An example: "O ye messengers! Eat of the good things (*tayyibât*), and do right (*sâlihâ*). Lo! I am Aware of what ye do" (23:51). Now the meaning of this rather elliptical, and at first sight astonishing, verse is the following: "Let no one reproach Muhammad in particular, nor any of the Messengers in general, for not doing penance; being Prophets, they are dispensed therefrom by virtue of their preeminent perfection, which proceeds from a Divine Command (*amr*); and they act normatively—

99

Now, it must be said that Islam represents a particularly difficult case from the Christian point of view given that the Koran combines a perspective which differs from that of Christianity while employing a symbolism that is very similar to it; the resulting misunderstandings are doubtless providential since each religion has to be what it is and cannot be confused with other credos, just as each individual is a man without being able to be other individuals, even though they too are human.

This analogy, which is much more than a mere comparison, contains a doctrine that is crucial from our point of view: each Revelation is indeed "true man and true God", that is to say, "true ego and true Self", whence precisely the meaning of the divergences on the surface of Unity. A Revelation is a "means of salvation", and such a means is what Buddhists term an *upâya*, a "heavenly mirage",[3] without there being in this word the slightest pejorative connotation, except that the Absolute alone is purely real; this means is necessarily drawn from the cosmic or samsaric Substance, hence from *Mâyâ*; and the same meaning is understood or implied, not only in the *Shahâdah*, but also in the doctrine of the two natures of Christ, notably in this saying: "Why callest thou me good? None is good, save one, that is, God."

Space can be measured by means of a spiral as well as by means of a star, though neither measure is the other; the same is true of theologies inasmuch as they are measures of the Infinite. It is the function of esoterism to include the measures exoterism excludes, and cannot but exclude; however, the fact that esoterism is capable of knowing a given metaphysical measure does not mean that it can therefore understand the coincidence of this measure with a religion foreign to its frame of reference, for gnosis is an essential and qualitative science, and as such it is inde-

---

'doing right'—by their very nature by virtue of this very Command, since every quality comes from God; and God knows infinitely better than anyone the truth of the matter." Thus, the Divine Command has been given in eternity and before creation. One will recall here the response of Christ to those who reproached the disciples for not fasting; it is doubtless by analogy with this incident that the verse cited above comes after a passage concerning Jesus.

3. A "mirage" rendering pure Truth intelligible and without which it would remain inaccessible. The so to speak feminine complement is *Prajnâ*, liberating Knowledge.

pendent of the knowledge of facts not belonging to its own traditional framework.

Muslims consider Christ from the standpoint of the "concentric circle", which is that of the discontinuity between "Creator and creature"; Christians consider him from the standpoint of "radius" or "ray", which is that of metaphysical continuity; but they admit this relationship only for Christ, whereas Hindus apply it to all the *Avatâras* and even—but in an eminently different and less direct way—to all that is created. Sapiential esoterism[4] combines the "circle" with the "cross", whatever may be the "geometric type"—if one can so express it—of its religious context.

According to the Koran, the message of Jesus—Sayyidna Isa—comprises essentially three aspects, one of which corresponds to the past, one to the present, and one to the future: indeed the Koranic Christ presents himself as confirming what was revealed before him, namely, the Torah,[5] and as predicting what is to come after him, "a Messenger whose name is Ahmad";[6] as for the present, Jesus makes a gift of a meal come from Heaven, which one will immediately recognize as the Eucharist.[7]

---

4. This qualification is necessary because there is also an esoterism that defines itself as such by the liberties it takes—*de jure* and with respect to the letter—from the point of view of love and of the *unio mystica* alone.
5. "Think not that I am come to destroy the law, or the prophets: I am not come to destroy, but to fulfill" (Matt. 5:17).
6. "And when Jesus son of Mary said: O Children of Israel! Lo! I am the messenger of Allah unto you, confirming that which was (revealed) before me in the Torah, and bringing good tidings of a messenger who cometh after me, whose name is the Praised One" (Koran 61:6).
7. "Send down for us a table spread with food from heaven" (Koran 5:114). According to the commentators, this meal was a fish, which symbolizes the passage from one state to another, or a regenerating grace. It is well known that in the early Church, the fish is an emblem of Christ, the Greek word *ichthus*, "fish", being composed of the initial letters *Iesoûs Christos Theoû Uios Sotêr*, "Jesus Christ, Son of God, Savior". This symbolism is associated with the professions of the apostles Peter, Andrew, James, and John, and with the word of Christ calling them to apostleship; the regenerating grace is represented by the baptismal water, whence the term "pool" (*piscina*), "pond of fish". One will remember here the Koranic story of the fish of Moses which, having been touched by a drop from the Fountain of Immortality, returned to life and re-entered the sea; this too refers to the passage from one state to another by means of a vivifying grace. Finally, in Hinduism, the *Matsya-Avatâra*—Vishnu incar-

To understand the deeper, and thus universal, meaning of the prediction of Sayyidna Isa, it is necessary to know first of all that the ternary "past-present-future" also represents another ternary: "outward-center-inward"; it is this second ternary that provides the key to the properly esoteric message of Christ and thereby also to the esoteric meaning of the Koranic passages concerning Sayyidna Isa. According to this interpretation, the "Messenger who shall come after me" is none other than the at once transcendent and immanent Logos, and thus the "inward Prophet", or the Intellect understood in its dual aspect as both human and divine; it is the "Divine Spirit", whose mystery is touched upon more than once in the Koran.[8]

According to the most ordinary Muslim interpretation, this "Messenger whose name shall be Ahmad" is the Prophet; in order to understand the meaning of this correspondence, one needs to take into account two things: first, that in the cyclic unfolding of the monotheistic ternary, Islam corresponds to "knowledge" or "gnosis", while Christianity represents "love", and Judaism "action"; in this respect, the correspondence of the historical Muhammad to the dimension of gnosis is thus perfectly plausible. Secondly, the name Ahmad is the "heavenly name" of the Prophet; in the passage referred to, it is thus a matter not so much of an earthly reality as of its heavenly root, and this brings us back to the inward dimension just alluded to.

The "Paraclete" promised by Christ is the "Spirit of Truth"; it is not a "consoler", as a faulty translation would have it, but an "ever-present helper", which is to say that this Spirit assists believers "from within" in the absence of the "outward" presence

---

nated as a fish—marks also, in connection with the symbolism of the flood and the ark, the passage from one cycle to another.

8. "They will ask thee concerning the Spirit (*Rûh*). Say: The Spirit is by command of my Lord (*min Amrî Rabbî*), and of knowledge ye have been vouchsafed but little" (17:85). The fact that, in other passages, the Spirit is not included with the angels, but is named separately, indicates its near-divine quality, and this is precisely what the words "by command of my Lord" express; the end of the sentence just quoted indicates that the Spirit is a mystery, thus a reality that is not easily accessible to human understanding. It is traditionally taught that the Spirit is so great that It occupies the same expanse as all of the angels taken together, and also that It alone will not die before the Last Judgment.

of Jesus. One knows that Muslim commentators read *Perikletos*, the "Illustrious", for *Paraklêtos*, and that they see in the Greek word a translation of the name *Ahmad*, which is derived, like the name *Muhammad*, from the root *hamada*, to "praise" or "exalt"; some have Arabized *Perikletos* into *Faraqlît*, "he who distinguishes between truth and error", by referring to the root *faraqa*, to "separate" or "discern"—from which one of the names of the Koran, *Al-Furqân*, is derived; this belongs, not to etymology, of course, but to a method of phonetic interpretation that the Hindus term *nirukta*.[9] Be that as it may, if the Prophet of Islam is assimilated to the "Spirit of Truth" prophesied by Christ, it is precisely because he represents, together with the Islam which he manifests, the perspective of gnosis, expressed scripturally and dogmatically by the unitary Testimony, *Lâ ilaha illâ 'Llâh*; furthermore, this Spirit is essentially the Intellect, hence the "Inward", under its dual aspect of organ of Knowledge and dimension of the Infinite, the "Kingdom of God" which is "within you"; it is in connection with this perspective, or with this reality, that Sayyidna Isa is *Khâtam al-wilâyah*, "Seal of Sanctity".[10]

And this allows us to make the following point: Sayyidna Isa, according to the Koran, is "sent to the Children of Israel"; now, apart from the fact that the term "Israel" is open to the extension given it by St Paul,[11] Jesus had—and in principle has—a mission regarding the Jews as such, a mission that is purifying on the one hand and esoteric on the other, the two things being moreover linked; this is to say that Jesus is "Seal of Sanctity", not only from the point of view of the Muslims, but also, and even *a priori*, for the faithful of the Torah, at least *de jure*.

---

9. We will take the liberty here of mentioning in this context—though it is unrelated to our subject—that the apparently etymological interpretations of sacred names in *The Golden Legend* belong to this same method; they are thus far from the gratuitous fantasies some have supposed.

10. Sayyidatna Maryam—the Virgin Mary—shares in this pre-eminence; she is the queen of the saints in the Muslim Paradise.

11. The incident of the centurion of Capernaum, or more precisely the words of Jesus that lend it its doctrinal substance, carry the same meaning of universality. It may be added that, according to the visions of Anne-Catherine Emmerich, Christ had more than one meeting with pagans.

From another point of view, the very expression *Khâtam al-wilâyah* indicates that the triple message of the Koranic Christ has the meaning, not only of a unique and particular message, but also of a type of message, and that there is therefore a place in Islam, as in any other traditional framework, for an "Isan" wisdom, a *hikmah 'issâwîyah*, characterized precisely by the three-dimensionality discussed above. In summary, the Isan wisdom manifests first of all its agreement with the "antecedent", hence primordial and underlying, Truth—the *Religio perennis*; secondly, it offers a heavenly manna, an ambrosia or nectar; and thirdly, it opens the way towards "immanent Prophecy", that is, to sanctity or gnosis. If it is objected that such a schema applies to every religion, one can respond that this is evident and that every Revelation offers a schema which, while being characteristic for itself, can be applied to every other Revelation; such an observation might merely be a playing with words, were it not for the fact that it answers a certain need for causality and therefore has a place here.[12]

A striking characteristic of the Isan message is its Marian or Maryamian[13] dimension: in the Koran, Jesus and Mary are indeed so closely associated that they appear almost as a unique and indivisible manifestation; Christ is "Jesus Son of Mary"—Isa bin Maryam[14]—and the Koran expresses this unity of "Jesus-Mary" in

12. In other words, the Isan perspective can be understood in three different ways: first, it is the historical message of Jesus; secondly, it is the specifically Isan wisdom, such as we have defined it; and thirdly, this is the Isan aspect found in every religion. According to the last of these meanings, every spiritual tradition presents in one way or another the three dimensions found in the Koranic Christ, in the same way as there is, for instance, a Muhammadan wisdom of universal character and thus, by the same token, a Muhammadan aspect in each religion—that of original purity, synthesis, equilibrium, and non-temporal "Platonism".

13. The use of adjectives derived from Arabic names serves as a reminder that this is a perspective rooted in the Koran and not one beholden *a priori* to Christian theology.

14. "(And remember) when the angels said: O Mary! Lo! Allah giveth thee glad tidings of a word from him (*bi-Kalimatin minhu*), whose name is the Messiah, Jesus, son of Mary, illustrious in the world and the Hereafter, and one of those brought near (*Muqarrabûn*)" (3:45). This announcement—which might seem commonplace from the Christian point of view—contains in reality a "symmetrism" that is characteristic of the Koranic language and of the Arab spirit in general: Jesus is *a priori* a

these terms: "And We made the son of Mary and his mother a portent, and We gave them refuge on a height, a place of flocks and watersprings" (23:50).[15] This association of the *Avatâra* and his *Shaktî*[16], to speak in Hindu terms, appears even in the trinity "God-Jesus-Mary" which the Koran attributes to Christianity, thus referring on the one hand—in part by way of reproach—to a psychological fact and on the other hand, by way of esoteric allusion, to a mystery inherent in what we have termed the "Isan message"; for this message is equally, and by definition, a Maryamian message by virtue of the fact that the Virgin is the "Spouse of the Holy Spirit" and that she is an aspect of the Way and the Life. We have in mind here the integration of the soul (*nafs*) into the "Marian substance"; the Spirit (*rûh*), for its part, is breathed in by the "Christic principle". This aspect of spirituality has been highlighted by St Bernard, then by Dante[17], and later by St Louis-Marie Grignion de Montfort,[18] to mention only these three

"word" of God, which means that he will be *a posteriori* near Him, like the closing of a circle; he is "illustrious", that is to say, great and venerated, *a priori* in this life and *a posteriori* in the next. According to Baidawi, Jesus is "Prophet in this world and Intercessor in the next". The word *muqarrab* ("brought near") contains an allusion to the loftiest angelic perfection— fashioned of "luminosity" and of "proximity"—that of *Ar-Rûh*, the "Divine Spirit", of which it cannot be said humanly whether It is created or uncreated. It is said that the "Word" breathed into the body of Mary was none other than the creative word *kun*, "Be!", out of which Adam and the whole world proceeded.

15. Or again: "And she who was chaste, therefor We breathed into her (something) of Our Spirit and made her and her son a token for (all) peoples" (21:91).

16. According to a *hadîth*, "no child is born but the devil toucheth it and maketh it to cry, except Mary and her son Jesus."

17. "The name of the beautiful flower (Mary) which I always invoke, morning and evening, brought my spirit to contemplating the greatest light (*il maggior fuoco*, the Virgin). And when my two eyes had made known to me the dimensions (of goodness and of beauty) of the living star . . . from the depths of Heaven I saw descend a flame forming a circle like a crown, which girt the star (of the Virgin) and moved round her" (*Paradiso* 23:88-96).

18. "Mary was very hidden in her life: this is why she is called by the Holy Spirit . . . *Alma Mater*, hidden and secret Mother. . . . The divine Mary is the earthly paradise of the new Adam. . . . The Blessed Virgin is the means by which our Lord has come to us; she is also the means that we must avail ourselves of to return to Him. . . . In truth, one may arrive at

names. It is proper to add that this perspective is independent of the distinction between the path of love and the path of gnosis, and that it is found in the one as in the other, as is shown by the "Marian" or "shaktic" aspect in the path of Ibn Arabi.

*

* *

In Islamic language, the distinction between the terms *salât*, "blessing", and *salâm*, "peace", as well as that between the corresponding verbs *sallâ* and *sallam*, used by way of eulogy after the names of the Prophet, helps one to specify what the respective natures of the "Isan" and "Maryamian", or Christic and Marian, realities are—the first corresponding to *salât* and the second to *salâm*. Mention can be made of a point that we have already brought up elsewhere,[19] namely, that—according to the Shaykh al-Alawi—the divine act (*tajallî*) expressed by the word *salli*, "bless", is like lightning and implies the extinction of the human receptacle, whereas the divine act expressed by the word *sallim*, "greet", spreads the divine influence in the substance of the individual in the manner of water, which conserves, not in that of fire, which burns; therein lies the difference between the Marian and Christic graces. The latter are "vertical" and the former "hori-

divine union by other paths. . . . But by the path of Mary, one arrives more gently and peacefully. . . . St Augustine calls the Blessed Virgin "the mold of God". . . . He who is cast into this divine mold is soon formed and shaped in Jesus Christ, and Jesus Christ in him: at little cost and in a short time, he will become God, since he is cast into the same mold that formed God. . . . But remember that one casts into a mold that alone which is melted and liquid. . . ." (St Louis-Marie Grignion de Montfort, *True Devotion to the Blessed Virgin*). It may be surprising to learn of a path that is "easy" and "quick", but it is necessary to understand that this possibility presupposes particular qualities and requires attitudes which, in fact, are far from being within everyone's reach; the difficulty lies here less in the "doing" than in the "being". The Marian, or "*shaktic*", perfection is to be as God has created us. Let us also quote, because of their aptness, these words by the same author: "Do not become encumbered, without a special calling thereto, with outward and temporal things, be they seemingly ever so charitable, for the outward exercise of charity towards one's neighbor has caused some to lose the spirit of prayer. . . . Understand that the great things that are done on earth are done inwardly" (*Spiritual Instructions*).
19. *Understanding Islam*, "The Prophet".

zontal"; the feminine influence predisposes to the balanced and harmonious reception of the virile influx; in other words, the soul, which is both hardened and dispersed, takes on in a certain fashion the bounty, beauty,[20] purity, and humility[21] of the Virgin in order to be pleasing to God.[22] There is an evident relationship here between, on the one hand, rebirth "of water and of the Spirit"—water corresponding to the virginal principle—and, on the other hand, the eucharistic species, where bread represents what might be termed "Marian homogeneity"; in Islamic terms, this homogeneity is the influence of *salâm* which completes and "fixes" that of *salât*. The Virginal principle thus assumes apparently opposite functions, depending on the aspect it manifests: it is both receptive, hence passive or plastic, and conservative or coagulating; from a higher point of view, it assumes an aspect of "fluid" or "nectar-filled inwardness", according to its reality as supreme *Shakti*.

The manifested Divine Spirit is comparable, in certain respects, to the reflected image of the sun on a lake; now there is, in this image, a feminine or "horizontal" element, and this is the potential luminosity inherent in water, and the perfect calm of a surface unruffled by any wind; and since these qualities enable the perfect reverberation of the solar orb, they already share something of its nature; so it is that the Primordial Recipient is a providential projection, or a type of duplicate image, of the Divine Content. "When He prepared the heavens, I was there," Primordial Femininity is made to say; "when He set a compass upon the face of the depth; when He established the clouds

20. For "the Buddhas also save by their superhuman beauty"; this meaning is found in the "Song of Solomon". The Golden Legend specifies that Mary, though exceedingly beautiful, extinguished all passion in those who beheld her.
21. Awareness of one's existential naught before God, and effacement before men. The Virgin dwelt in effacement and refused to perform miracles; the near silence of the Gospels concerning her manifests this effacement, which is profoundly significant in more than one respect; Maryam is thus identified with the esoteric Truth (*Haqîqah*) in that she is a secret Revelation corresponding to the "Wine" in the *Khamrîyah*.
22. One will recall in this context that for Vishnuism each soul is a *gopî*, a servant—and lover—of Krishna, and is thus identified with Radha who is their summit and their quintessence.

above: when He strengthened the fountains of the deep; when He gave to the sea His decree, that the waters should not pass His commandment; when He appointed the foundations of the earth" (Prov. 8:27-29). Now, the qualities of this *Materia Prima* or this *Prakriti* are purity and transparence, and then receptivity towards Heaven and intimate union with it. Sayyidatna Maryam, the Virgin, is in fact described as being "chosen and made pure",[23] and being "submissive"[24], and "believing the Words of her Lord".[25] She does not exist without the Divine Word, nor the Divine Word without her; together, with this Word, she is all.

*

* *

When a Muslim saint refers to Sayyidna Isa or his Mother—or to Sayyidna Idris (Enoch) for example, or to Sayyidna Al-Khidr (Elias)—this reference pertains to the *tawfîq* ("divine succor") or *maqâm* ("station") of a spirituality of a very elevated nature[26] and

---

23. "O Mary! Lo! Allah hath chosen thee and made thee pure, and hath preferred thee above (all) the women of creation" (3:42). The first election is intrinsic: Allah chose the Virgin in herself and for herself; the second choice is extrinsic: He chose her in regard to the world and for a divine plan.

24. "O Mary! Be obedient (*uqnutî*—"devout in prayer") to thy Lord, prostrate (*usjudî*) thyself and bow (*arka'î*) with those who bow (in worship)" (3:43). As is the case in other passages, the command given to the avataric creature does no more than express the nature of this creature, cosmic perfections always deriving from a divine Command (*amr*); in pronouncing His order in eternity, God created the nature of the Virgin. The angels repeat this command only to the glory of Mary. It is worthy of note that this verse indicates, in summary, that the motions of Muslim prayer derive from the Marian nature.

25. "And Mary, daughter of Imran, whose body was chaste, therefor We breathed therein something of Our Spirit (*min Rûhinâ*). And she put faith (*saddaqat*) in the words of her Lord and His scriptures, and was of the obedient" (66:12). It is fitting to note that in the Koran, as in other Scriptures, there are parabolic passages whose function is less to relate facts than to depict a character, an attitude, or a situation, depending on what is paramount for the "Divine Intention".

26. This point is indispensable, for in Islamic spirituality there is no anticipated reference to a "Pole" other than the Founder of Islam. It is on the basis of his *maqâm* that Ibn Arabi could have inner contacts with Sayyidna Îsa.

not to that of a religious schema; in Islam, such a schema is purely Koranic and Muhammadan, by the logic of things.[27]

In the foregoing we have seen what is implied in a spiritual reference to the reality "Isa-Maryam"; to further specify the nature of this reference, the conversation between Jesus and Nicodemus may be recalled—a conversation that took place "at night", which evokes the *Laylah* or the *Haqîqah* of the Sufis— where it was said that "except a man be born of water and of the Spirit, he cannot enter into the Kingdom of God." Now Water, leaving aside other more contingent meanings, represents perfection according to Maryam, and the Spirit is perfection according to Isa, their cosmogonic prototype being "the Spirit of God" that "moved upon the face of the waters";[28] there is in an analogous reference in the Song of Solomon spoken by the Beloved: "I sleep, but my heart waketh." Holy sleep, or *apatheia*, refers to the first of these two mysteries and holy wakefulness to the second; their combination gives rise to a spiritual alchemy found, in a variety of forms, in the heart of all initiatic methods. The mind is in a state of sleep insofar as it is detached from the world, which is ephemeral and which disperses; thought thus remains in a calm and pure disposition, in parallel with acuity of discernment, for serenity is all the more precious insofar as its substance is intelligent.[29] The heart, for its part, is in a state of

27. But this is independent of the prestige enjoyed by Mary in Islam. We would like to recall here that Ephesus, near Smyrna, where the Assumption took place, is a place of pilgrimage where the Virgin performs miracles for Muslims as well as Christians.
28. "The Waters" must not be confused with the primordial chaos, made of "desert and void" (*tohu wa bohu*), but must be interpreted as meaning the "Divine Passivity", or the Universal Substance, which is always virgin; in Hindu terms, this is the aspect of *sattva* in *Prakriti*, and in fact constitutes its very essence. The *Mânava-Dharmashâstra* mentions the "benevolence" of the quality of *sattva*; St Bernard extolled the "gentleness" and the "sweetness" of the Virgin, which Dante in his turn has sung in these terms: "Whatever melody soundeth sweetest here below, and most doth draw the soul into itself, would seem a rent cloud thundering, compared unto the sound of that lyre wherewith was crowned the beauteous sapphire (Mary) by which the brightest heaven is made more limpid (*del quale il ciel più chiaro s'inzaffira*)" (*Paradiso* 23: 97-102).
29. Thus Christian tradition makes mention of the wisdom of the Virgin and of the infused nature of her learning; her strength lies in her quality of

wakefulness, for, having overcome its hardness and heaviness by means of faith and the virtues—or through gnosis—it receives and transmits the Divine Reality which is *Verbum, Lux,* and *Vita.*

adamantine inviolability. Inversely, the masculine pole must possess the virginal qualities in order to be identified with Intelligence and Power.

The Virginal Doctrine

In speaking of the "virginal doctrine" we want to allude to the teachings of the Blessed Virgin as they appear not only in the *Magnificat*, but also in various passages in the Koran; in other words, we are considering Mary not only in her Christian aspect, but also in her capacity as Prophetess[1] of the whole Abrahamic lineage.

The *Magnificat* (Luke 1:46-55) contains the following teachings: holy joy in God; humility—"poverty" or "childlikeness"—as a condition for Grace; the holiness of the Divine Name; inexhaustible Mercy and its connection with fear; immanent and universal Justice; the merciful assistance granted to Israel, this name having to be extended to the Church since it is, according to St Paul, the prolongation and the supra-racial renewing of the Chosen People.[2] This name must also be extended, owing to the same principle, to the Islamic Community since it too belongs to

---

1. A Prophetess, not in the role of a law-giver and founder of a religion, but one who bestows enlightenment. There is among Muslims a divergence of opinion concerning whether Mary—Sayyidatna Maryam—was a Prophetess (*nabîyah*) or simply a saint (*walîyah*); the first opinion is based on the spiritual eminence of the Virgin, that is to say, on her rank in the hierarchy of the most prominent spiritual figures, whereas the second opinion, stemming from an ultra-critical and fearful theology, takes account only of the fact that Mary had no law-giving function; this "administrative" point of view misses the nature of things.
2. "His servant Israel", says the Canticle of Mary, thus specifying that sacred servitude enters into the very definition of Israel, to the extent that an Israel without this servitude is no longer the Chosen People, whereas inversely a non-Israelite monotheistic community is identifiable with Israel—"in spirit and in truth"—by the fact that it realizes servitude toward God.

111

the Abrahamic lineage. For the *Magnificat* speaks also of the favor granted to "Abraham and his seed", and not exclusively to Isaac and his seed; Abraham includes all of the monotheistic Semites, both racially and spiritually, an inclusion that extends beyond the mere fact of physical races.

The connection—enunciated in the *Magnificat*—between fear and Mercy is of capital importance; this doctrine cuts short the illusion of a superficial and easy religiosity—very much in vogue among today's "believers"—that confuses Divine Goodness with the weaknesses of humanism and psychologism, and even of democracy, and that is completely in line with modern narcissism and the desecration it entails. It is particularly noteworthy that the traditional doctrines which insist the most on Mercy— Amidism for instance—take for their starting point the conviction that we deserve to go to hell and that we are saved only by the Goodness of Heaven; the way will then consist, not in saving ourselves by our own merits, since this is considered to be something impossible, but in conforming ourselves morally, intellectually, and ritually to the requirements of a Mercy that wishes to save us and with respect to which all we need do is open ourselves. The whole Canticle of Mary is impregnated with elements of Mercy and elements of Wrath, which thus refer to love and fear, and which make it forever impossible to be mistaken about the laws governing Divine Bounty. The mildness of the Virgin is accompanied by an implacable purity; one finds in her a strength that recalls the songs of triumph of the prophetesses Miriam and Deborah; in fact, the *Magnificat* sings of a great victory of Heaven, and of an overflowing of "Israel" beyond its ancient frontiers.

The severities of the Marian Canticle towards the proud, the mighty, and the rich, and the consolations directed to the humble, the oppressed, and the poor, refer—apart from their literal meaning—to the equilibrium-restoring power of the Beyond; and this insistence on cosmic alternations is easy to understand if one remembers that the Virgin herself personifies Equilibrium since she is identified with the Cosmic Substance which is both maternal and virginal, a Substance made of Harmony and Beauty which is thereby opposed to all disruptions of equilibrium. In the Marian teaching, such disequilibria come essentially from pride, injustice, and attachment to riches;[3] one could further specify: love of self, contempt for one's neighbor, and the desire to possess, which includes insatiability and avarice.

As for the joy mentioned in the Virgin's Canticle, it goes hand in hand with humility—the consciousness of our ontological nothingness before the Absolute—or more precisely with the Divine Response to this humility; what is emptiness for God will thereby be filled, as Meister Eckhart explains by the example of a lowered hand open upward. And the virginal message according to the Koran is, as will be seen, a message of divine generosity.

*

* *

The Marian teaching as it appears in the Koran insists on Mercy on the one hand and on immanent and cosmic Justice on the other, or on the alternations resulting from the universal Equilibrium. One finds the idea of Mercy—as a teaching of the Virgin—in the following passage: "And her Lord (the Lord of St Anne: "spouse of Imran") accepted her (Mary) with full acceptance and vouchsafed to her a goodly growth;[4] and made Zachariah her guardian.[5] Whenever Zachariah went into the sanctuary (*mihrâb*)[6] where she was, he found that she had food.[7] He

---

3. And not the mere fact of being rich, because an outward situation is nothing in itself; a monarch is necessarily rich, and there have been holy monarchs. There is justification, nonetheless, in condemning the "rich" because, on average, possessors become attached to what they possess; conversely, only he is "poor" who is content with little.
4. An allusion to the avataric beauty of the Virgin and also, according to the commentators, to the growth of graces in her.
5. One will note that the name of Zachariah, which in Hebrew means "God remembers" (*Zekaryah*), contains in Arabic (*Zakarîyâ*) the root *zakara*, thus the meaning of "plenitude" and "abundance". The Arabic equivalent for the Hebrew *zekar* is *dhakara*, whence the word *dhikr*, "remembrance" (of God).
6. The reference here is to a place in the Temple of Jerusalem, reserved for the Blessed Virgin. The association of ideas between Mary and the prayer niche in mosques is commonly found among Muslims: in many mosques one finds the verse of Zachariah and Mary inscribed above the *mihrâb*, such is the case, notably, in Hagia Sophia, which thus remains dedicated to the Virgin even after the Byzantine era and under the Turks.
7. Winter fruits in summer and summer fruits in winter, as is specified by tradition; it likewise relates that Mary's apartment was closed by

said: O Mary! Whence cometh unto thee this (food)? She answered: It is from Allah. Allah giveth without stint to whom He will" (*Sûrah* of "The Family of Imran", 3:37).

This response is the very symbol of the Marian message according to the Koran; and even in other passages, where the name of Mary is not mentioned, this sentence in fact indicates an aspect of this message. "Beautified is the life of the world for those who disbelieve;[8] they make a jest of the believers. But those who keep their duty to Allah will be above them on the Day of Resurrection. Allah giveth without stint to whom He will" (*Sûrah* of "The Cow", 2:212). In this passage, one finds the key-phrase regarding Divine Generosity combined with the ideas—enunciated in the *Magnificat*—of the necessity of fear and of cosmic alternations, of the compensatory and the counterbalancing relationship between the here-below and the hereafter.

An analogous passage taken from the previously mentioned *Sûrah* ("The Family of Imran") is the following: "Say: O Allah (*Allâhumma*)! Owner of Sovereignty! Thou givest sovereignty unto whom Thou wilt, and Thou withdrawest sovereignty from whom Thou wilt. Thou exaltest whom Thou wilt, and Thou abasest whom Thou wilt. In Thy hand is the good. Lo! Thou art Able to do all things. Thou causest the night to pass into the day, and Thou causest the day to pass into the night. And Thou bringest forth the living from the dead, and Thou bringest forth the dead from the living. And Thou givest sustenance to whom Thou choosest, without stint" (26-27). One finds once again, along with the key-phrase, the idea of cosmic alternations.

Another passage: "O my people! Lo! This life of the world is but a passing comfort, and lo! the Hereafter, that is the enduring home. Whoso doeth an ill-deed, he will be repaid the like thereof, while whoso doeth right, whether male or female, and is a believer,[9] (all) such will enter the Garden, where they

seven doors, which evokes the symbolism of the "book seven times sealed".

8. Literally: "who cover (*kafarû*)", that is to say, who cover the Truth; these words contain an allusion to innate knowledge, though "covered" by passion and pride.

9. This qualification is crucial. It is faith that saves, not the deed as such; nonetheless, both faith and works are susceptible to complex and subtle, sometimes even paradoxical, assessments.

will be nourished without stint" (*Sûrah* of "The Believer", 40:39-40).

*

* *

One of the most important passages, both from the generally Islamic as well as from the specifically Marian point of view, is the Verse of Light along with the three verses that follow it: "Allah is the Light of the heavens and the earth. The similitude of His light is as a niche wherein is a lamp.[10] The lamp is in a glass. The glass is as it were a shining star. (This lamp is) kindled from a blessed tree, an olive neither of the East nor of the West, whose oil would almost glow forth (of itself) though no fire touched it. Light upon light Allah guideth unto His light whom He will. And Allah speaketh to mankind in allegories, for Allah is Knower of all things." Then, after this famous passage, come the following verses: "(This lamp is found) in houses which Allah hath allowed to be exalted and that His name shall be remembered therein. Therein do offer praise to Him at morn and evening. Men whom neither merchandise nor sale beguileth from remembrance of Allah and constancy in prayer and paying to the poor their due; who fear a day when hearts and eyeballs will be overturned; That Allah may reward them with the best of what they did, and increase reward for them of His bounty. Allah giveth blessings without stint to whom He will" (*Sûrah* of "Light", 24:35-8).

This group of verses evokes first of all the symbolism of the prayer-niche—a symbol itself of the mysteries of the Divine Light and of its modes of presence or immanence—and closes with the key-phrase of the Marian message, the words on Generosity. One likewise encounters an allusion to the Name of God and another to fear; finally, the Verse of Light contains the virginal symbols of the crystal, the star, the blessed tree,[11] and oil, which refer respectively to purity or the virginal body, to the *Stella Matutina* or the

---

10. It is actually a burning wick, and not a "lamp".
11. Within the framework of this particular symbolism, the words "neither of the East nor of the West" seem to indicate that the Virgin, in that she personifies both the universal *Shakti* and the *Sophia Perennis*, belongs exclusively neither to Christianity nor to Islam, but to both religions at the same time, or that she constitutes the link between the two.

115

Stella Maris, to spiritual maternity, and to the luminous fruitfulness or the blood of Mary—blood which, pertaining to the Divine Substance, shines by its own nature.

In its intrinsic meaning, the Verse of Light refers to the doctrine of the Self and Its refractions in cosmic manifestation; the connection with the Virgin is plausible since she personifies the receptive or passive aspects of Universal Intellection, and thus Beauty and Goodness; but she likewise incarnates—by virtue of the formless and indefinite nature of the Divine *Prakriti*—the ineffable essence of wisdom or sanctity and as a result the supraformal and primordial reality, at once virginal and maternal, of the saving coagulations of the Spirit.[12]

The Virgin is associated, in the consciousness of Muslims, not only with the prayer-niche, but also with the palm-tree: Mary finds herself beside a withered palm-tree in the wilderness; a voice cries out to her: "Shake the trunk of the palm-tree toward thee, thou wilt cause ripe dates to fall upon thee" (*Sûrah* of "Maryam", 19:25). The miracle of the palm-tree is a counterpart to the miracle of the niche: in both instances, Mary is nourished by God; however, in the first case, the fruits come without her having to do anything other than invoke God in the prayer-niche, whereas, in the second case, she must participate in the miracle; the first miracle is one of pure grace, and the second is one of active faith. It is easy to transpose this imagery onto the spiritual plane: these graces of orison rest either on a static and contemplative base, or on one that is dynamic and active. Invocation may arise from contentment or from distress; the soul is involved in these two modes so long as her exile lasts. To the perfection of quietude must be added the perfection of fervor; fervor entails an awareness of our existential distress, just as quietude entails our sense of immortality, of ontological beatitude, of infinitude in God.

12. According to Ruzbihan Baqli, a commentator of the Koran and patron saint of Shiraz, "Mary's substance is the substance of original sanctity". A Maghrebi Shaykh, who had no non-Koranic knowledge of Christianity, told us that Maryam personifies Clemency-Mercy (*Rahmah*) and that, for this reason, our era is especially dedicated to her. The essence of Mary—her "coronation"—is the Names *Rahmân* and *Rahîm*; she is thus the human manifestation of the *Basmalah* ("In the Name of God, the Beneficent, the Merciful").

*

* *

The Koran contains a particularly synthetic passage concerning less the "doctrine" of the Virgin than her "mystery": "And Mary, daughter of Imran,[13] whose body was chaste, therefor We breathed into her something of Our Spirit. And she believed in the words of her Lord and in His scriptures, and was of the obedient" (*Sûrah* of the "Banning", 66:12).

"Whose body was chaste": the Arabic term, which is very concrete, implies a symbolism of the heart: God introduced into the virgin heart an element of His Nature, which is to say that in reality He "opened" this heart to the transcendentally omnipresent Divine Spirit; but this Spirit remains in fact unknown to hearts because of their hardening, which is also the cause of their dissipation and impurity.

"We breathed therein something of Our Spirit": the image of breath evokes both the intimacy and the subtleness of the gift, its profundity, if one will. "Of Our Spirit": no divine manifestation can involve the Divine Spirit as such, or else this Spirit would henceforth be in the manifestation in question and no longer in God.

"And she had faith in the Words of her Lord and His Scriptures": the Words are inward certainties, the contents of the Intellect, which include essentially the metaphysical truths; the Scriptures are the revelations that come from the outside.[14] "To

---

13. The triliteral root of this name contains among other meanings that of "prosperity" and of "flowering", which well become her whom God "vouchsafed a goodly growth" and to whom He gave His sustenance "without stint" (*Sûrah* "The Family of Imran", 3:37). It should be noted that the words "daughter of Imran" link Mary, not only to her direct father but also to her ancestor, the father of Moses and of Aaron, whence the description "sister of Aaron" which the Koran likewise uses, meaning thereby to highlight that the spiritual, sacerdotal, and esoteric super-eminence of the brother of Moses is remanifested in Mary; in other words, the purpose is to show, on the one hand, that the Holy Virgin is of the same race as the two brother prophets and, on the other hand, that she is a prophetess, not law-giving and exoteric like Moses, but contemplative and esoteric like Aaron.

14. These specifications are made so as to forestall the objection that Mary accepted only the Scriptures, or only the Words, or that she remained passive without accepting anything in a positive way; these caveats are far from superfluous in a Semitic climate and in view of theology.

have faith" or "to accept as true" (*saddaqa*) means here, not to admit with difficulty and to retain superficially with the mind only, but to recognize immediately and to believe "sincerely", that is to say, by heeding the consequences, both outward and inward, that the truth implies and demands, whence the designation of *Siddîqah* that Islam confers upon the Blessed Virgin: "She who believes sincerely, totally".

"And she was of the obedient" (*qânitîn*): the Arabic term implies the meaning, not only of constant submission to God, but also absorption in prayer and invocation, meanings that coincide with the image of Mary spending her childhood in the prayer-niche; in this way, she personifies prayer and contemplation.

Muhyiddin Ibn Arabi, after declaring that his heart "has opened itself to all forms", and that it is "a cloister for monks, a temple of idols, the Kaaba",[15] adds: "I practice the religion of Love";[16] now it is over this formless religion that, Semitically speaking, Sayyidatna Maryam presides, thus identifying herself with the Supreme *Shakti* or the Celestial *Prajnâpâramitâ* of the Asian traditions.[17]

15. In "The Interpreter of Desires" (*Tarjumân al-Ashwâq*).
16. It is true that the author specifies in his commentary that this religion is "Islam", but he was doubtless obliged to do so in order to avoid a charge of heresy, and he could do so in good conscience by understanding the term *islâm* in its direct and universal meaning.
17. At the time of the persecution of Christianity in Japan, the Christians did not hesitate to make their devotions in front of statues of Kuan-Yin, the Buddhist goddess of Mercy. Another example of Marian universality, if one may so call it, is the following: the basilica of Our Lady of Guadalupe, near Mexico City—a famous place of pilgrimage—is built on a hill which in ancient times was consecrated to the mother-goddess Tonantzin, a divinity of the Earth and the Moon; this divinity appeared herself, in the form of an Aztec princess of great beauty, to a poor Indian, telling him that she was the "Mother of God" and that she wished to have a church on this spot. Another example: above the principal gate of Cordoba, now no longer extant, there was a statue of the Virgin; archaeologists think that it was the image of a Roman goddess identified by the Christians as Mary; the Muslims, when they came, respected the statue and in their turn venerated the statue of the Virgin-Mother as the patroness of Cordoba. But above all the following coincidence must be mentioned: it is not by chance that the town of Ephesus, where Mary was assumed into Heaven, was dedicated to Artemis, goddess of light, in that she was the sister of Apollo, and goddess of the moon, in view of her femininity, and identified by the Ionians with a foster-mother-goddess of perhaps Ori-

*

* *

The fact that the Islamic tradition records the super-eminent dignity of the Blessed Virgin presents a problem: if on the one hand the Logos is necessarily and self-evidently identified in Islam with the Founder of this religion,[18] and if on the other hand the feminine aspect of the Logos—inasmuch as it is taken into consideration—can be personified only by Maryam owing to her incomparable quality as attested to by the Koran and the *Sunnah*, then why did this personification have to appear outside the Arab world and in connection with the Founder of the Christian religion?[19] The reason for this is the following: it is precisely because Maryam is, in the world of monotheistic Semites, the only "feminization of the Divine", if one may say—or, in Hindu terms, the only avataric *Shakti* of Vishnu[20]—that she had to appear in all three of the monotheistic religions, and consequently on the threshold of Christianity. Had she been an Arab, she would have remained a stranger to the other two religions; had she lived in Israel before the time of Jesus, she would have remained a stranger to the Christian religion, or she would have anticipated this religion in some fashion;[21] being unique and incomparable both in Judaism—by virtue of her concrete personality as a Prophetess, whether understood or not—as well as in Christianity, by virtue of her function as Co-Redemptress, was *ipso facto* unique

ental origin; let us likewise recall that Artemis is the protectress of virginity and the beneficent guardian of the sea, and that she is thus both *virgo* and *stella maris*, and that her favorite animal is the hart, which in Christian symbolism represents the soul thirsting for the heavenly fatherland: "As the hart panteth after the water brooks, so panteth my soul after thee, O God" (Ps. 42:1).

18. But nonetheless without excluding, in the esoteric order, interferences by other manifestations of the Logos, notably that of Jesus, "Seal of Sanctity".

19. This is a question that makes no sense from the specifically Christian point of view; but what is at issue here is the Semitic and monotheistic world, taken both as a whole and with its three great traditional dimensions.

20. One *hadîth* places Mary by the side of Adam and above Eve, because of the privilege of having been breathed into by the Divine Spirit.

21. In itself a contradictory idea, but not devoid of sense or function—though provisional—in the present context.

and incomparable for Islam and therefore entitled to full rights of "spiritual citizenship" in this religion, like all the Semitic Prophets up to and including Christ. There was therefore no necessity, nor even any possibility, from the point of view of Islam—this question not arising for the other two religions—that Maryam should have a function in the genesis of the Muslim world; in her quality as the sole major *Shakti* in the monotheistic world, she held the one historical place she could have, and took on the one religious role she could assume.

Or again: if Maryam could appear neither in the Arab world nor in the Jewish world before Christ, it is because, owing to the very incomparability of her nature, she had to be linked to a masculine manifestation of "human Divinity";[22] now this manifestation, in the Semitic world, is precisely Christ; in other words, the possibility of such a manifestation in the Semitic world is the sufficient reason for the existence of Christianity from the point of view under consideration here.

Maryam belongs to Judaism by the fact of her personality, to Christianity by her particular function, and to Islam by her supereminence in the entire Abrahamic cosmos. The Jewish message of the Virgin is precisely the *Magnificat* inasmuch as it refers to Israel; this Canticle is at the same time her Christian message inasmuch as "Israel" is the Church and her Islamic message by the reference to the "seed of Abraham"; and this, as we have seen, is a message formulated in the Koran in the terms appropriate for Islam. In a word: Maryam fits into the Abrahamic-Muhammadan cycle by the fact that she belongs to the Sinaitic-Christic cycle, which for its part constitutes from the Muslim point of view, an internal dimension of the first cycle.[23]

---

22. Brahmanically speaking, an avataric woman is necessarily the *Shakti* of an *Avatâra*; thus she has to appear with him; she could appear neither alone nor, quite clearly, in a spiritual climate whose perspective providentially excludes the notion of "Divine Descents".
23. Moses and Aaron open the Sinaitic cycle; Jesus and Mary complete it. From another point of view, however, this cycle is perpetuated in the form of Jewish orthodoxy, which as a matter of fact would lose none of its specific orthodoxy—established on the perpetuity of the Law—if in the general context of its message it accepted Jesus as a prophet of esoterism and a spiritual renewer, or if at least it left the question open; for Jesus does not "destroy" the Law, but "fulfills" it. Be that as it may, the Koranic

The Virginal Doctrine

This having been said, it is relevant to add that the Marian wisdom is necessarily an expression of Christic wisdom, to which it adds—or from which it extracts—an aspect proper to itself, and it is precisely this aspect that is enunciated in the verse of the prayer-niche;[24] whereas the doctrine of cosmic or human alternations is Marian because it is Christic, the doctrine of sustenance received from God—or "from the Inward"—is properly Marian, along with the virginal and maternal graces emanating from the very person of the Blessed Virgin. The following saying of Jesus is Marian in spirit: "Man shall not live by bread alone, but by every word that proceedeth out of the mouth of God" (Matt. 4:4); and likewise this saying: "My yoke is easy, and my burden is light" (Matt. 11:30). With regard to the *Magnificat* and to its Biblical anticipations, it is in no wise contradictory to term "Christic" a teaching formulated even before the birth of Christ, given on the one hand the cosmic and spiritual inseparability of Jesus and Mary, and on the other the unity or timelessness of the Logos considered here in its Semitic and monotheistic manifestation.[25]

The spirituality that is properly Marian could be summarized in these terms: to become pure prayer, or pure receptivity before God—*Gratia plena*—so as to be nourished by Him alone; for Maryam, the Divine Quintessence of this bread—or of this "sustenance" (*rizq*)[26]—was Isa, "Word of God" (*Kalîmatu 'Llâh*) and "Spirit of God" (*Rûhu 'Llâh*), this Bread on which she lives in Eternity and on which she was already living, inwardly, during her childhood in the Temple.

*
* *

designation "sister of Aaron" given to Mary indicates in its way the complementary relationship shared by these two cosmic miracles that were Sinai and Christ.
24. The most direct Koranic expression of this aspect, or of this Marian mystery, is probably the following verse: "And Allah is the best of providers" (*Sûrah* of "The Congregation", 62:11). The Divine Name that corresponds to this idea is "the Provider" (*Ar-Razzâq*), whence the Muslim name "Servant of the Provider", *'Abd Ar-Razzâq*, which has something of a Marian connotation.
25. See the preceding chapter in this book, "The Koranic Message of Sayyidna Isa".
26. The same verbal root as *Razzâq*, the above-mentioned Divine Name.

121

That the Blessed Virgin, speaking spontaneously, would express herself in Biblical terms will be easy to understand for anyone who has an idea of what the relationship can be between innate knowledge and formal Revelation in the soul of a being such as Mary. We would now like to quote the main Biblical passages in which the words of the *Magnificat* are in some fashion prefigured—if it is permitted to express oneself thus[27]—and we shall do so in the same order as the ideas appear in this Canticle.

"Yet I will rejoice in the Lord, I will joy in the God of my salvation" (Hab 3:18).

"Who is like unto the Lord our God, who dwelleth on high, who humbleth himself to behold the things that are in heaven, and in the earth! He raiseth up the poor out of the dust, and lifteth the needy out of the dunghill" (Ps. 113:5-7).

"The Lord hath done great things for us; whereof we are glad. . . . They that sow in tears shall reap in joy" (Ps.126:3, 5).

"He sent redemption unto his people: he hath commanded his covenant for ever: holy and reverend is his name. The fear of the Lord is the beginning of wisdom" (Ps. 111:9-10).

"Like as a father pitieth his children, so the Lord pitieth them that fear him. . . . But the mercy of the Lord is from everlasting to everlasting upon them that fear him, and his righteousness unto children's children; to such as keep his covenant,[28] and to those that remember his commandments to do them" (Ps. 103:13, 17-18).

"Thou hast broken Rahab[29] in pieces, as one that is slain; thou hast scattered thine enemies with thy strong arm" (Ps. 89:10).

---

27. It is permissible precisely in the sense that this orison is an inspiration in its turn, and not, as some have imagined, an improvisation based on prior readings.
28. This reservation is crucial; it indicates at one and the same time both the relativity and universality of the notion of "Israel".
29. This name is synonymous with Leviathan: this is a monster which personifies the primordial chaos under its "watery" aspect, if one will, and which in fact is killed by God, by the *Fiat Lux*. The name of Rahab is also applicable to the Egypt of tyranny, idolatry, and the practice of magic, the only one the Hebrews knew. The flight into Egypt by the Holy Family is like an homage to the other Egypt, that of the sages; and it is not without significance that it took place in the footsteps of the first Joseph, the patriarch, who found there blessing and glory.

"And the afflicted people thou wilt save: but thine eyes are upon the haughty, that thou mayest bring them down" (2 Sam. 22:28).

"Awake, awake, put on strength, O arm of the Lord; awake, as in the ancient days, in the generations of old. Art Thou not it that hath cut Rahab, and wounded the dragon?" (Isa. 51:9).

"The voice of him that crieth in the wilderness, Prepare ye the way of the Lord, make straight in the desert a highway for our God. Every valley shall be exalted, and every mountain and hill shall be made low: and the crooked shall be made straight, and the rough places plain. And the glory of the Lord shall be revealed, and all flesh shall see it together: for the mouth of the Lord hath spoken it" (Isa. 40:3-5).[30]

"To set up on high those that be low; that those which mourn may be exalted to safety. He disappointeth the devices of the crafty, so that their hands cannot perform their enterprise" (Job 5:11-12).

"For he satisfieth the longing soul, and filleth the hungry soul with goodness" (Ps. 107:9).

"But thou, Israel, art my servant, Jacob whom I have chosen, the seed of Abraham my friend. Thou whom I have taken from the ends of the earth, and called thee from the chief men thereof, and said unto thee, Thou art my servant; I have chosen thee, and not cast thee away. Fear thou not; for I am with thee: be not dismayed; for I am thy God: I will strengthen thee; yea, I will help thee; yea, I will uphold thee with the right hand of my righteousness" (Isa. 41:8-10).

"He hath remembered his mercy and his truth toward the house of Israel: all the ends of the earth have seen the salvation of our God" (Ps. 98:3).

"And I will establish my covenant between me and thee and thy seed after thee in their generations for an everlasting

---

30. This passage, taken up again by St Luke (3:4-6), evokes the equilibrium-restoring function of the Principle; that is to say, there is a reference here both to Divine Justice, which is immanent in a certain sense, and to Universal Harmony (the *Prakriti* of the Hindus), which is benefic as well as implacable; it is this Harmony that she who has been called the "divine Mary" incarnates.

covenant, to be a God unto thee, and to thy seed after thee" (Gen. 17:7).

Finally, the canticle of Hannah, mother of Samuel, summarizes the whole doctrine of the *Magnificat*: "My heart rejoiceth in the Lord, mine horn is exalted in the Lord. . . ."[31] The bows of the mighty men are broken, and they that stumbled are girded with strength. They that were full have hired out themselves for bread; and they that were hungry ceased. . . . The Lord killeth, and maketh alive: he bringeth down to the grave, and bringeth up.[32] The Lord maketh poor, and maketh rich: he bringeth low, and lifteth up. He raiseth up the poor out of the dust, and lifteth up the beggar from the dunghill. . . . He will keep the feet of his saints, and the wicked shall be silent in darkness. . . . He shall give strength unto his king, and exalt the horn of his anointed" (1 Sam. 2:1, 4-10).

31. The horn symbolizes strength; the exaltation of the horn is success, prosperity, and the victory given by God.
32. "I kill, and I make alive; I wound, and I heal: neither is there any that can deliver out of my hand" (Deut. 32:39).

Synthesis of the *Pâramitâs*

When considering the most prominent thesis of the *Mahâyâna*, that which distinguishes it most characteristically from *Theravâda* Buddhism, one might be inclined to suppose that, in its general form, it is a way of love, analogous to the *bhakti* of India or of Christianity; it is important, however, not to isolate this appearance from its total context, and to know that *Mahâyâna* comprises essentially two poles, first the thesis of the universal charity of the *Bodhisattva*, and second the metaphysics of the "Void", which, despite some differences in perspective that led to the opposition between Shankara and Nagarjuna, corresponds strictly to *Advaita-Vedânta*. Far from appearing only in the guise of an implicit gnosis, and veiled by a language typical of a mysticism of love, this metaphysics asserts itself directly in numerous Sutras and makes itself known as the reason for being of the whole *Mahâyâna*; it determines its entire doctrinal corpus to such a degree that the charity, which is its point of departure, finds itself infused by this metaphysics. The point of departure of the way— the *Bodhisattvayâna*—corresponds to an awareness of the "void-ness" of all things, and not merely to a moral option; the ego of the aspirant identifies itself at the outset with the whole *samsâra*; in understanding the nature of the *samsâra*, the soul frees itself from its error and begins the realization of the universal Body of the Buddha.

Before proceeding further, we want to respond to a question concerning a phenomenon, at first sight paradoxical, which seems to lie at the root of *Mahayâna* alone: what is the meaning of the assertion, made by the Northern Buddhists, that in the early days of Buddhism the times were not yet "ripe" for the public preaching of the Mahayanist Sutras and that, until then—that is, until the epoch of Nagarjuna—these Sutras had remained either hidden or secret, and protected by the genii, the *nâgas*, against all profanation?[1] The key to the enigma lies in the fact that some aspects of a Revelation require an appropriate field of resonance; this is to say that tradition has the role, not only of communicating vital truths, but also of creating a setting adapted to the manifestation of modes of a particular character.

This is a phenomenon that occurs to one degree or another in all religions. In every religion, several centuries after its foundation, one sees a new flowering or a kind of second youth; and this is due to the fact that the presence of a collective and material ambience, realized by the religion itself, creates conditions allowing, or requiring, the unfolding of an apparently new kind: in the West, the Middle Ages, with its great saints of a particular type, its chivalry, and its sacred art—fully developed and perfected, and thus definitive and irreplaceable—was the Christian epoch par excellence; and this was so in a manner different from the first centuries of Christianity, which, in another respect, clearly retain the superiority of their original perfection. In Islam, likewise, the epoch of Ibn Arabi—who was the "pole" of his age—coincides with a world elaborated over several centuries of Islam and presents, on the plane of esoterism, a very ample and profound flowering, at times close to the initial prophetic atmosphere.

In Buddhism, this law or this possibility appears on an order of magnitude unknown elsewhere, and this is what establishes the originality of the *Mahâyâna*, not from the point of view of the content, but as a phenomenon: far from constituting just a perplexing enigma, this unfolding of the Buddhist Revelation is in fact a perfectly limpid possibility which was bound to manifest in its place and time with the full plenitude of its potential. In speaking of the *Mahâyâna*, we mean to include the *Vajrayâna*—Buddhist Tantrism—which is sometimes presented as a "third setting in motion of the Law", and which repeats in its own fashion, within the framework of *Mahâyâna* itself, the same unfolding we have just mentioned. But whether it is the one or the other, or

---

1. The *nâgas* are represented as serpents; their symbolism—like that of dragons—as guardians of treasures or sacred precincts is well known.

whether—in *Mahâyâna* terminology—it is the *Hinâyâna*, it is important to understand that there can be no effect without a cause: what we wish to say is that the sole possible cause of the values traditionally connected with the Buddha is the Buddha himself and no other; the homage granted him by Brahmanists, including Shankara, is one more indication among many other signs of the avataric scope of the personage.

In order to better characterize the profound intention or the meaning of the *Mahâyâna*, we would like to draw attention to the following factors: Buddhism, without ever forsaking its serenity, has something vertiginously quantitative in one of its aspects, something desperately riveted to "horizontal" causality, or to action and merit, and something moreover radically misogynist, if such an expression is permissible: one has the impression of losing oneself in myriads of *kalpas* and in accumulations of seemingly limitless merits and demerits. Buddhism intends thus to suggest the nature of the *Samsâra*, which is a bottomless abyss, a measureless system of concentric circles and at the same time a spiral motion without beginning or end,[2] or with no other beginning or end than that which limits it metaphysically, and this is the *Nirvâna* that envelops all, absorbs all, extinguishes all. Now in esoterism, the hopeless number of quantities is reduced to mere mirages, femininity is grasped in its universal essence, and Deliverance becomes a flash of lightning; what is thus affirmed is the eternal truth that our Deliverance was ever before us, and that in the apparently insuperable difficulty there is a secret point where all becomes easy— mystery of intellection according to Zen, *Shingon*, and *Tendai*, mystery of grace according to *Jôdo*. After countless efforts worth no more than a gesture, man is breathed in by the Heavens and falls upwards, as it were, into his own Deliverance; our merits have no positive value: they do but eliminate—more symbolically than effectively—the obstacles that cut us off from celestial attraction.

Every spiritual cycle, whatever its order of magnitude, comprises such alternations. On earth, Rigor appears before Mercy, if only to prepare the advent of the latter; in the celestial regions,

---

2. All of this is of course related to the extreme precariousness of the chances of entering the human state, which is to the other states what the center is to the periphery, or the point to extension.

however, Mercy precedes Rigor and coincides in its substance with the beatific dimension of the Absolute Itself.

*

* *

"Charity" (*dâna*), which constitutes as it were the framework or the periphery of the *Mahâyâna*, is the first of the six *pâramitâs* or virtues of the *Bodhisattva*; "wisdom" (*prajnâ*) is the sixth and their completion. The four other *pâramitâs* appear as intermediary virtues: these are "renunciation" (*shîla*), "virility" (*vîrya*), "patience" (*kshânti*), and "contemplation" (*dhyâna*); these spiritual modes amount to so many paths, at once simultaneous and successive—a single one being able to determine a whole life, but without either needing or being able to exclude the daily practice of the others. Moreover, the first five *pâramitâs* are not really separate from the virtue of *prajnâ*, of which they are secondary aspects whose function is to contribute in their way to the awakening of liberating Knowledge.

The essence of the *Mahâyâna* as a method is really the "transfer of our merits to others" (*parinâmana*): "Enlightenment" as well as "Salvation" embrace, in their moral intention and in the metaphysical scheme of things, all beings of the visible and invisible universe. If the *Bodhisattva* is supposed to "refuse to enter *Nirvâna* so long as a single blade of grass remains undelivered", this means two things: first—and this is the cosmic viewpoint— that the function of the *Bodhisattva* coincides with what in Western language would be termed the permanent "angelic presence" in the world, a presence disappearing only with the world itself, at the time of the final reintegration known by Western gnosis as the *apocatastasis*; and second—and this is the metaphysical viewpoint—that the *Bodhisattva*, in realizing the "nothingness" of things, realizes thereby not only the "void" of the *Samsâra* as such but, by the same token, its nirvanic quality. For if on the one hand everything is "void", on the other hand everything is *Nirvâna*, the Buddhist notion of emptiness being both negative and positive as is expressed in the saying: "Form is void and Void is form". The *Samsâra*, which seems at first to be inexhaustible, so much so that the Bodhisattvic vow appears to have something excessive or even demented about it, is "instantly" reduced—in the timeless instantaneity of *prajnâ*—to "universal Enlightenment" (*Sambodhi*); on this plane, all antinomy is transcended and as it were consumed. "Delivering the last blade of grass" amounts in this respect to seeing it in its nirvanic essence, or to seeing the unreality of its non-deliverance.

Since *Prajnâ* is the synthesis of the five other *pâramitâs*, the *Mahâyâna* is reducible in principle to *prajnâ*; in other words, the inward union with the transcendent "Void" could suffice in principle as a spiritual viaticum; however, because human nature is in fact contrary to unity and simplicity, the method of regeneration will therefore have to take account of all aspects of our samsaric imprisonment, whence the necessity for a path which, while presenting at the outset an element of unity and simplicity, proceeds from the multiple to the one and from the complex to the simple.[3]

It is not hard to see how the first five virtues or spiritual methods are contained in the sixth: first of all, there is no possible gnosis without an element of renunciation or detachment; outwardly, gnosis of necessity comprises a factor of moral alternative on which it can base itself and which enables it to unfold. Likewise, gnosis requires virility or "heroicalness": it comprises, indeed, an aspect of battle against samsaric seductions, both inward and outward; there is no spiritual victory without "the fight with the dragon". To the virtues of rigor, the virtues of mildness are adjoined, namely, charity and patience; just as patience is, by its nature, the *shakti*—the complementary power—of renunciation, so charity is the *shakti* of virility. Gnosis requires, if one may put it this way, an element of generosity and another of beauty: the "mathematical" and "masculine" aspect has need of a "musical" and "feminine" complement, the whole universe being woven of this warp and woof; without beauty, truth cannot manifest itself and still remain true to itself and yield its full message. Referring to the canonical image of the Buddha, we could express ourselves in the following manner: if the Buddha represents renunciation, the lotus supporting him will be patience; if he represents virility,

---

3. This is what—let it be said in passing—neither pseudo-Zenists nor pseudo-Vedantists want to understand: they fancy that it is possible to make our nature disappear with mental reductions that are as pretentious as they are unavailing.

the lotus will be charity; if he is Supreme Knowledge, the lotus will be contemplation, with all the virtues this entails.

*

* *

Amidism, which was taught in China by Tan-Luan, Tao-Cho, and Shan-Tao, then in Japan by Honen and Shinran, appears in some respects as a merciful synthesis of the six *pâramitâs*: "Universal Enlightenment" is latent in everything since each thing, being "void", "is none other than the Void"; now this Enlightenment can as it were sweep the individual into its embrace through the merciful *upâya* that is the remembrance of Amitabha as actualized by the formula *Namo'mitâbhaya Buddhâya*; since spiritual realization exist "prior" to man, man, who possesses no more reality of his own than foam possesses in relation to water, "falls" into his preexisting *Nirvâna*, which takes the initiative, so to speak, in its capacity as *Bodhi*, "Enlightenment". In these conditions—strange as it may seem—it is *Nirvâna* "in act" that assumes the *pâramitâs*; this is what is known in the tradition as the "power of the Other", in contrast with the "power of Oneself", which is the spiritual principle of ordinary Buddhism as also for those esoterisms that are independent of the cult of Amitabha, such as Zen or *Shingon*.

This celestial gift of *pâramitâs* that are fulfilled in advance— or this saving grace bestowed in function of their prior realization by Amitabha, who is at once the projection both of the universal Buddha and the historical Buddha—is included in the Buddha's "Original Vow", in reality a cosmic or divine act upon which the whole doctrine of the "Pure Land" is erected.[4] Partic-

---

4. There are forty-eight vows (*pranidhânas*); only the eighteenth, which is by far the most important and which Honen qualified as the "king of vows", is the "Original Vow": "When I shall have attained the state of a Buddha, if the beings of the ten regions (of the universe) shall have believed in me with serene thoughts and shall have wished to be born in my Country and shall have thought of me be it only ten times—if these beings are not to be reborn there, then may I not obtain perfect Knowledge; none are excepted save those who shall have committed the five mortal sins and shall have blasphemed the Good Law" (The greater *Sukhâvatî-Vyûha-Sûtra* 8:18, according to the Chinese translation, the surviving Sanskrit texts being incomplete). The "ten times" of the text also has the meaning of "ten modes", such as thought, speech, vision, gesture.

ipation by devotees in the *pâramitâs* is then reduced essentially to faith, three aspects of which, or three "mental states", are distinguishable: "truthful thought" or a "sincere spirit", "deeply believing thought", the "desire to be reborn in the Pure Land".[5]

However, the *pâramitâs* are not contained in these mental attitudes alone; they are above all inherent in the "remembrance of the Buddha" (*buddhânusmriti*) itself:[6] this is to say that perpetual remembrance is at once renunciation or purity, virility or persevering activity, patience or peace, generosity or fervor, contemplation or discernment, wisdom or union. Indeed, to abide in this single remembrance, or in the act that fixes it in duration by reducing time to an eternal instant, does not go without renunciation of the world and of oneself; this allows us, by the same token, to understand what role the *pâramitâ* of virility plays here: if renunciation (*shîla*) is a participation in Eternity, virility (*vîrya*), for its part, will be situated under the sign of the Eternal Present, like the lightning bolt or the "third Eye". As for patience (*kshânti*), it consists, within the context of "remembrance", in abiding calmly in the Center, in the grace of Amitabha, whereas charity (*dâna*) is on the contrary a projecting of the ego into the distance, or the extending of the will outside the individual shell: if patience is founded on our awareness of possessing everything in grace, charity will be our awareness of living in all things, and of extending our spiritual activity to all creation. The remembrance of Amitabha also

5. According to the *Amitâyur-Dhyâna-Sûtra*, 22, the first-named state excludes all dissimulation and all lukewarmness; the second state, according to Honen, implies an awareness on the one hand of our misery and helplessness, and on the other hand of the saving power of Amitabha and his wish to save us if we invoke him with faith. The third mental state means that we offer all of our merits for the sole intention of being born in the "Pure Land", and that at the same time, within the scope of this intention itself, we take pleasure in the merits of others as if those others were ourselves; this attitude confers on our path a secret radiance and a kind of impersonal amplitude.

6. It should be pointed out here that, despite its divergent form, the Tibetan invocatory formula *Om Mani Padme Hum*, by virtue of its homage to the "Jewel" and the "Lotus", is equivalent to the Japanese *Namu Amida Butsu*; it is in effect addressed to the *Bodhisattva* Avalokiteshvara and for that reason also to the Buddha Amitabha of whom this *Bodhisattva* is an extension.

implies, with all the more reason, contemplation (*dhyâna*) and Knowledge (*prajnâ*); the latter corresponds in some respect to Plenitude and the former to the Void. We have already seen that the "Void" has both a negative and a positive meaning; in its positive meaning it can be termed "Plenitude". The "Void" is "Plenitude" inasmuch as It is opposed to the samsaric "nothingness", not inasmuch as It constitutes its Quintessence, for in this respect all is Plenitude and all is Void.

These relationships could be described even more simply by specifying that the synthesis of the *pâramitâs* finds its most distinct realization in the two conditions *sine qua non* of the *nembutsu* which are "faith" and "action": action summarizes the active virtues and faith the contemplative virtues, though both the one and the other comprise static and dynamic elements, such as abstention in the case of action and ardor in the case of faith. Moreover, these two categories bring us back to the twin pillars of all spirituality: "discernment" and "concentration", or doctrine and method; in fact, all possible intellectual, psychic, and moral qualities are to be found under these two denominators for they pertain either to intelligence or to the will, and thus describe—by indicating what we should be—what we are in our innate and eternal "Buddhahood".

*
* *

According to a spatial symbolism in use in the *Mahâyâna*, the universal Buddhas or the *Dhyâni-Buddha*s, also called *Jinas*, the "Victorious Ones", come forth by projection from the *Âdi-Buddha*: they are five in number and each rules over a cardinal point—the most eminent of them being Vairochana who is situated at the Center.[7] To Vairochana corresponds analogically the element ether; to Akshobhya, who is in the East, corresponds the element air; to Amitabha, the West and water; to Amoghasiddhi, the North and earth; to Ratnasambhava, the South and fire. Now ether is everywhere, and everywhere it is central and immutable, like truth

---

7. Depending on the school, it is either Vairochana, or Vajradhara, or Amitabha, who is identified with the Supreme; many another fluctuation could be mentioned, especially where the quaternary is divided into two or is multiplied, each time with its attendant *Bodhisattva*s and *Shakti*s.

or contemplation; the sun rises in the East, invincible like a sword unsheathed, and invincible is air unleashed as a hurricane; the West indicates repose, as does water, which gathers tranquilly and endures all things; the North is cold like purity, and the earth is firm like renunciation; and the South possesses warmth and life, and it is generous like charity. The *Âdhi-Buddha*—or *Prajnâpâramitâ*—is symbolically situated at the Zenith or beyond space; with respect to the sensible elements, including ether, he rules over the supra-sensible element, namely consciousness, which means that he is to be identified, not with the cosmic principles or, to be more precise, with modes of relative knowledge as is the case with the *Dhyâni-Buddhas*,[8] but with Absolute Knowledge, which embraces all relativities while remaining outside them.

In *Shingon* esoterism, the open fan of the five elements is closed again within "Consciousness", which is the sixth and superior element: to be *Buddha* is to know totally the nature of apparently external phenomena; it is therefore to know that they have no substance different from ourselves. To affirm that the Bodhisattva sees nothing but the "void" (*shûnya*) means that he perceives only the "emptiness" (*shûnyatâ*) of things, or that he beholds things in their aseity, which is identical with that of consciousness;[9] the elements are like the outward diversification, or like crystallized aspects, of this single consciousness; he who beholds the world beholds himself, and he who realizes the depths of the heart contains the world. The synthesis of the five objective elements in the sixth, which is subjective, prefigures in its own way the spiritual synthesis of the *pâramitâs*: in other words, earth, water, air, fire, ether—taken in their broadest meaning—are, all told, the outward and cosmic appearances of the first five *pâramitâs*, while the sixth element—*chitta* or consciousness—is by the same token the natural prefiguration of the sixth virtue, *prajnâ*.[10] An analogous

---

8. Who correspond to the four archangels of Islam, Vairochana—at the Center—being the equivalent of *Ar-Rûh*.
9. This vision of the "emptiness" of things is not unrelated to the fact that a noble man sees in every phenomenon the essential, whereas a vile man sees the accidental; now the "essence" of things rejoins their "voidness" in that it is an opening toward the non-manifested or the manifestation of an archetype.
10. Esoterically, the lotus on which the Buddha is enthroned represents innate and latent knowledge, whereas the halo expresses the effective Knowledge realized by the *Tathâgata*.

synthesis is achieved in Zen, where the path consists in discovering the infinite aseity of the heart and thereby in realizing, as in a lightning flash, "that which is".

But let us return to the synthesis brought about by the Vow of Amitabha: this synthesis has a special relationship not only with the symbolism of the West, the setting sun, and the element water, but thereby also with the virtue of patience; at the same time, this perspective of *bhaktic* esoterism[11] identifies Amitabha with the *Âdi-Buddha*, so that the symbolism of the evening or of freshness, and also of patience, is granted a preponderant and somehow central significance; trusting abandonment to the "Power of the Other" and to salvific grace pertains indeed to the nature of water and to "passive Perfection". The man whose heart rests in the supernatural certitude of salvific grace need only await, humanly speaking, the dissipation of all *karmic* effects; he is patient under the weight of the *Samsâra* which he must still bear and which, for him, will exhaust itself like his own earthly destiny. Clearly, this perfection of trust or quietude cannot be a matter purely and simply of passivity; in other words, it would amount to nothing if it did not comprise, quite essentially, the complementary aspects of activity and impassivity; each *pâramitâ* is like a mirror that reflects objects without ceasing to be what it is; there is no spiritual patience without a concomitant renunciation and strength. This is the unmistakable meaning of *Amidist* texts, as seen in these words from the illustrious Honen:[12] "The man who longs for Paradise and who sets his whole mind on this single intention will behave like someone who detests or even abhors the world."—"As for the passage (in the book of Shan-Tao) on a heart strong as a diamond, which allows nothing to either trouble or vanquish it . . . it means that we must not let our merits[13] be squandered in any direction whatsoever. . . . Seeing that diamond is an indestructible substance, may it serve then as an example to show us that neither should the heart allow itself to be broken in its resolve to reach the goal."

---

11. Hence of relative esoterism, which does not exclude, in its kernel, the profoundest gnosis for whosoever has the calling to discover it.
12. *Honen: The Buddhist Saint* (Kyoto, 1949), Vol. 3, Ch. 21:8, 22:10.
13. That is, the benefic forces emanating from the accumulation of our past merits, or good *karma*.

A Note on the Feminine Element in *Mahâyâna*

"Transcendent Wisdom" (*prajnâ*), the most exalted of the six spiritual disciplines (*pâramitâs*), is personified in a divinity bearing the very name of Prajnaparamita; if man becomes wise, it is in fact owing to pre-existing Wisdom whose function, at once virginal and maternal, is Its inherent Beatitude and Mercy. This divinity is the "Mother of all the Buddhas" and thus is not without analogy to the goddess Tara or more specifically to the "White Tara", who is also equated with "Transcendent Wisdom" (*Prajnâ*); Mongols call her "Mother Tara" (*Dara Eke*) and designate her as "Mother of all the Buddhas and *Boddhisattvas*", whereas Tibetans give her the name of "Savior" (*Döl-Ma*). Seen from the point of view of the human support or of the "glorious body",[1] one can recognize Prajnaparamita or Tara in queen Maya, mother of the historical Buddha:[2] just as the Buddha can be said to be a mani-

---

1. This is the *sambhoga-kâya*, or beatific body, which is situated between the earthly body, *nirmâna-kâya*, and the divine body, *dharma-kâya*.
2. "He (the king Shakya) had a queen called Maya, as if to say that she was free from all illusion (*mâyâ*): a splendor proceeding from his splendor, like the sun's magnificence when it is free from any obscuring influence; a queen supreme in the assembly of all queens. Like a mother for her subjects . . . she was the most eminent of goddesses for the whole world. But queen Maya, having beheld the great glory of her newborn child . . . could not sustain the joy he brought to her; and so as not to die of it, she ascended to Heaven" (The *Buddha-Karita* of Ashvagosha, 1:15–16; 2:18). According to one *Jâtaka*, "the mother of a Buddha . . . is a person who has realized perfections throughout a hundred thousand *kalpas* and who has been faithful to the five precepts from the day of her birth." Guénon has remarked that "the mother of the Buddha is called *Mâyâ-Devî* and that,

festation of the Absolute Buddha—the *Ādi-Buddha* or Vajradhara, or Mahavairochana depending on the various terminologies—so does his august Mother manifest the complementary power of the universal Buddha, or the saving grace inherent in *Nirvāna* and emanating from It.[3]

Since "extremes meet", it is telling that the most intellectual and most ascetic attitude, thus in a way the most "virile" possible, namely Knowledge (*prajnā-pāramitā*), coincides with a feminine principle, as if, at the very height or depth of abstraction or annihilation, there occurred a kind of compensatory reversal; in Vedantin terms, one would say that *Ātmā*, while being perfectly *Sat* and *Chit*, Being and Knowledge, comprises thereby—and necessarily so—*Ānanda*, Beatitude. The use of the symbolism of femininity may seem surprising in a Buddhist climate; though it is true that feminine symbols refer in the first instance, quite evidently, to universal realities that have nothing human about them, the human concomitances of the symbol nonetheless are what they are: in other words, the immediate human significance of the image retains all of its rights without there being any reason to fear irreducible antinomies or moral conflicts. Sages are the first to understand that femininity itself is independent of earthly accidentality or of the contingent, samsaric aspects of the carnal creature; though it be opportune to turn away from seductions and, in some respects, from the enfettering chain of attachments, regardless of the nature of their supports, it is however neither possible nor desirable to escape from the principle of femininity,

with the Greeks and Romans, Maïa was also the mother of Hermes or Mercury." – "The Annunciation takes the form of 'Maha Maya's dream', in which she sees a glorious white elephant descending from the skies to enter her womb. . . . It is not explicit, but can be presumed, that the birth was 'virgin'; in any case it is interesting that the story was already known to Hieronymus, who mentions it in a discussion of virginity and in connection with the miraculous births of Plato and Christ" (Ananda K. Coomaraswamy, *Hinduism and Buddhism*, "The Myth").

3. Analogous remarks could be made about Gopa Yashodhara, the spouse of Shakyamuni, and about their son Rahula. All the nobility of this wife shines forth in the fact that she grieved, not for the simple reason that Shakyamuni had left her, but because he had not taken her with him in his exile so as to share in his austerities; she understood the reason for this later and entered the Buddha's community.

which is nirvanic in essence and hence divine. The more or less asexual nature of the divinities of the *Mahâyâna* pertains only to privative contingent possibilities and not to their positive substance; thus the fluctuations found in Mahayanist imagery and in its eso-exoteric interpretations indicate in their own way the complexity of all these relationships and the human embarrassment in the face of this complexity. If a woman is supposed to "despise her femininity"[4] in the paradise of Amitabha, this means that she is entirely freed from the physiological and psychological servitude of her earthly condition, but not from her heavenly substance; otherwise the power of taking on a "feminine form" attributed to divinities described as either "masculine" or "asexual" would be meaningless; the ostracism of the dogmatic formulation is proportional to the sincerity of the renunciation. We have here two perspectives that intertwine and modulate each other: in the first, woman is considered as the principal factor of seduction chaining one to the *samsâra*, so much so as to appear to be the very genius of the latter; the second perspective, which is so to speak the opposite side of the same circle, femininity reveals itself instead in its positive reality as maternity, virginity, beauty, and mercy;[5] this is the Christian opposition—or complemen-

---

4. According to the greater *Sukhâvati-Vyûha* which, together with the lesser *Sukhâvati-Vyûha* and the *Amitâyur-Dhyâna-Sûtra*, is the chief scriptural authority for Amidism. Christian symbolism according to which "one neither marries nor is given in marriage" in Heaven, refers to this aspect of things, whereas the Muslim symbolism of the houris derives from the same perspective as Tantrism.

5. It should be noted in the present context that the whole *Amitâyur-Dhyâna-Sûtra* is addressed by the Buddha to a woman, the queen Vaidehi, just as the lesser *Sukhâvati-Vyûha* does not fail to specify that it is addressed to women as well as men, even though at first the admission of women into the fold of Buddhism did not take place without some difficulty. "Whatever son or daughter of a family shall hear the name of the blessed Amitayus (an aspect of Amitabha), the *Tathâgata* ("He thus come"), and having heard it shall keep it in mind . . . when that son or daughter of a family comes to die, then that Amitayus, the *Tathâgata*, surrounded by an assembly of disciples and followed by a host of *Bodhisattvas*, will stand before them at their hour of death, and they will depart this life with tranquil minds. After their death they will be reborn in the Sukhavati world, in the Buddha country of the same Amitayus, the *Tathâgata*. Therefore then, O Sariputra . . . every son and every daughter of a family ought with his whole mind to make fervent prayers in view of that Buddha country."

137

tarity—between Eve and Mary. And this is important: in regard to Heaven, each creature is considered to have a "feminine" character; this is why it is said that each soul is a *gopî* in love with Krishna; however, from the point of view of participatory analogy—not of complementary opposition—each soul is considered instead to have something "masculine", and this is what Buddhism has in mind when it seems to want to forbid women access to Heaven. This, we must insist again, is independent of the question of the "glorious body", which belongs to an altogether different order, cosmic and not spiritual.

In certain sectors of Buddhism there exists, incontestably and even of necessity, a direct or indirect tendency to interiorize femininity and sexuality, and not simply to reject it—whence the possibility of marriage, unthinkable at the origin, for some adepts in certain branches of the *Mahâyâna*, in Tibet and especially in Japan; the example of Shinran, disciple of Honen, is particularly noteworthy.[6] Leaving aside all the requirements of ascetic and disciplinary dogmatism, Buddhist asexualism is really but a means of affirming the idea of "voidness", or one might say that asexuality expresses an aspect of the "void";[7] hence it is said that the Bodhisattva sees nothing but the "void", which must be understood in a negative or samsaric sense as well as in a positive or nirvanic sense.[8]

– "Every son or daughter of a family who shall hear the name of that Enunciation of the Law and keep in memory the names of those blessed Buddhas will be favored by the Buddhas and will never again return, being once in possession of the transcendent Wisdom" (The lesser *Sukhâvatî-Vyûha*, 10, 17).

6. We could mention here the visit Honen received on his deathbed from Queen Vaidehi, the famous woman disciple of the Buddha, a supernatural occurrence proving that celestial asexuality is manifested, not in the "glorious body", but in the absence of samsaric passion and in the beatitude of inward union.

7. It is only too obvious that modern views about woman, due to a generalized egalitarianism, and then to a certain—strictly negative—feminization of man combined with an artificial virilization of woman, are here null and void. However, one must take into account a compensatory phenomenon at the "end of times", which is that piety and spiritual gifts are more frequently found among women than men.

8. "Where there is form"—the Buddha said—"there is void, and where there is void, there is form. Thus, void and form are not distinct."

A Note on the Feminime Element in Mahâyâna

An important aspect of the symbolism of femininity is, in the *Vajrayâna*, the couple *upâya-prajnâ*, represented in Lamaism by two embracing deities: one knows that *upâya* is the "means"—or the "mirage"—which reveals the Truth in the most efficient way, whereas *prajnâ* is the liberating knowledge thus awakened; this sexual symbolism also applies, in principle, to the coupling of "void-form" (*shûnya-rupâ*) or "*Nirvâna-Samsâra*", for the reciprocity is analogous or even fundamentally identical. Though such a symbolism may appear to be at the antipodes of Buddhist asexualism, in reality it coincides with it in the sense that all polarity is transcended in union and as if extinguished in a common infinitude, or in supreme non-duality.[9] In order to grasp well the relationship between this image and the concepts of *upâya* and *prajnâ*, one must know that the second element is "ourselves", for it is our transpersonal essence, whereas the first element is the Logos, which, across the *samsâric* darkness, awakens and actualizes That which we are. Each creature, Shingon emphatically asserts, is a Buddha unawares.

---

9. It is said that the Buddha, before dying, ascended to Heaven to preach the *Dharma* to Maya; and this meeting can well symbolize the supreme Union, for it is really the celestial complement—in a positively converse way—of the *Tathâgata*'s earthly birth; this was the divine birth of Maya in Prajnaparamita.

The Mystery of the Two Natures

A strange fact to note in the history of Christianity is that Pope Honorius I, though an impeccable pontiff, was expelled from the Church by the Sixth Ecumenical Council for the sole reason of having hesitated in the question of the "two wills" of Christ. A century and a half after this pope's death, the Seventh Ecumenical Council considered it useful or necessary to ratify the excommunication of Honorius I and to include his name in the anathema of all known heresies.

This ostracism is logically surprising when one is aware of the complexity of the issue at stake. For some, Christ has two wills since he is "true man and true God"; for others, these two wills are but one since—as Honorius himself said—Christ's human will cannot operate in contradiction to his divine will. One could say *grosso modo* that Christ possesses two wills in principle and one in fact; or again, one could use the image of two overlapping circles and express oneself thus: if it goes without saying that Christ possesses *a priori* two distinct wills, given his two incommensurable natures, there nonetheless is a region in his person where the two wills blend, as is seen precisely in the geometric symbolism of two intersecting circles.

What can be said concerning the two wills applies above all and with all the more reason to the two natures: if it is true that Christ is at the same time both man and God, two things are then incontrovertible, namely, the duality and the unity of his nature. We are not saying that the monophysites, who admit only the unity of Christ's nature, are right against the Orthodox and Catholics, but neither do we say that they are intrinsically wrong from their point of view; and the same holds, as a result, for the

141

monothelites, who simply apply the monophysite principle to a particular aspect of the nature of the God-Man. The legitimate right of the monophysites appears, quite paradoxically, in the Catholic doctrine of transubstantiation: it seems to us that it would be appropriate to apply to the Eucharistic elements what is affirmed dogmatically of Christ, namely, that he is "true man and true God"; if this is so, one could equally admit that the Eucharist is "true bread and true Body" or "true wine and true Blood" without compromising its divinity. To say that the bread is but an appearance is to apply to the Eucharist the doctrine—judged heretical—of the monophysites, for whom Christ is, precisely, only apparently a man since he is really God; now just as the quality of "true man" in Catholic and Orthodox doctrine does not preclude Christ from being "true God", so should the quality of "true bread" not preclude the host from being "true Body" in the minds of theologians, all the more as both things—the created and the Uncreated—are incommensurable, which means that the physical reality of the elements does not exclude their divine content, any more than the real corporeality of Christ prevents the presence of the divine nature.

It must be said again that monophysitism and therefore also transubstantialism are not intrinsically wrong—the opposite would in fact be astonishing—and for the following reason: to acknowledge that Christ's humanity is a vehicle of the divine nature amounts to saying that if, in one respect, the human side is really human, it is so in a way that is nonetheless different from the humanity of ordinary men; the Divine Presence transfigures or transubstantiates in a certain way, and *a priori*, the human nature; Christ's body is already here below what heavenly bodies are, with the sole difference that it is nevertheless affected by some of the accidents of earthly life. The same is true for the Eucharist: if in one respect it is "real bread" and "real wine", in another—which does not abolish the first—it is in fact substantially more than ordinary matter; metaphysically, this does not oblige one to pretend that this matter is "only an appearance", but theologically, from the point of view of uni-dimensional—we might say "planar"—alternatives, the negation of real matter is probably the only means for a certain mentality of affirming effectively and enduringly the transcendence of the Eucharist.

Nonetheless, this doctrine is bound to be a "double-edged sword", the dangers of which can be neutralized only by esoteric truth, or "theosophy" in the ancient and true sense of the word.

Theologians seem to think that bread and wine are, as natural substances, unworthy of the Divine Presence, a sentiment recalling a thesis of St Gregory of Nyssa which is not irrelevant here. Hellenists[1] deemed the Incarnation to be unworthy of God owing to the frailty and impurity of earthly bodies; in his "Great Catechesis", St Gregory answers that sin alone, not fleshly materiality, is unworthy of God. The Greeks might have responded that corporeal miseries, being traces of original sin and the Fall, partake in the indignity of sin and unquestionably manifest it; and the Bishop of Nyssa could have retorted that a proof of the compatibility between the human body and a Divine inherence is provided by the inherence of the Intellect, which is of a heavenly order and whose transcendence the Greeks are the first to acknowledge. The decisive argument is that these two orders, the created and the Uncreated, share no common measure and that nothing that is merely natural—whatever its distant cause may be—can oppose itself to the Presence of God.

*
* *

The uninformed reader who finds in the Koran that Jesus was "one of those brought nigh" (*muqarrabûn*) and "one of the righteous" (*sâlihûn*)—*Sûrah* of "The Family of Imran", 45, 46—has the following reaction: that Christ is "one of those brought nigh" is evident from every point of view, for if the greatest Prophets are not "close" to God, who then could be? And that Christ was "one of the righteous" is evident *a fortiori* and by several orders of magnitude, mathematically speaking. In reality, both seeming pleonasms are merely ellipses meant to illustrate a doctrinal position directed against the Christian thesis of the twofold nature of Christ; generally speaking, when the Koran appears to make statements that are

---

1. We are referring here to the partisans of Hellenism, that is to say, of the Hellenist tradition, which we cannot term "pagan" since we are envisaging it with respect to its spiritual values, though the word "Hellenist" more often designates, on the one hand, the Hellenized Jews of Antiquity and, on the other, scholars versed in Greek language and literature.

all too obvious, and disappointing in their context, it is engaging in implicit polemics; in other words, it is aiming at a particular opinion which it does not enunciate and which needs to be known in order for one to understand the passage. What Islam intends to affirm, in its way and according to its perspective, is that Jesus is "true man and true God": instead of saying "man", the Koran says "righteous" so as to define immediately the nature of this man; and since its intention is to specify that no man is God, it suggests what in Christian terms is called the "divine nature" of Christ by using the expression "brought nigh", which denotes the most elevated station Islam can attribute to a human being.

Be that as it may, the twofold nature of Christ is sufficiently specified in the following verse: "Jesus the Messiah, son of Mary, is the Messenger of God and His Word, which He (God) placed in Mary, and (Jesus is) of His Spirit (the Spirit of God)" (*Sûrah* of "Women", 171). In admitting the Immaculate Conception and the Virgin Birth, Islam accepts in its way the divine nature of Jesus;[2] "in its way", that is, with the obvious reservation that it always intends to dissociate the divine from the human, and therefore that the Christic phenomenon is for it no more than a particular marvel of Omnipotence.

*
* *

We have said above that the ostracism by the two Councils of Honorius I in particular and of the monophysites-monothelites in general is logically surprising; now to say "logically" is to imply a reservation, for it is no surprise from an exoteric point of view that a too fragmentary or in some respect inopportune formulation should be considered a crime;[3] this shows that one is dealing

2. According to a *hadîth*, Jesus and Mary were the only human beings the devil did not touch with his claw at their birth, and who therefore did not utter a cry.

3. Let it be said in passing that the anathematization of Honorius I proves, moreover, not that he was heretical, but that he was considered as such and that, as a result, the Church admits that a pope can lapse into heresy—except, of course, when promulgating a dogmatic or moral definition *ex cathedra*; one might reject this by proposing that Honorius I did no more than sin against discipline; but in that case, the anathemas

with a domain that must be distinguished from that of pure, hence disinterested, knowledge, which admits the interplay of aspects and points of view without ever getting locked in artificial alternatives or in issues that might cause offense. It is important, however, not to confuse theological elaborations, which are fluid and produce scissions, with the dogmas themselves, which are fixed; such elaborations—though also providential on their level—appear in their turn as dogmatic systematizations, but far more contingently so than those within which they are situated as modalities; these are minor *upâyas*, if one will, that is, "saving mirages" or "spiritual means" designed to render more accessible that major *upâya* which is religion. Now it is essential to keep in mind the idea of "lesser truth" or of "relative error" contained in this Buddhist notion; there is thus on the part of Heaven "tolerance out of Mercy" and not "plenary approbation". For man is a form, and he needs forms; but since he also—and even above all—needs the Essence, which religion or wisdom is supposed to communicate to him, he really needs a "form of the Essence" or a "manifestation of the Void" (*shûnyamûrti*). If in one respect form is a prolongation of the Essence, in another it contradicts it, which accounts on the one hand for the ambiguity of the exoteric *upâya*, and on the other hand for the two aspects of esoterism— one of which extends and intensifies the dogmatic *upâya* while the other, on the contrary, is independent of the former to the point of being able to contradict it. To the objection that esoterism also belongs to the formal order, one must respond that esoterism is aware of this and that it tends to transcend the accidentality of its own form, whereas exoterism is totally and heavily identified with its form.

heaped upon him canonically would be inexplicable. Be that as it may, there is nothing in principle to prevent a pope from ruining the Church without in the least having to make an *ex cathedra* pronouncement; the greatest theologians admit the possibility of a pope lapsing into heresy, and the whole problem for them then becomes whether the heretical pope is deposed *ipso facto* or must be deposed canonically. However, the possibility at issue here—of which Honorius I is not at all an example— occurs in so severe a degree only under utterly abnormal circumstances, which the twentieth century in fact offers; moreover, it remains to be seen whether the pope who might be incriminated is a legitimate pope with regard to the conditions of his election.

What results from this, in an altogether self-evident way, is that the dividing line between orthodoxy and apparent, and therefore merely extrinsic, heresy depends on psychological or moral contingencies of an ethnic or cultural provenance; while the fundamental *upâya*, quite clearly, transmits total truth through its symbolism, the same cannot be said of this minor *upâya* that theology represents; its relativity—with respect to total truth—is moreover proven, in the Christian sphere, by the notion of "theological progress", which contains an admission at once candid and dreadful.[4] It is true that every theology can lead incidentally to the profoundest insights, but it cannot, in its general and official doctrine, draw the conclusions such insights entail.

It is a radical error to believe that the greatest spokesmen of theology, were they even canonized saints, hold *ipso facto* all the keys to supreme wisdom;[5] they are instruments of Providence and are not called upon to go beyond certain limits; on the contrary, their role is to formulate what these limits are, according to a perspective willed directly or indirectly by Heaven. By "indirectly" we mean those cases where Heaven tolerates a limitation required— or made desirable—by a particular human predisposition, perhaps not well-defined *a priori*, but nonetheless proving to be predominant; this explains the majority of the differences or

4. Either one of two things: either there is theological progress, in which case theology is of little importance; or theology is important, in which case there can be no theological progress.
5. Thus the "wisdom of the saints", which some seek to set in opposition to metaphysics, is but an abuse of language; the "wisdom" of Ecclesiasticus is not, after all, of the same order as that of the Upanishads. It should be noted in this connection that if the Semitic Scriptures, even the most fundamental, do not have the tenor of the *Vedânta*, this is because, unlike the *Vedânta*, they are not directed exclusively to an intellectual elite, but have a function that obliges them to take account of possibilities found in the collective soul and to forestall the most diverse of reactions. To this it must be added that a sacred book, like the Gospel for example, which seems to speak to sinners, at least at the outset, really addresses any man insofar as he sins; this confers upon the notion of sin the widest significance possible—that of a centrifugal motion, whether compressive or dispersing—even when there is properly speaking no objective transgression. Sacred language, even if directed at first to specific men, is finally directed to man as such.

divergences—in most cases unilateral[6]—between the Western and Eastern Churches. Some of these differentiations may seem a gratuitous luxury, but they are nonetheless unavoidable and finally opportune, collective mentalities being what they are. Even so, the opportuneness has nothing absolute about it and cannot prevent a kind of poison, concealed in a such and such a theological particularism, from manifesting itself in the course of history, belatedly and upon contact with false ideas whose possibility theologians could not foresee.

In considering the most general factors of the issue, we shall say that Semitic dogmatisms, as well as Hindu *darshana*s like Ramanujan Vishnuism, pertain to the chivalrous and heroic spirit,[7] which necessarily tends toward voluntarism and individualism, and thus to moralizing anthropomorphism. It is in view of such a temperament, and because of it, that exclusivist dogmas[8] are crystallized and their corresponding theologies elaborated, which clearly implies that this temperament or this manner of seeing and feeling is acceptable to God as the "raw material" of the *upâya*; however, since each religion is by definition a totality—as is

6. For the spirit of innovation is to be found with the Latins, a fact resulting moreover from the paradoxical coincidence between the prophetism and the caesarism of the papacy.

7. The fact that Ramanuja was a *brahman* and not a *kshatriya* is not grounds for an objection since all castes—inasmuch as they are particular predispositions—are reflected or repeated in each single caste, so that a *brahman* of a *kshatriya* type is individually equivalent to a *kshatriya* of a *brahman* type. Furthermore, every human collectivity produces a human type with no affinity for speculative thought; it is all the more paradoxical and significant that this is the type or mentality—which a Hindu would call a *shûdra* outlook—that determines all the so-called "new theology" and constitutes its sole originality and sole mystery.

8. Such an adjective is not a pleonasm, for a metaphysical axiom itself can also have a dogmatic character, practically speaking, but without therefore having to exclude formulations diverging from it. On the other hand, there are metaphysical axioms whose conditional character is recognized *a priori*, depending on the degree of relativity of the idea expressed: hence, archetypes contained in the Creator Intellect are more real than their cosmic manifestation while being illusory with respect to the Divine Essence; such and such Hindu Divinities are dogmatically inviolable, but they vanish before *Paramâtmâ* or, rather, are reabsorbed therein, so that it may be possible to deny without heresy their existence, provided of course that by the same token one deny all beings that are even more relative.

proven by its imperative and unconditional character—and since God could never impose absolute limits, the religious phenomenon by definition comprises the esoteric phenomenon, which is transmitted in principle and preferably—in different degrees—by vocations that favor contemplation, including sacred art.

A certain underlying warrior or knightly mentality[9] accounts for many of the theological oscillations and their ensuing disputes—the nature of Christ and the structure of the Trinity having been the notable issues at stake in the Christian world— just as it accounts also for such forms of narrow-mindedness as the incomprehension and intolerance of ancient theologians toward the metaphysics and mysteries of Hellenism. It is, moreover, this same mentality that produced the divergence, in the very heart of the Greek tradition, of Aristotle from Plato, who personified in essence the *brahmâna* spirit inherent in the Orphic and Pythagorean tradition,[10] whereas the Stagirite formulated a metaphysics that was in some way centrifugal and perilously open to the world of phenomena, actions, experiences, and adventures.[11]

After this parenthesis, which the general context of the case of Honorius I permits or even demands, let us return to our doctrinal subject.

*
* *

9. One cannot lose sight of the fact that, in all climates, the same causes produce the same effects—in highly diverse proportions—and that India is no exception; the quarrels of sectarian Vishnuism are a case in point.

10. It goes without saying that the classical period—with its grave intellectual and artistic deviation—and its reoccurrence at the time of the Renaissance are patent examples of warrior or knightly, and hence *kshatriya*, Luciferianism; however, we do not have in mind here deviations as such since, on the contrary, we are speaking of normal manifestations, which are acceptable to Heaven; otherwise there could be no question of voluntarist and emotional *upâyas*.

11. However, let us not make Aristotelianism responsible for the modern world, which is due to a convergence of various factors, such as the abuses—and all subsequent reactions—provoked by the unrealistic idealism of Catholicism, and also by the diverging and irreconcilable demands of the Latin and Germanic mentalities, all of which end up precisely with scientism and the profane mentality.

The problem of the two natures of Christ can be reduced, in the last analysis, to the relationship between the relative and the Absolute: if Christ is the Absolute entered into relativity, it follows, not only that the relative should return thereby to Absoluteness, but also and above all else that the relative should be prefigured in the Absolute; this is the meaning of the Uncreated Word, which manifests Itself in the human order, not only in the form of Christ or the *Avatâra*, but also and *a priori* in the form of the immanent Intellect, and this brings us back to the complementarity between Revelation and Intellection. The Absolute manifested in the human world is at once Truth and Presence, or either one or the other of these two elements, but without being able to exclude its complement. The element "Presence" takes precedence in Christianity, hence the sacraments and the emphasis on the volitive aspect of man; in other climates, and above all in universal Gnosis, which retains its rights everywhere, it is the element "Truth" that determines the means of the path, in diverse ways and on diverse levels.

In order to be as clear as possible, it is necessary to insist on the following principle: there is no possible relationship between the Absolute as such and relativity; for such a relationship to exist, there must be something relative in the Absolute and something absolute in the relative. In other words: if one admits that the world is distinct from God, one must also admit that this distinction is prefigured in God Himself, which means that His unity of Essence—which is never in question—comprises degrees; not to admit this polarization *in divinis* is to leave the existence of the world without a cause, or it is to admit that there are two distinct realities and thus two "Gods", namely, God and the world. For either one of two things: either the world is explained starting from God, in which case there is in God prefiguration and creative act, and thus relativity; or else there is in God no relativity, in which case the world is unexplainable and becomes thereby godlike. We shall once again emphasize that Divine Relativity, the cause of the world, fulfills the role of the Absolute in relation to the world; in this sense, theologians are right to uphold, as the case may be, the absoluteness of all that is divine; absoluteness is then, for them, synonymous with Divinity.

149

At the risk of repeating ourselves, we could express this as follows: whoever admits the presence of the Absolute in the world, in the form of Christ for instance, must admit equally the presence of the relative in God, in the form of the Word, precisely; whoever denies that there can be any relativity in God must consider the Creator, or the Revealer, or the Redeemer as being situated beneath God, in the manner of the demiurge; for the Absolute as such neither creates, nor reveals, nor saves. In the refusal to admit the relativity of the hypostases, there is an element of confusion between the absolute and the sublime: since the Divinity deserves or demands worship, there are some who want the Divinity to be "absolutely absolute" in every possible respect, if we may express ourselves, provisionally and incidentally, in such a manner. Now God is deserving of the worship of *latria*, not inasmuch as He comprises no relativity—for in this respect He is humanly inaccessible—but inasmuch as He is absolute with respect to the relativity of the world, while comprising an aspect of relativity in view of this very contact.

One could object that the thesis of reciprocity between the Absolute and the relative does not take into account the incommensurability, and hence the asymmetry, between the two terms; this is both true and false. If one wants to place emphasis on the incommensurable nature of God, one cannot do so simply by denying relativity within the Divine Principle; one can do so adequately only by separating the creative Principle from the intrinsic Absolute, which takes us back to the alternative between *Paramâtma* and *Mâyâ*, and then to the absorption of the second term by the first, precisely as a result of their incommensurability. This reduction of the real to the One without a second is exactly what those who deny relativity *in divinis* do not want, all the more as they hold fiercely to the unconditional and in some way massive reality of the world; in wanting an "absolutely absolute" God situated above an unconditionally real world, they seek to keep "both feet on the ground" without sacrificing anything of transcendence. In reality, however, the Universe is no more than an inward and, as it were, dreamlike dimension of God: it reflects divine qualities in a contrasted, changing, and privative mode, thereby realizing the possibility for God to be other than God, a possibility contained in the Divine Infinitude itself.

The Question of Theodicies

"God does what He wills": this affirmation in the Koran all too readily evokes the unfortunate image of a more or less arbitrary Divine Will, when in fact it simply means that man is in general ignorant of the motives of that Will, particularly with regard to the multiple contradictions the world displays. According to theologians, God does not "will" sin since He forbids it, but He does "will" it since sin is possible and nothing happens without God "willing" it or even "creating" it; otherwise one would have to admit, it appears, that God is unable to prevent what He does not will, *quod absit*. The core of the problem here is to be found in the confusion between Being and Beyond-Being, or between the ontological and existentiating Principle and the supra-ontological Essence,[1] a confusion resulting from the fact that on the one hand theology envisages God in an anthropomorphic manner, thus as if He were a human subject, and on the other aims to give account of the whole of the Divine Nature, even though this is incompatible with the preceding point of view.

What the Essence "wills" in virtue of its infinitude—and since "the good tends essentially to communicate itself", according to the Augustinian formulation—is its own radiance and, consequently, the world as such and in its totality; now this manifestation implies by definition remoteness from its Source, so that in

---

1. The *Ungrund* (the "ground without a ground") of Boehme or the Brahma *nirguna* ("without attributes") of the Vedantins, whereas Being as such, hence existentiating, is *saguna* ("with attributes"). The scholastic distinction between an *Infinitum absolutum* and an *Infinitum secundum quid* can apply to this initial metaphysical difference, the creative Principle corresponding to the second term of the alternative.

151

"willing" Manifestation the Essence implicitly and indirectly wills the penalty one calls evil, at the risk, precisely, of not wanting to shine or to "diffuse Itself". However, the Divine Will that wants the moral good, and for this reason forbids sin, is not the same that wills the world: the Will of Beyond-Being, or the Essence, wills the world in itself, whereas the Will of Being—already more relative, even though it prolongs Beyond-Being—presupposes the world and exerts itself only within the world. In other words, Beyond-Being desires the good as radiance, manifestation, or world, whereas Being desires the good as participation of things in the Divine Good; in the first respect, the world is a good since it manifests the Supreme Good, whereas in the second, obedience to the Divine Law—or to any norm or natural quality—is a good because it enables participation in the Supreme Good. In the first case, the Divine Will is affirmed through ontological Radiance, or *Mâyâ*; and in the second, it is affirmed through the Norm, the Law, or Revelation; we thus find ourselves in the presence of two Divine Subjectivities, one pertaining to the Absolute and the other already determined by Relativity; while they are intrinsically identical, they apply extrinsically to two different planes, whence the possible appearance of contradiction. This being so, there is absolutely no reason for wondering why God "wills" this or that, and why, in the case in point, He "wills" sin while forbidding it.

Taken as a whole, the world is good inasmuch as it manifests God; but it contains a partial and contingent aspect of perverseness, since in not being God while nonetheless existing, it opposes itself to God or tends to be the equal of God; since this is impossible, all phenomena—and finally the world itself—are marked by impermanence: they always fall back, as it were, into the void, like arrows shot toward the sun in the mad hope of reaching it.

*

* *

According to Epicurus, and those who have followed him, no theodicy is possible for the following reasons: either God wants to eliminate evil but cannot, in which case He is not powerful while being good; or God can eliminate evil but does not want to, in which case He is not good while being powerful; or He neither can nor wants to eliminate evil, in which case He is neither mighty nor good; or He can and wants to, in which case evil does not exist. And yet evil does exist.

Epicurean reasoning is based on ambiguities regarding the very notions of "evil", "willing", and "power". First of all: will and power are inherent in the Divine Nature, which is Absoluteness and Infinitude; this means that God can neither go against His nature nor will anything that is contrary to it on pain of contradiction, hence of absurdity. It is impossible, because absurd, that God would have the power to be other than God, to be neither absolute nor infinite, or not to be at all; and He cannot will what lies outside His power in that it is contrary to Being. God is all-powerful in relation to the world, His creation or His manifestation; but Omnipotence can in no way act on the Divine Being Itself, given that this Being is the source of Omnipotence and not conversely.

Now Infinitude, which is an aspect of the Divine Nature, implies unlimited Possibility and consequently Relativity, Manifestation, the world. To speak of the world is to speak of separation from the Principle, and to speak of separation is to speak of the possibility—and necessity—of evil; seen from this angle, what we term evil is thus indirectly a result of Infinitude, hence of the Divine Nature; in this respect, God cannot wish to suppress it; likewise, in this respect—and only in this respect—evil ceases to be evil, being no more than an indirect and distant manifestation of a mysterious aspect of the Divine Nature, precisely that of Infinitude or of All-Possibility.

One could also say that Infinitude engenders Possibility, and Possibility engenders Relativity; now Relativity contains by definition what we could term the principle of contrast. Insofar as a quality is relative—or is reflected in Relativity—it has ontological need of a contrast, not intrinsically or in virtue of its content, but extrinsically and in virtue of its mode, thus because of its contingency. Indeed, it is the relative or contingent character of a quality that requires or brings about the existence of the corresponding privative manifestation, with all its possible gradations and as a result, its defect, vice, evil. Evil is the possibility of the impossible, since relative good is the Possible approaching impossibility; for it is from this paradoxical combination of Possibility with impossibility—impossibility becoming real only in and through Possibility—that Contingency or Relativity originates, if one may be allowed an ellipsis that is complex and daring, but difficult to avoid at this point.

If God cannot eliminate evil as a possibility, it is because in this respect evil is a function of His Nature and, being so, it ceases as a result to be evil; and what God cannot do, on pain of contradiction or absurdity, He could never will. However, the Divine Will opposes evil inasmuch as it is contrary to the Divine Nature, which is Goodness or Perfection; in this relationship of opposition—and in this alone—evil is intrinsically evil. God fights this evil perfectly since, on all planes, it is the good that is finally victorious; evil is never more than a fragment or a transition, whether we are in a position to see this or not.

The foundation of any theodicy should thus essentially be: first, that Divine Omnipotence does not extend to the Divine Nature, which could never be the object of the former; second, that the Divine Will accords with Power and could never, as a result, oppose the Divine Nature, which is the source of its faculties or functions; third, that evil is evil only insofar as it opposes the Divine Nature, but not insofar as it results indirectly from It as an instrument of separativity or diversity, both of which issue from Divine All-Possibility and thus, ultimately, from Infinity itself.

The reasoning of Epicurus has been eagerly adopted, not just by those who deem it in their interest not to believe in God, but also by those who have succumbed to the hypnosis of the world termed "real" and "concrete"; from the point of view of metaphysical intellection, the world contains far less evidence and intelligibility than the transcendent Invisible. Epicurean reasoning is the classic example, as it were, of a logical operation that works impeccably in the absence of information required by its content: one speaks of "evil", but fails to realize that evil is by definition evil only in one respect and not in another, which is proven at the outset by the fact that there is no absolute evil and that evil is never a substance; one speaks of "God", but fails to realize that God, being infinite, carries in His Nature the cause of an unfolding that necessarily contains an element of contradiction by reason of His very Infinitude; and one speaks of "power" and "willing", but fails to realize that the Divine Nature is the Sub-

154

ject of these and not the Object, which amounts to saying that these two faculties, while being unlimited by virtue of Divine Unlimitedness and in the direction of contingency, are limited at their "peak" by Divine Absoluteness, which no will and no power could ever act upon.

Every theologian will acknowledge that God is free to create the world; none will admit that God is free not to possess Freedom, or not to be God, or not to be at all. Thus the whole problem of theodicy, so rashly and crudely taken up by Epicurus, is concerned mainly with the question of the Divine Nature, that is, with the characteristics of the Substance which is both absolute and infinite.

*
* *

For the Stoics, evil is a necessary concomitant of the good; and likewise for Leibnitz: the world is perfect in its totality, but things are imperfect; God has allowed moral evil because without it there would be no virtue.[2] This is in fact the common opinion of theologians: the role of evil is to cooperate with the created good; as a result, evil is no more than an indirect aspect of the good. This argument is based on the principle of contrast we alluded to earlier: in order to be actualized, the good requires a contrary element to the very degree that the level of actualization is relative; what is thus at issue here is an internal law of relativity.

For Plato, the terminal point of the cosmogonic fall is matter, which makes concrete the principle of centrifugal coagulation; for Christians, this "matter" becomes "flesh" and, with it, pleasure,[3] whereas for Islam, as for Judaism, evil is polytheism,

---

2. As for the "best of all possible worlds" of Leibnitz, the "principle of the best" is not even conceivable since it evaporates into the indefinite. The existent world as a whole is "the best" by the fact of its very existence, and only because of it, which is to say that such an evaluation is meaningless, or that it amounts to no more than the axiomatic conclusion that Being is the Good.
3. Contrary to a too widely held opinion, the moral doctrine of Aristotle, who advocated the golden mean inasmuch as this is situated between two excesses, is not an invitation to mediocrity, nor is it responsible for the tendency toward the bourgeois secularism that it may have occasioned. However, this moral doctrine is to be distinguished from Christian

idolatry, and disobedience, and thus finally duality, which at its ontological root has no connection—to say the least—with what we call sin. The same is true of Plato's "matter" and the "flesh" of the Christians when we trace them back to their respective roots, which are Substance and Beatitude.

For Plotinus, absolute Being is the source of what *a posteriori* we call evil, in the sense that emanated Being, which will create the world, mixes with possibility due to this very emanation—or this issuance—and thus becomes predisposed to all the falls which make up the descending diversity of the world; emanated Being—the creative or demiurgic Principle—produces privation indirectly, not insofar as it is Being, but on the contrary insofar as emerging from Absolute Being or Beyond-Being, it limits itself and thus takes on an aspect of lesser reality.

Origen envisages above all moral evil, of which natural ills in every order are in fact the consequences; for man has drawn along with him in his fall all the realms of nature. Thus Origen perceives the source of evil in the misuse of free will; free will has been given to man because, without freedom, man would have been immutable like God. One can object that God possesses freedom before man and better than man, but does not misuse it; if man abuses this gift, this is because his nature is not fully suited to it, and because the cause of evil is not freedom but corruptibility. Origen's argument nonetheless has the merit of showing, though by way of a detour, that creation implies imperfection, by metaphysical necessity; the possibility of a choice between the Substance and the accident, or between the Real and the illusory, operates as the motive force of the cosmogonic descent.

According to St Thomas, evil results from the diversity of creatures and the gradation of their qualities, the compensation for evil being the total Order in view of which it is tolerated; physical ills are the privation of Being in relation to the substance of creatures; moral evil is this same privation with respect to their activity. In order to escape from Manichean dualism, which ruins the notion of the Supreme Good, St Thomas concludes that evil does

morality, which sees in morals a spiritual means—whence its sacrificial character—whereas for the Greeks, as for most Orientals, moral equilibrium is spiritually a basis and not a means.

not have its cause in Being—it does not in fact have its direct cause there—and that it simply attaches itself to the good by depriving it of a particular quality; evil "is" not, but it "exists" or, in other words, it is an evil, whereas its existence is a good with respect to—and because of—universal totality. In referring to an Augustinian formula previously mentioned, we might add that the cause of evil—but not inasmuch as it is evil—is the innate need of the Good to impart itself, for it is this need that produces the world, and it is this production—or this unfolding of Being— that requires differentiation, vertical as well as horizontal; now differentiation entails modes of privation of Being, hence what we are entitled to call evil.

*

* *

Whether one speaks of "matter", of the "flesh", or of misused "freedom", it is always, from the point of view of the ultimate cause, a question of Possibility, which is the *Shakti* or the Power of *Âtmâ*, and which coincides with Relativity and thereby with the process that is both cosmogonic and individualizing. "Sin is the ego", some Hinduizing idealists preach, which, incidentally, exempts them from any objective discernment and from any uncomfortable option; now the ego as such derives from the Divine Self, not only directly and by participation and analogy, but also in an indirect way and by separation and inversion; it is in this last respect that it manifests sin or evil, or, if one prefers, Luciferianism. This aspect notwithstanding, the ego is as innocent as matter, or flesh, or pleasure in their existential and virtually spiritual purity, as is proven by the fact that holiness does not necessarily exclude these elements.

If man is the handiwork of a Principle that is sovereignly good, then why, more than one philosopher has asked, is he exposed to evil? But precisely: he is the handiwork, not the Principle; not being the Principle, which alone is good, he can neither be the good nor be subjected to the good alone; he is a good when manifesting the Principle, but he is not a good when separating himself from It. Eve is an aspect of Adam, and the fall brought about by Eve is equally so. In a certain sense, the role of evil in the world is to recall that "that God alone is good"; otherwise the world

157

would be God, which is to say that it would not be; this, however, is contrary to the nature of the Principle which, being the Infinite, tends to manifest Itself in inexhaustible diversity, or which, being the Good, tends to impart Itself to one "other than Itself". It would moreover be naïve to believe that all would be perfect if man no longer suffered and if he no longer committed crimes, for the average man of the "dark age", even when his moral behavior is correct, is far from representing a pure good, and his manner of envisaging both evil and good is on a level with his degeneration: that is, it has nothing to do with man's ultimate interests.

One point that seems to have been overlooked in most theodicies is the extreme limitation of evil itself in space and time when these are considered in their full extension, and all the more so when taken in the context of total Existence; it is true that the authors of these doctrines do not ask whether evil is big or small, but merely note its existence; however, this is precisely the reason why they give too much the impression of establishing a kind of symmetry between good and evil, when in fact there is no common measure between them in the cosmic cycles any more than in the total universe. It must be acknowledged that Aryan as well as Semitic eschatologies share some responsibility in creating this impression of symmetry, but this is because they are disposed in view of the actual state of earthly man, and not because they are meant to do justice to the overall proportion of things.

Some have sought to see an "optimism" in theodicy, which is entirely to misunderstand its point of view, which is essentially objective. For optimism, according to the current use of this term, is a matter of subjectivity and not of objectivity; its error is to deny an evil that really exists, just as pessimism is wrong, not in recognizing an evil, but in denying a real good.

*
* *

The Power of cosmogonic propulsion, upon contact with certain cosmic planes which it itself unfolds, gives rise to the privative and subversive principle that we call evil; it is this ultimate consequence which, as the Gnostics see it, redounds upon the creative Power itself, and which leads them to attribute to Plato's demiurge a negative and quasi-malefic significance, similar to that assumed by Ahriman in Zoroastrianism. If Christianity for its part sees in Lucifer a fallen angel, this is because it is referring to the Power of a propulsion become tenebrous upon its entry into the animic state; and if Islam, on the contrary, specifies that the devil, Iblis, is a jinn and not an angel, hence a being created out of fire and not light—the Koran insists on this—it is because the propulsive Power becomes negative and subversive only upon its entry into the animic and subtle substance, so that in defining the *Princeps hujus mundis*, there is no need to take into account superior cosmic antecedents.

If the Power of divine attraction is personified upon contact with man, the perverted propulsive Power is no less so; the fact that it is *a priori* impersonal in no wise prevents it from becoming personal in its relations with the human world. This personification of the malefic power has induced some, in Islam as well as in Christianity, not only to see in the devil a quasi-human individual, but even to envisage his ultimate reintegration into Divine Mercy; if such an opinion is inadmissible in this anthropomorphist form, it nonetheless holds some metaphysical import to the extent that it refers finally to the *apocatastasis*: evil will be resorbed into its original and neutral substance; fire and darkness will be transmuted into light.

To summarize: Divine Freedom means that God is free not to create a particular world, but not that He is free not to create at all. This is to say that Divine Freedom—that of Being (*Brahma saguna*, "with attributes")—acts on the modes and forms of universal Manifestation and not on its immutable principles; God is free—and He has the power—to eliminate a specific evil, but not evil as such,[4] given that evil as such is a necessary penalty for the full unfolding of Manifestation, and that this unfolding—like Manifestation itself—results necessarily from the Infinitude of the Divine Essence. Now for the Essence, the question of Manifestation, and all the more so that of evil, does not arise; from the perspective of the eternal Wakefulness of the Absolute, the universal

---

4. Christ cured the sick, but he did not abolish sickness, and he thus demonstrated or illustrated the doctrine of which we have just given a brief survey.

Dream has never been,[5] for the accident, whatever its quality, can never add anything to the Substance. But one could also contend that the accident is nothing other than the Substance, or that it partakes of the latter's reality; or yet, that it possesses all the reality corresponding to its nature or possibility.

*
* *

It goes without saying that even the best possible metaphysical argument could never convince us if there were not within us some trace of what this argument is meant to communicate, or if the certitude that it aims to awaken in us were not already contained in the very substance of our spirit; this certitude is virtual in some, while for others it is merely potential and inoperative. It is in any case impossible for an argument concerning the Invisible and the Transcendent to convince anyone in the manner of a demonstration whose particulars are all sensorially or mathematically verifiable.

The classic error rationalists make with respect to metaphysical demonstrations is to believe that a metaphysician assumes his thesis as a result of the arguments he propounds, and that this thesis is therefore no more than a mere conclusion, and that it falls apart as soon as one denounces the weak points that some excel in discovering—which is not difficult to do since the facts of the demonstration elude ordinary experience; in reality, as we have said more than once, metaphysical arguments are not the causes of certitude, but its effects; in other words, the certitude at issue, while being a subjective phenomenon, is made of objectivity since it pertains entirely to a Reality that is independent of our mind.

As for theodicy, it is necessary to know that the Intellect perceives the Universal or Divine Good *a priori*; that is, it may perceive It before understanding—or wanting to understand—the nature of evil; and if a contemplative metaphysician may be able to overlook the doctrine of evil, it is precisely because he is certain

---

5. And this is why the Dream not only unfolds but is resorbed; its unfolding manifests its participation in the Essence, whereas its resorption on the contrary manifests its illusory nature in relation to the Absolute.

from the outset, in an unconditional and in some fashion primordial way, of the infinite primacy of the Good under the three aspects of "pure Being", "pure Spirit", "pure Beatitude".[6] For him a theodicy can serve the secondary function of an "appeasing of the heart", as the Sufis would say, but it will never play the role of a proof *sine qua non.*

St Anselm's *credo ut intelligam* means that faith is an anticipation, by our whole being and not by reason alone, of the quintessential certitude we have just mentioned; by anticipating this intellection, faith partakes of it already without it always being possible to ascertain where faith, in the basic sense of the term, ends and where direct knowledge begins. This is also one of the meanings of the blessing pronounced upon those "that have not seen, and yet have believed"; but in virtue of its sacred character, this saying applies to all levels and therefore encompasses the level of gnosis, for, indeed, "to believe" is not only to admit volitively and emotively; it is also to draw, on the very plane of plenary and intellective certitude, the consequences of what one knows; it is thus to know "as if one saw" and with the awareness of being seen by Him whom we see not;[7] in this sense, faith is more than mere comprehension; or, if one prefers, faith is the dimension of amplitude or of unfolding in understanding, the dimension that allows a consciousness that is *a priori* only speculative—though sufficient, certainly, on the plane of concepts—to become operative, together with its concomitants of detachment and generosity. And this allows us to note that many doctrinal explanations—in the category of theodicies—lose much of their importance, practically and subjectively, in relation to the intuition of the Essence, for this intuition enables us to place within parentheses questions for which we have only a virtual answer, questions, in other words, for which we possess the solution not in detail, but in principle; for those who know that God is sovereignly good—though obvi-

---

6. To speak of "Being" is to speak of "Spirit" and "Beatitude"; and one will recall that "Beatitude" coincides with "Goodness", "Beauty", and "Mercy".
7. Mutilated intelligence, deprived of its volitive and moral complement, is a consequence of the Fall. Objectively speaking, intellection suffices unto itself; but we are subjects or microcosms and must therefore adapt integrally to our objective knowledge on pain of perdition, for a "house divided against itself shall not stand".

ously they are not unaware of evil—know as a result that evil cannot have the last word and that it must have a cause that is compatible with Divine Goodness,[8] even if they do not know what this cause is. Whatever our degree of doctrinal knowledge or of ignorance may be, the best way to grasp the metaphysical limits of evil is to conquer evil in ourselves, and this is possible, precisely, only on the basis of an intuition of the Divine Essence, which coincides with the Infinite Good.

*

* *

He who has the intuition of the Absolute—which does not solve the problem of evil dialectically, but places it within parentheses by removing all its poison—possesses *ipso facto* the sense of the relationship between the Substance and accidents, so that he is unable to see the accidents outside of the Substance. An accident, that is, a phenomenon or a being of whatever kind, is good insofar as it manifests the Substance, or what amounts to the same: insofar as it manifests the resorption of the accidental within the Substance. And conversely, a phenomenon is bad—in some respect or other—inasmuch as it manifests the separation of the accidental from the Substance, which amounts to saying that it tends to manifest the absence of the Substance, but without succeeding wholly in doing so, for existence testifies to the Substance.

God and the world: the Substance and the accidents; or the Essence and the forms. The accident, or the form, manifests the Substance, or the Essence,[9] and proclaims Its glory; evil is the

8. According to the meaning of the Sanskrit term *Ânanda*, "consisting of Beatitude"; the effect of Beatitude, on the plane of creatures, is what we call in human terms goodness. When Buddhists say that there is in the center of each grain of sand a Buddha, they mean that the world, the *Samsâra*, is in some fashion woven out of Beatitude, of *Nirvâna*, which allows them moreover to affirm that the *Samsâra* is none other than *Nirvâna*; and the latter appears then as the Substance of the *dharmas*, of the accidents.

9. In the relationship between the "accidents" and the "Substance", one can discern a kind of continuity, whereas the relationship between "form" and "Essence" is conceived rather in a discontinuous mode; the first relationship refers more particularly, though not exclusively, to the Infinite

ransom of accidentality inasmuch as the latter is separative and privative, not inasmuch as it is participatory and communicative. Knowledge of the immanent Substance is victory over the accidents of the soul—hence over privative accidentality as such since there is an analogy between the microcosm and the macrocosm—and it is for that reason the best of theodicies.

and to the Feminine, whereas the second evokes the Absolute and the Masculine. According to the first relationship, there is resorption, and according to the second extinction; or again, according to the first relationship, the soul meets the Substance by crossing, without concupiscence, through the accident-symbol, whereas in the second relationship, the soul renounces, but without bitterness, the accident-illusion. All this is a question of emphasis, for the notions of "Essence" and "Substance", or of "form" and "accident", are in fact broadly interchangeable.

Some Difficulties Found
in Sacred Scriptures

To read the sacred Scriptures of mankind with unreserved admiration is one thing and to recognize that one is not always capable of appreciating them is something else; we may indeed know that a given text, being sacred, must be perfect both in content and in form, without being able to understand why; this is the case when our ignorance comes up against certain passages that only traditional commentary, and in some cases the original language, would make intelligible to us. To accept with veneration "every word which proceedeth out of the mouth of God" does not therefore in the least require any sort of pious hypocrisy, which is to say that our acquiescing, not just in principle but in fact, is intelligent and sincere only when based on real motives; otherwise we should be compelled to accept every incongruity resulting from errors in translation, so long as we were unaware of their inaccuracy.[1]

It is true, and even inevitable, that pious illusions of this and similar kinds do occur, even within the fold of the great orthodoxies; as an example we may take the affirmation, not infrequently heard among Muslims, that the Koran possesses not merely a perfect form, which would be plausible and even

---

1. The Bible would be much more comprehensible and much less vulnerable if one did not systematically ignore rabbinical exegesis, which does not mean that Christian authors have always ignored it, and one could well dispense with "scientific" and other forms of logomachy. Meister Eckhart, for instance, knew the exegesis of Maimonides, whom he called "the Rabbi" just as Aristotle was called "the Philosopher".

obvious, but also a superhuman and inimitable style; and one hears stories of men who tried to imitate the Koran but failed lamentably. That they failed is not hard to believe, but this was not because of the inimitability of the style, for the Koran is formulated in human language, and the gamut of possibilities of perfection on this level is of necessity fairly restricted; language can scarcely be more than language. That the Koran is perfect and normative from the point of grammar and syntax is incontestable—the contrary would be inconceivable for a revealed Book—but it is not unique in this; that its language is sometimes of an unsurpassable poetic quality is no less certain, but to say that it cannot be surpassed is not necessarily to say that it cannot be equaled; finally, that it contains all necessary truths, to say the least, is likewise not in itself a pure miracle. The divine quality of a revealed Book cannot be apparent in an absolute fashion from its earthly form, nor from its conceptual content alone; in reality, the divine and therefore supernatural, miraculous, and inimitable quality, which only pious prejudice could attribute abusively to words, is in fact of an altogether different order from that of the most perfect dialectic or the most brilliant poetry: it shows itself first of all in a richness of meanings—a feature that is incapable of being imitated—and also in what might be called the underlying divine substance perceptible through the formal expression and especially manifested in its results in souls,[2] and in the world, in space, and in time.[3] Only this divine substance can explain both the spiritual and the theurgic efficacy of the Koranic verses, with its consequences in the lightning-like expansion of primitive Islam in the conditions in which it took place, as well as in the stability of Muslim institutions and the extraordinary fruitfulness of Islamic doctrine and the power of the spirituality, not

2. "Charms have a certain natural force: and any one who comes under the influence of the charm, even if he does not understand it, gets something from it, according to the nature of the sounds thereof. . . . Just so is it with the giving of names in the divine Scriptures, only they are stronger than any charms" (*The Philokalia of Origen*, 12:1).
3. "And this Koran is not such as could ever be invented in despite of Allah" (10:37). "If We had caused this Koran to descend upon a mountain, thou (O Muhammad) verily hadst seen it humbled, rent asunder by the fear of Allah" (59:21).

forgetting the profound originality of architectural and ornamental art, whatever its "original materials" were; and only this non-human substance can account for the monolithic conviction that characterizes Muslim faith, whose causes could never be found in the ideas alone or in the style.[4]

It goes without saying that the style of the Koran, from a certain point of view, cannot be imitated; but this is so in the case of every masterpiece. As for the elliptical and as it were super-saturated style that the Koran owes to its celestial origin, it cannot be claimed that this is a linguistic or literary perfection. One might almost say that the sacred Scriptures wish to make us realize that their perfection is difficult of access from all points of view, and that human expressions cannot but be imperfect in certain respects. Moreover, Muslims, like the exegetes of other religions, have not failed to emphasize the providentially harsh and uncompromising character of revealed Scripture, a character at variance, not of course with the perfection of language, but with the opinion of those who would uphold the formal and as it were "massive" sublimity of the revealed Book.[5] There is indeed in the Koranic style something of a special concern not to indulge in poetry—which does not prevent certain passages from attaining the most powerful beauty of expression.

The specific character of the Koran doubtless reveals itself more directly in some passages than in others, notably in the eschatological Meccan *sûrahs* or in passages such as the Throne verse (2:255) or the Light verse (24:35), but the zealots we have in mind seek to extend this manifest divine sublimity to the whole Book, even to stipulations on civil law. Moreover, the distinction that has just been established between degrees of expressivity does not resolve the following crucial question: is there a style of language that is necessarily divine, or in other words, are there formal or literary criteria directly proving the divine provenance

4. For ideas are also to be found in the great theological treatises, just as beauty can be found equally in Sufi poems; but neither the one nor the other could have conquered—and preserved—a whole part of the world.
5. Moreover, the sublimism in question has had various effects: thus it has given rise, in a certain "specialized" psalmody of the Koran, to a curious super-saturation, an idolatry of sound that robs the reading of its spiritual as well as sonorous beauty.

of a text? The problem is basically the same as that of the super-human beauty of the *Avatâra*, which may also be miraculous in its effects:[6] where visual beauty alone is concerned, the face and body of the heavenly Messenger cannot be either more or other than summits of human and racial beauty—admittedly summits that are extremely rare and even unique in virtue of a providential originality which is compounded of elements that altogether elude our powers of assessment—and it is only with the soul, the expression, and the attitudes that a strictly superhuman beauty first appears. Neither in the divine Messenger nor in the Message can there be any monstrousness of perfection, that is, something violating the norm.[7] If those skeptical Arabs who tried to imitate the Koran failed, it was not literary impossibility so much as the supernatural reality that made their effort vain, and the more inexorably so in that they were Muslims "by right" if not "in fact"; their sin was that of Prometheus, or Icarus, or the Titans. This is an order of things that literary criticism, either Eastern or Western, could never explain.[8]

In order to read a sacred Book without difficulties, one must be aware, among other things, of the associations of ideas that a given word evokes in a given language, and of the metonymies

6. Tradition emphasizes this feature especially in the cases of Krishna and the Buddha; in the latter case the central role of the sacred image illustrates this truth. In Christianity the importance of icons indicates the same reality, not only for Christ, but also for the Virgin. As for Islam, the beauty of the Prophet is the subject of a dogma, and this is reflected in the general cult of the beauty of things and of the soul. The generosity of man should be able to repose in the harmony of things, which should be like a mirror of that generosity.

7. Lest we forget, the norm by definition is divine.

8. To illustrate this, let us suppose for a moment that the Koran were a part of the Bible, and that it had been written several centuries before our era. There can be no doubt that there would have been "criticisms" to the effect that the Koran had been written at different periods and thus also by different authors; that certain passages were much more recent than tradition alleged, not to speak of later interpolations by copyists—a never-failing argument in the arsenal of the destructive "exegetes" of the Scriptures.

which are common usage in it. This brings us to the following distinction: there are sacred Scriptures in which the original language is of capital importance, whence the more or less express prohibition against translating them for canonical usage—this is so in the case of the Torah, the Koran, and the Vedas, and perhaps also the Tao Te Ching; and there are others in which the whole meaning is contained in the imagery and in the direct expression of thought—such is the case of the Gospels and the Buddhist Books—and where translations into popular but noble languages are even traditionally anticipated. Reference is made to "noble" languages in order to emphasize that modern Western languages represent languages that have become more or less trivial—with respect to the sacred—as a result of several centuries of irreligious literature and democratic mentality; thus they are hardly suited to convey the Scriptures, when all the canonical, liturgical, and psychological aspects are taken into account, whereas these same languages could still do so in the Middle Ages. We speak of "traditionally anticipated translations" in order to recall that the possibility of translating Scripture is already prefigured in the "gift of tongues" and, as regards Buddhism, in the original parallelism between Pali and Sanskrit. But once it has become liturgical, the language is crystallized and does not change further, even if it undergoes modification in profane usage.[9] It is noteworthy that these two forms of Revelation, the Buddhist and the Christian, are founded on a humanization of the Divine—the impersonal Divine in the first case and the personal Divine in the second—whereas in the Jewish, Islamic, and Hindu traditions, the Revelation takes on above all and essentially the form of Scriptures; Hindu avatarism does not alter this fact,

---

9. As Joseph de Maistre wrote, "Any changing language is not well suited to an unchanging religion. The natural movement of things constantly attacks living languages and, aside from these great changes that alter them absolutely, there are also changes which may not seem important but which in fact are very much so. Every day the corruption of the age seizes words and spoils them for its own amusement. If the Church spoke our language, the most sacred words of the liturgy would be at the mercy of the first brazen-faced wit who had the effrontery to ridicule them or make them indecent. For every conceivable reason, the language of religion must be kept out of the domain of man" (*Du Pape*, Book 1, Ch. 20).

for the Vedas are prior to the *Avatâras*; it is not they who reveal the *Sanâtana-Dharma*, or who create it, so to speak.

Detailed understanding of the Torah, the Koran, and the Brahmanical Books presupposes a knowledge not only of the associations of ideas evoked by the Hebrew, Arabic, or Sanskrit terms, but also of the implicit propositions furnished by the commentators, either precisely in virtue of their learning, or through inspiration; as for the symbolism that is so important in all Scriptures, including the Gospels, it is necessary to distinguish between a direct, complete, and essential symbolism and one that is indirect, partial, and accidental: when Christ raises his eyes towards Heaven in prayer, the symbolism is direct, for Heaven or "that which is above" represents by its spatial situation and also its cosmic nature the "divine dimension"; but when, in the parable of the sower, the birds that carry away the seed represent the devil, the symbolism is quite indirect and provisional, for it is only insofar as they remove the seed and fly about in all directions that birds, which in themselves symbolize the celestial states, can assume this negative meaning. Another example can also be noted here, this time of a symbolism that is both partial and direct: the Koran compares the braying of a donkey to the voice of Satan, but the donkey in itself is not involved, even though its cry can never lend itself to a positive interpretation.[10] These different levels of symbolism are frequently encountered in the Law

---

10. It was to a she-ass—that of Balaam—that God gave speech, and it was an ass that carried the Virgin and Child on their flight into Egypt, and also Christ on his triumphal entry into Jerusalem. Let us remember too that the ass bears on its back the mark of a cross. The ass symbolizes humility, in contrast with the princely pride of the horse, and indeed it incarnates, alongside its noble fellow creature, the peaceful, modest, and touching— we might almost say childlike—character of creatures without glory, but nonetheless good; as for its braying, this seems to manifest an ambition to equal the neighing of a horse, as if there were here the caricatural mark of the temptation of the small to play at being great, and thus of the sin of pride. One could accept that the ass at the manger has a lower, if not malefic meaning—in view of its braying and its reputation for stubbornness—but according to another interpretation, which is much more adequate and which is corroborated by the *Golden Legend*, the ass at the manger represents the presence of the small and the humble, those who are despised by the world but received by the Lord.

of Manu, which it is impossible to understand in detail without knowing the implicit ramifications of the various symbols.

For the unprepared reader, many passages of the Scriptures contain surprising repetitions and pleonasms, if indeed they are not altogether unintelligible or apparently absurd. Thus, for example, the Koran says of Abraham: "We have chosen him in the world here below, and in truth he is in the world beyond, amongst the just" (2:130). One may wonder what the function is of the second proposition, which in any case is obvious. In fact it is rendered necessary by the preceding words: "in this world"; if the Scripture had said simply: "We have chosen him", it would have been unnecessary to elaborate further; but since it adds "in the world here below", it is obliged to say also "and in the world beyond", so as to prevent the first phrase being interpreted in a limitative sense.[11] From the Islamic point of view, the second phrase was all the more necessary in view of the fact that Christianity placed Abraham in the "limbo of the Fathers" and because Christ described himself as being "prior" to the Patriarch.[12]

Here is another example: Jesus said, "I shall announce to you what ye will eat and what ye will store up in your houses" (Koran 3:49). This passage alludes first to the Eucharist, and secondly to the amassing of treasures in the world to come[13]—two elements of the Christ-given message; but these associations are not obvious at first sight and on mere reading. An analogous passage is the following: "Jesus, son of Mary, made this prayer: O God our Lord, send down upon us a table spread with food from Heaven, that it may be a feast for the first and the last of us, and a sign of Thy power" (5:114). The words "the first and the last of us" refer respectively to the saint and to the man of sufficient virtue, and also in a different connection to the gnostic and to the simple

---

11. This verse is not unconnected with the following one: "We showed Abraham the kingdom of heaven and of the earth so that he might be among those who possess certainty" (6:75). Here "heaven" means both the stars and the heavenly worlds, or, according to Ghazzali, "inward vision".

12. This Christ did in that he was an actual and concrete manifestation of the Logos, one which was central for a given world.

13. "Sell that ye have, and give alms; provide yourselves bags which wax not old, a treasure in the heavens that faileth not, where no thief approacheth, neither moth corrupteth. For where your treasure is, there will your heart be also" (Luke 12:33-34).

believer; the remainder of the passage contains a divine threat against the unworthy, which recalls the analogous threat of St. Paul: "Whosoever shall eat this bread unworthily eateth damnation to himself" (1 Cor. 11:27-29).

On an entirely different plane, and in a passage concerning the pilgrimage (2:198), the Koran remarks, to the amazement of the unprepared reader, that "it is not a sin for you if you seek some favor from your Lord", which means: it is permitted to you during the pilgrimage to gain some subsistence by means of commerce; it is enough to know this, but this meaning is not clear from the words themselves. Of an analogous kind is the following difficulty: "There is no sin for those who believe and do good works, in what they have eaten, if they fear God and are believing, and do good works, and again fear God and believe, and again fear Him and excel in good" (5:93). The sum and substance of this is that in the case of true believers, no trace remains of any sin they may have committed by ignorance before the revelation of the corresponding prescription, or before their entry into Islam; and this also includes the case of the true believers—but not of the hypocrites—who died before this revelation. As for the repetitions contained in this passage, they refer according to the commentators to the divisions of time—past, present, and future—and also to the degree of application—ego, God, neighbor—of our moral duties and of the spiritual attitudes corresponding to them. But this verse also has a meaning both more literal and more general, namely that in exceptional circumstances the alimentary prescriptions are subordinated to the intrinsic principles, which is to say that the observance of the latter may, in case of need, compensate for the lack of observance of the former.

One detail in the Koran which may cause surprise is that often, without transition or logical connection, some legal stipulation or other is followed by a phrase such as: "And Allah is Mighty, Wise". The reason for this is that the Koran contains several superimposed "layers", as it were; after pronouncing on a temporal matter, the veil of contingency is torn, and the immutable foundation reappears.

But, one may ask, if the reading of the Koran is so arduous and precarious, even for men who know Arabic, how is it that Islam can peaceably win so many followers among peoples who do not know this language, and are as far removed from the Arabs as the Negroes, the Chinese, and the Malays? The reason that Islam expands is not by the reading of the Koran, but by its human, spiritual, psychological, and social manifestation: if African Negroes embrace the Arab religion, it is because they observe the kind of life led by Muslims, see them praying, hear the call of the muezzin, observe a certain generosity common to believers, as also the serenity of the pious; it is only afterwards that they learn the minimum of Arabic necessary for the canonical prayers. The immense majority of non-Arab Muslims will never be able to read the Koran, still less appreciate its literary qualities; they live with the effects without knowing the cause. It is easy to understand the importance in Islam of the *'ulamâ* when one knows that they are the guardians and, as it were, the reservoirs, not only of the verses of the Koran—very often sibylline[14]—but also and above all of the implicit meanings derived from either the *Sunnah* or the traditional commentaries.

Certain enigmas in the Koran result from a purely metaphysical intention: "Dost thou not see how thy Lord hath spread the shade—And had He willed He could have made it motionless—then We (Allah) have made the sun to be its indicator; then We withdraw it unto Us, a gradual withdrawal" (25:45). In this passage, what is striking in the first instance is that the shade is not described as indicating the movement of the sun by its movement, but on the contrary the sun is described as indicating the shade. According to some exegetes this expresses, or confirms, the fact that God is the direct cause of every phenomenon—that there are thus no intermediate causes;[15] others relate the term "shade" (*zill*)[16] to the twilight, that is to say, brightness without sun—this

---

14. This characteristic belongs much more to the "parabolic" (*mutashâbihât*) than to the "confirmed" (*mukhamât*) verses (3:7), the latter constituting the "Mother of the Book" (*Umm al-Kitâb*); the former contain a multiplicity of meanings and the latter one single meaning; the "confirmed" verses may comprise gradations, but they are parallel and not divergent. The "Mother of the Book" is basically the dogmas together with the essential precepts and prohibitions.
15. On this subject see the formulation of Fudali, quoted in the present author's *Stations of Wisdom*.
16. The meaning of this word is to be distinguished from that of *zulmah*, "darkness" or "obscurity", and from that of *fai'*, "projected shadow".

is the hour that corresponds to the heavenly state,[17] free both from darkness and the burning sun. Finally, according to another interpretation of the verse,[18] the shade represents relative existence, which is an absence of Being or a void (*'adam*), the shade itself being an absence of light; and indeed relative existence[19] cannot be known except by virtue of absolute Being[20] which here corresponds to the sun.[21]

Another passage of the Koran that calls for mention here is the following: when Satan says that he will seduce men "from in front, from behind, on their right and on their left" (7:17), the commentators observe that neither above nor below is mentioned and conclude that this verse expresses in its fashion the limitation of the power of Satan; now the two inviolable dimensions are essentially "greatness" and "littleness"; that is, man is saved either because he remains "little" like a child, or because he rises above things like an eagle.[22] These two states, moreover, can and must be combined, as is indicated for example by the name of Lao-Tzu, the "Child-Elder"; in other words, one can be either "too little" or "too great"[23]—too humble or too elevated—for mortal sin and the final disgrace; the very type of the Promethean or titanic sinner is the impassioned and ambitious adult who,

17. The "companions of the right" (the saved) will be found "amongst thornless lote-trees, and clustered plantains, and spreading shade . . ." (56:27-30).
18. Mentioned, like the foregoing, in the famous compilation of *Rûh al-Bayân*.
19. This is a pleonasm, but the term is used for the sake of greater clarity.
20. Or "relatively absolute", in keeping with a very important metaphysical nuance referred to several times in the author's works.
21. It has been remarked to the author that in Sufi symbolism, the creation of shade precedes that of light, because the shade—the negative of Being, or ignorance—represents relativization, manifestation, or the first objectification of the Essence.
22. The same passage affirms that the majority of men are ungrateful, thus emphasizing that what lures man into Satan's net is lack of gratitude toward God—a statement calling for much development. It is indeed by a kind of ingratitude—or by a thousand kinds of ingratitude and culpable unawareness—that man removes himself from the Center-Origin; it is the gift of existence, or intelligence, profaned and squandered, and finally trodden underfoot.
23. The innocent littleness of children does not need wisdom, but wisdom—being a totality—is impossible without this littleness.

being neither child nor old man, has neither the humble and trusting innocence of the little, nor the detached and serene wisdom of the great. But "height" is also the adamantine Truth, just as "depth" is the unalterable nature of things. The devil has no hold on either the incorruptibility of pure knowledge or on the innocence of pure Being.

In the sacred Texts there may be symbolical or dialectical antinomies, but not contradictions; it is always a difference of point of view or aspect that provides the key, even in cases like that of divergent Gospel narratives. For example, when according to St. Luke one of the thieves is bad and the other good, it is obviously a case of simple opposition between evil and good, unbelief and faith, vice and virtue.[24] On the other hand, when according to St Matthew and St Mark the two thieves abuse Christ, they are identifiable with the two poles of vice—one mental and one moral—found in the human soul, where Christ appears as the Intellect and on a lower level as the voice of conscience, which is a prolongation or a reflection of the pure Intellect. Moreover, if good and evil as such are to be found in the soul, there is also evil under the guise of virtues and good spoiled by vices. Let us remember also that if one of the thieves was good, he was nonetheless, as a thief, an offence to Christ, so that the narratives of Matthew and Mark coincide from a certain point of view with that of Luke. Nevertheless, it is Luke's version that takes prece-

---

24. Tauler compares the crucifixion of the first thief to the vain repentance of people who put all their faith in outward austerities and penances born of pride, which only bring them damnation in return for their sufferings; this is the "zeal of bitterness" of which St Benedict speaks. The second cross is that of the sinner who has really turned away from the world, who has sacrificed everything for God, and joyously accepts the sufferings deserved for his sins, with a firm hope in the love and mercy of God. The central cross is that of the perfect man who has chosen to follow Christ in all things, and who must be crucified in the flesh in order to attain the "cross of the divine nature of Christ". From the point of view of Hermetic symbolism, this image can be identified with the caduceus, wherein the central axis or the "tree of the world" comprises two cycles, one ascending and one descending, which relates it to the *janua coeli* and the *janua inferni*, and also, in Hindu terms, to the *deva-yâna* and the *pitri-yâna*.

dence, wherever this alternative exists, for Mercy has priority over Rigor, according to an Islamic formula.[25]

This style of interpretation—whose origins, as far as Christianity is concerned, are to be found in Origen, St Ambrose, St Augustine, St John Cassian, St Gregory, and others—is profoundly rooted in the nature of things, and consequently it occurs in all traditional settings; but what is important here is that many of the images contained in the sacred Scriptures would remain unintelligible without their transposition onto the metaphysical, macrocosmic or microcosmic planes.[26]

Contrary to what is generally believed today, the people of antiquity were in no way blind to the strangeness, as far as the literal sense is concerned, of certain passages in the Scriptures. Origen noted, quite justifiably, that a blow given by the right hand falls on the left cheek, and that it is thus surprising that Christ enjoins offering the left cheek after the right, not inversely;[27] or again, that the eyes look at one object together, not separately, and thus it is impossible to take literally Christ's counsel to pluck out one's right eye, if it has looked with concupiscence, quite apart from the fact that the counsel itself can scarcely be meant literally, and so on.[28] Again, Origen remarks that if there are Israelites "in spirit", there must also be Egyptians and Babylonians "in spirit", and that the Biblical passages concerning Pharaoh and

25. This is the inscription on the Throne of Allah: "Verily, My Mercy hath precedence over My Wrath."
26. There is also a diabolical pseudo-exegesis on the part of modernistic sectarians, for example the affirmation by the Ahmadis of Lahore—a heresy founded in the nineteenth century—that the "resurrection of the dead" means the present day "awakening of peoples"! This is false twice over, first because the resurrection concerns the dead and not the living and takes place at the Last Judgment, and secondly because people are not awakening, to say the least; what is awakening is something quite different. In exactly the same category are those Christian exegetes whose sole concern is to empty the Scriptures of their content, for example by "psychologizing" the angels, who in reality are perfectly objective and concrete beings, as well as being at the same time "higher states", a difference corresponding to that between the Boddhisattvic function and the corresponding nirvanic level.
27. The Gospel indicates a logical and moral hierarchy, and not a succession of physical situations.
28. Here the logical and moral meaning is as clear as can be, in spite of the physical impossibility of the image.

176

Nebuchadnezzar cannot all be applied to the monarchs bearing these names; consequently some of them are applicable only to the "types" that these names designate. [29]

As regards the apparent contradictions of the sacred Scriptures, a further example from the Bhagavad-Gita may be quoted: "All this universe is permeated by Me, My form [nevertheless] remaining unmanifested. All beings dwell in Me [but] I do not dwell in them. And yet these beings do not dwell in Me. Behold my divine *yoga*! Supporting all beings without dwelling in them— that is My Self (*Âtmâ*), the cause of beings" (9:4, 5). One might think that this passage contains a flagrant contradiction, but the relationships envisaged change from one sentence to the next, as Shankara explains in his commentary: "No being deprived (by hypothesis) of the Self can become an object of experience. Thus they dwell in Me, that is to say, they exist by Me, the Self. . . . I am certainly the ultimate Essence, even of ether . . . but these things—beginning with *Brahmâ* (and down to the smallest of creatures)—do not dwell in Me. . . . The *shruti* speaks of the nonattachment of the Self, seeing that It has no connection with any object: void (of the limitative condition) of attachment. It is never attached." *Âtmâ* cannot comprise in Its infinite nature any factors of attachment or of limitation.[30]

---

29. Analogously, but on another plane, when Christ declares that "no man cometh unto the Father but by me", it is a question not only of one particular manifestation of the Logos, but of the Logos as such, and thus of every illuminating and law-giving manifestation of the eternal Word. The intrinsic truth of the great revelations of humanity forces us to this conclusion, just as other objective facts force us to interpret—and thus limit—certain scriptural passages, for example the prohibition of killing, or the injunction to turn the other cheek, which no one takes in an unconditional or absolute sense.

30. It may be remarked in passing that in some respects the European feels closer to the mentality of Hindus than to that of Arabs. In other respects, however, he is closer to the Arabs and Islam—even if he does not admit it—than to the Hindus and Brahmanism. The former affinity is explained by the fact that Europe, apart from tiny exceptions, is Aryan, and this is not merely a matter of language, though one should remember that there is no language without a corresponding mentality. The latter affinity is explained by the fact that Europe, being Christian with Jewish and Muslim minorities, is spiritually Semitic, at least by heredity. This observation is not unconnected with the general question now being considered.

Sometimes divergences in sacred texts—and *a fortiori* between texts of different provenance—are more or less comparable to the divergence between exact astronomy and that of Ptolemy, the former founded upon the objective, but in a way "extra-human", nature of facts, and the latter upon human experience, of necessity limited but symbolically and spiritually adequate, because "natural".[31] A spiritual perspective may, in a given case, opt for one or the other of these solutions—analogically speaking—according to its internal logic and to the opportunity it gives rise to. For example, in the fundamental divergence between the Christian and Muslim theses regarding Jesus' end on earth, there is a mystery which the Gospel does not take account of explicitly, and of which each of the two viewpoints providentially conveys a somewhat extreme aspect, in keeping with the respective demands or interests of each spirituality.[32]

The greatest possible divergence in this realm is probably to be found in the opposition between the non-theism—or nirvanism—of the Buddhists and the monotheism of Semitic origin, the former being founded on the dream-like and impermanent character of the cosmos in connection with the negative or "void-like" appearance of Absolute Reality, and the latter on the reality

---

31. We shall note that traditional India admits both a flat and a spherical earth: for the *Puranas*, the earth is a disc supported by Vishnu as a tortoise, whereas for the *Sûrya-Siddhânta* it is a sphere suspended in the void.
32. Docetism and monophysitism have exhibited various aspects of this mystery; the term "aspects" is used because the whole question is one of great complexity, and it is even probable that it cannot be solved in earthly terms. At all events it is this mystery that explains, on the one hand, the superhuman and supernatural heroism of the martyrs integrated into the nature of Christ and, on the other hand—on a completely different plane—the profusion of divergent doctrines concerning his nature from the very beginning of Christianity. However that may be, one must not lose sight of the fact that the Koranic passage in question, which while affirming the reality of the Ascension allows the Crucifixion only the semblance of reality (4:157-8), can have—and indeed of necessity does have—a meaning that concerns a "spiritual type" and not a historical personage, and that it is sometimes difficult, and perhaps even impossible in a scriptural passage of this kind, to know where the limit between history and symbolism lies. This is so especially in those cases where the literal meaning is a matter of indifference as regards the "Divine Intention" of a given Revelation, and from the point of view at which the religion in question must place itself.

178

of experience of the world and on the positive and active manifestation of the creative Principle. These definitions, inadequate as they may be in some respects, illustrate in their fashion the non-contradiction—or the profound coherence—of the heavenly universal Word.[33]

Here we may stop, as our purpose was merely to show that the apparent deficiencies found within the same sacred Book are in fact syntheses or ellipses, and also to emphasize that in order to be in conformity with the truth and orthodoxy, it is not at all necessary to find sublime something that one is unable to understand and appreciate. To be respectful without hypocrisy and sincere without disrespect, it is enough to know that the Divine Word is necessarily perfect, whether at the moment we are capable of recognizing it or not. Be that as it may, since it is impossible to make the Sacred Texts the subject of a demonstration, which finally is of secondary importance, without exceeding the limits of such a demonstration—for its contents inevitably open up horizons that take us singularly far from the original intention –it is fitting to conclude with a quotation that brings the question back to its essence and at the same time serves as a justification for the present study: "Say: if the sea were ink for the writing of the Words of my Lord, the sea would be exhausted before those Words, even if We (Allah) were to add a further sea to augment it" (Koran 18:109).[34]

33. As the author has remarked elsewhere, "theism" is to be found in a certain fashion within the framework of Buddhism, notably in the form of Amidism, even though it is "non-theistic", and "non-theism" is in turn to be found in the monotheistic esoterisms in the concept of the "impersonal Essence" of Divinity (*Treasures of Buddhism*, World Wisdom Books, 1993).
34. Likewise: "And if all the trees on the earth were pens, and the sea, with seven more seas to help it, were ink, the words of Allah could not be exhausted. Lo! Allah is Mighty, Wise" (31:27).

Paradoxes of Spiritual Expression

When the notion of dialectic is applied to the domain of spirituality, it must be amplified to include more than the art of reasoning correctly, for what is at stake now is the whole problem of spiritual expression itself; before knowing how to reason, it is necessary to know how to express oneself, because spiritual dialectic is first and foremost the capacity to give account in human language of realities that transcend, if not man's mind, at least his earthly experience and his ordinary psychology. In other words, dialectic is not only a question of logic, it is also a question of verbal adequation; both things require principles and experience. Now a man can be the beneficiary of the loftiest spiritual knowledge without possessing the art of expressing himself from the point of view both of the content and of the form, if only because he is a victim of the mental habits of his social surroundings; thus prudence of the most basic kind obliges us to take into account this margin of contingency when considering a sage whose dialectic disappoints us, provided of course that we have some grounds for believing he is a genuine sage. In any case, it is a fact that traditional metaphysicians too often accept theological patchwork in the mental expression of their infused science, while otherwise proving that their knowledge is not bound to this framework or level.

The Semitic religions of Abrahamic lineage appear as gifts come down from Heaven at a particular moment in history; now in order to convince whole collectivities, that is, in order to convert and to integrate them, these religions must appeal to volitive and emotional factors; and this, quite obviously, has nothing to do with pure intellection, nor with nuanced dialectic. Monotheists needed Hellenism finally, not only for the sake of learning how to give a more explicit account of their intellectual intentions, but also to favor the flourishing of intellection itself, by availing themselves precisely of a suppler means of expression than that offered by the symbols and ellipses of the Scriptures.

It could be said *grosso modo* that the vice of the Greeks was not that they could not think, but that they no longer knew what to use thinking for; the mistake of the monotheists was to accuse Greek truth of falsity for having been thought out, instead of accusing particular thinkers of being unable to make truth operative, that is, of an inability to detach it from mere mental processes; this reproach would nevertheless presuppose identifying truth itself, wherever it exists and in spite of the framework. In accusing the philosophers of spiritual sterility, if not always of error, the mistake was made of attributing the vices of the sophists to the Neoplatonists, schematically speaking; both Plotinus and his truth were accused of the shortcomings of paganism, namely, of worldly and unworkable intellectualism.

But this background situation could not stop the ancient Christians—consciously or not—from thinking along lines inherited from the philosophers, nor finally from using their philosophy to shore up their own theological speculations.

$$*$$
$$*\quad*$$

If intellectually lacking, or even disappointing, formulations encountered among saints can be explained either by an intellectual or doctrinal limitation,[1] or simply by a lack of dialectical skill—which is a matter of instrumental inadequacy—there is yet a third possible factor that must be taken into account here, namely, that of a moralizing intention or, to be more precise, the function of righting or re-establishing an equilibrium. Saints dwell in the midst of a religious humanity of which they are a part; however, this collectivity, according to the natural—and cyclical— law of gravity and degeneration, is sliding downwards so that reli-

---

1. A doctrinal limitation does not always denote a corresponding intellectual limitation since it can be situated on the level of mental articulation and not on that of pure intellection.

gion tends to be corrupted in its collective support. Parallel to this trend, society is governed by leaders who follow their passions and ambitions; thus to the coagulating heaviness of the collectivity is added the dissipating and exteriorizing restlessness of those who govern; each vice not only colludes with the other, but conjures it. It is in the context of this fatality that one must situate the ascetic extravagance of many saints, whose moralism may strike one at first as flat and obsessive; from the point of view of the pure and simple truth, all of this may seem paltry and excessive, but in the face of a concrete human reality, it is useful and even indispensable, for one cannot neglect the possibility of opposing a gross and negative disequilibrium with another disequilibrium, also gross but positive.

It is the function of most saints to set a good example to the point of excess, and it is a truly sacrificial function: by exaggerating to the point of absurdity, the saint takes upon himself, in some fashion, all the sins of society. It is certainly regrettable that such a function too often presents spirituality from an angle that disfigures it, just as it is regrettable that, on an altogether different plane, metaphysical dialectic readily makes use of the crutches of theology, and thus involves itself in a voluntarist and sentimental anthropomorphism; but these are the unavoidable effects of pressures from the milieu.

It is a fact that religions attach little importance to intelligence while, on the other hand, insisting on faith, virtue, and works; this is not difficult to understand since every man has an immortal soul in need of salvation even though he may not be intelligent, whereas, conversely, not every intelligent man is saved, to say the least. On the one hand, intelligence has no effective worth unless its contents are expressly the fundamental and saving truths; on the other hand, intelligence must be balanced by virtue and faith, because without the aid of these two elements, it is not fully in conformity with its nature nor, consequently, with its vocation. Faith is the quality that converts into deeds—positive or negative depending on the case—the facts provided by truth; and virtue is the aptitude of our will and sensibility to conform ourselves to what truth and faith demand. Faith is to be distinguished from rational certitude in that it brings together the acceptance of the true with the love of the true and the will to realize it; thus it is a certitude that is not just mental, but that encompasses and engages every fiber of our being.

Faith and virtue do not produce intelligence, as is only too obvious; but they do confer upon even the most modest of intelligence the maximum of purity and acuity that lie in its power; conversely, if intelligence in the ordinary sense of the term does not produce *de facto* either virtue or faith, this is simply because it is not fully itself, for the pure Intellect possesses both of these powers in its very substance and actualizes them inasmuch as it is fully realized. But this realization, precisely, presupposes the collaboration of an active faith and of an effort toward virtue, as is proven by all spiritual methods, even those that are most free from all voluntarist and sentimental elements.

The well-known corruptibility of intelligence allows one to excuse, to a large extent, the familiar—and specifically voluntarist—equation of intelligence with pride:[2] it could never be a question here of intelligence as such, of an intelligence that is fully itself and, as a result, includes in its nature the roots of both faith and virtue, and thereby also their necessary manifestations; on the contrary, it is a question of intelligence as it is in fact encountered in most cases, namely as a freely available capacity for coordination that, most often, is offered to the world and denied to God.

If it can be admitted without difficulty that, from the point of view of piety, virtue takes precedence over intelligence, it will be much harder to admit that it does this sometimes to the detriment of truth, though, in this case, it is merely a question of truths that are not important for salvation;[3] it might be tempting to object that if intelligence is capable of deviating, virtue can no

2. There are other such pious equations, notably that between beauty and sin or, inversely, between ugliness and virtue; often cleanliness suffers the same verdict as beauty, and uncleanliness benefits from the same favorable prejudice as ugliness. One finds in every religious climate—*de facto* if not *de jure*—such excesses dictated by a concern both for efficacy and simplification.

3. In the piety of some zealots, virtue readily defies common sense: basic logic may perish, so long as humility is safe. In all justice, truth—or the

less, but this would be an inexact comparison since a corrupted virtue is no longer a virtue, whereas deviated intelligence is still intelligence, unless one were to deny this with the help of some new term, which would define intelligence only in terms of truth, just as virtue is defined by the good it manifests. The opposite of virtue is vice; now according to what is commonly taught vice is, with respect to virtue, either a privation or an excess; error for its part is not necessarily a lack of intelligence nor, above all, an excess of intelligence, though it is possible to call a lack of pure intellection a "lack of intelligence" and to call an abuse of philosophizing thought unbalanced, because severed from intellection, an "excess of intelligence"; but this would not conform to current usage, in which intelligence is by no means synonymous with metaphysical adequation.

The root of this problem of terminology, in short, is the fact that intelligence appears in two forms—notwithstanding all secondary modes—namely, intellection and reasoning; now it is possible to reason very cleverly in the absence, first, of intellection and, second, of the facts required by the subject at hand, while maintaining that this is undeniably an operation of the intelligence. Be that as it may, stupidity and intelligence can be quite congenial at the level of rationality, which alone is considered when speaking in the usual sense of "intelligent" men; even so, the term "rationality" is but a euphemism, especially when what passes for psychology gets involved.

Conversely, pure intellection can express itself naively, and can even go hand in hand outwardly with a logic that is more than feeble—this is often a matter of formation or training—without it being possible to deny that it is intelligence, and clearly much more fundamentally so than is a merely virtuoso rationality. As a result, one should not be too surprised that theologians and mystics can sometimes reason very poorly, if indeed they are reasoning at all; this deficiency can even reach absurd limits but without abandoning the minimal framework of saving truth. For if it is possible for intelligent people to accept error, the contrary must be equally possible, namely, for naïve people to accept the truth.

nature of things—sets the purview of virtue's rights; in other words, virtues are limited by truth, while being unlimited in sanctity.

A patent example of voluntarist thinking, more dynamic than logical, is the obligatory conviction that one is "the greatest sinner in the world"; this blame which the believer is meant to direct automatically against himself is a typically Christian formulation, for "he that humbleth himself shall be exalted"; clearly, this saying of Christ can be interpreted at various levels, but it had to be given a volitive and sentimental meaning, absolutely binding and effective, and therefore adjusted to the passional man and not the "pneumatic". At first sight, the absurdity of such a conviction is flagrant: first of all, the man who turns toward God believing himself a sinner cannot be the greatest of sinners; secondly, no one either knows all men or can know the extent and number of their sins; thirdly, it is highly improbable that there should be at any given moment one man on earth who alone would be the greatest sinner of all.[4] Such is the degree of absurdity here that one is obliged to seek for the plausible intention of the formula on another plane, and one succeeds in doing so by taking into account the theological context, which is that God alone possesses necessary Being; the reason for the human state is for man to become aware of this, which he can do, in an atmosphere of voluntarist individualism, only by means of a sentimental prejudice where the subjective intention is more important than the objective reality—in other words, where a drama of annihilation replaces the awareness of our nothingness.

In favor of this pious strategy, one could mention the merits of its age-old efficacy; in its disfavor, we must point out on the contrary its present-day ineffectiveness inasmuch as this results, not from the worldliness or the perversity of modern man, but simply from a certain critical sense which men have acquired from experience and which they can no longer overlook, whether they are good or bad. In other words, if the exaggerations of saints have

---

4. These objections are too obvious not to have been known in all times; yet here is the classic response of devotees: if notorious sinners were to enjoy the graces we have received, they would be better than us. Such a response only extends the limits of the problem while adding new difficulties to it.

lost in our age their power to convince,[5] this is largely due to the fact—aside from negative reasons—that people have learned how to think, as it were in spite of themselves and because of a historical fatality; now knowing how to "think" does not here mean, assuredly, knowing how to discern the value of things in depth, but simply subjecting phenomena as such to a certain minimum of logical analysis, to the detriment sometimes of the comprehension of their content, whereas men were formerly more sensitive to the contents and intentions and less to the logic of forms. This is in fact what the history of art teaches us: for primitive man, the most rudimentary design could be charged with a symbolic consciousness and an evocative power that is hard to imagine, whereas the artist formed by centuries of visual and technical experience is capable of reproducing with perfect exactitude the most complex form but perhaps without grasping any more of it than a kind of physical and accidental topography.

*
* *

"Allah does what He wills" and "He is without associates": these two principial statements explain the Islamic negation of the necessary succession of temporal phases, on the one hand, and of secondary or horizontal causes, on the other. In other words, for Muslim thought God alone is the cause, not natural laws, and God creates each thing anew at each instant, not because the existence of a tree—or its possibility or archetype—requires that it continue to be a tree throughout duration, but because "God wills" ever anew that the existing thing should be a tree and nothing else, for motives known to Him alone; time is thus reversible, and physical causes are but apparent; the world is a chaos that only an incomprehensible and unforeseeable divine "willing" holds together, not *a priori*, but by means of creative or causative acts ever renewed out of a perpetually resurging nothingness. To believe the contrary—in the opinion of these thinkers—amounts to denying that God "does what He wills" and

---

5. Those of a Benoît Labre, for example. What is objectively absurd can serve as a vehicle for what is subjectively plausible, that is, spiritually effective; but it remains a double-edged sword.

to asserting that He has "associates" who come to His assistance and without whom He cannot manage.

This doctrine, which is typically theological in its obstinate clinging to a single dimension of the Real—that is, in its refusal to combine divergent though complementary aspects—is founded, geometrically speaking, on a consideration of "vertical radii" to the exclusion of "concentric circles"; for this way of thinking, the "vertical" relationship excludes the "horizontal", just as, in trinitarian theology, the divinity of the *hypostasis* excludes the non-hypostatic nature of the Divinity, because the Trinity is conceived as the Absolute as such. In theology, aspects and points of view—objective and subjective situations—are frozen for the spiritual benefit of such and such a mental predisposition; only in pure metaphysics does the Real reveal diverse aspects—in themselves divergent—and intelligence shifts its position according to these divergences. Metaphysics alone knows how to reconcile the "vertical" dimension of causality with the "horizontal" dimension, or the absoluteness of the Divine Principle with Its aspects of relativity.

*
* *

Average Sufism identifies wisdom with moral attitudes, such as alms-giving and poverty, which, in themselves, have nothing to do with Knowledge. Gnosis implies the idea of universal illusion, and this idea, if truly understood, brings about detachment; now one may proceed in a reverse direction and provoke the understanding of illusion by imposing detachment on the soul; and this is imposed on the soul precisely by such measures as poverty, alms-giving, the breaking of profane habits. To admit the illusory nature of the world sincerely is, indeed, to be detached from it, and this detachment is proven by the attitudes that correspond to it; nonetheless, in spite of its justification, such a reasoning is problematic, for if on the one hand it indicates a way, on the other hand, it blurs the trail, and makes one lose sight of the metaphysical—hence esoteric—primacy of Knowledge.

But there is still another explanation for the ambiguity of average Sufism. Esoterism is directed in principle to any man of sound mind, but the moment it places itself on the level of this point of view, its methods become exteriorized, so to speak: rather than dissolving the shell of ignorance by means of intellection *ab intra*, it is broken by means of asceticism *ab extra*; metaphysical notions appear then only *a posteriori* and as no more than points of reference.

Be that as it may, we could present the paradox of average Sufism in the following way, at the risk perhaps of repeating ourselves on some points; but that is of little account, for the question has rarely been broached from this angle. It is important to make a distinction between esoterism as such and what could be called a "pre-esoterism":[6] this "pre-esoterism" is nothing more than an ascetic exoterism, excessive, subtle, interiorized, and pushed to the outermost limits of what is exorbitant and refined, whereas esoterism proper starts from superior concepts that exempt it, precisely, from moral and social extravagances. Since the doctrines and methods of esoterism are not directed to the naïve and worldy man, they could in no wise be individualistic, sentimental, and quantitative; this is demonstrated by Shadhilism, which requires on the part of its adherents no change in their social condition and which, as a result, allows neither mendicancy nor the tattered garb of ordinary and moralizing Sufism. "Pre-esoterism" puts in the place of the metaphysical truth the sincerity of faith, and in the place of direct and positive spiritual practices the quantity of pious and ascetic practices; but the two attitudes are often inextricably intertwined, either to the detriment of true esoterism or, on the contrary, in its wake. For if pre-esoterism has, strictly speaking, no logical connection with sapience, it nonetheless plays a kind of preparatory and disciplinary role in regard to it: indeed, it is a perfectly logical principle to submit man to moral trials before offering him, not some initiatic and operative treasure, but simply a superior truth, thus ensuring that this truth will be accepted, not as a dangerous and possibly impious play of the mind, but as a viaticum which engages the whole man in a

6. In the sense of an antecedent that is not historical, of course, but ascetic and preparatory. The symbolist and doctrinally unarticulated or implicit character of early Sufism's documents favors, however, the confusion between religious zeal and esoterism; it must not be forgotten that esoterism admitted, at the origin, only oral teaching.

definitive manner and which, consequently, cannot be dissociated from the virtues specific to piety.

If this preliminary function of quantitative asceticism has too often been taken as an end in itself, one must nonetheless take care not to confuse the popularizing abuse with an asceticism based on a purifying purpose; in the latter case, concepts appear as secondary since truth is seen from the point of view of its immanence; it will suffice then to break the shell to discover the kernel, which is immanent and liberating knowledge.

*
* *

What is characteristic in Islam of the "human margin", found in one degree or another in every traditional system, is hagiography;[7] we obviously have nothing against the didactic content of the legends, but it has to be admitted that their exaggerations and platitudes make them unreadable for anyone wishing to form a concrete and plausible image of what saints are. If everything is meant to be symbolic—and the symbolism is made incisive because of the sinful propensities presupposed in the average reader—what seems to be forgotten is that the absurdity of the detail or of the image ruins the symbol, if not for a particular pious subjectivity, then at least in principle; the isolating, magnifying, striking, and emotional quality of the language, which violates the outer logic of things, leads to unintelligibility when taken outside the psychological sector from which it is derived and which it addresses. This is as much as to say that the apologetic value of the stories of saints is nil; there is no point in showing them to a non-Muslim in order to foster his interest in Islam. What matters is that for an Easterner, who accepts this dialectic, the legends transmit in trenchant fashion their message of virtue.

Legalistic scruples for instance, examples of which make for nearly unbearable reading, refer to the crucial virtue of sincerity: the aim is to educate man, not in view of a cringing punctiliousness, which actually offends God—as the Western reader readily

---

7. By "hagiography" we mean neither the canonical account of the Life of the Prophet (*Sîrat an-Nabî*), nor the personal recollections or testimonies of the Sufis.

presumes—but for the sake of a perfect veracity in deeds and thoughts, which is a means of realizing a certain unity in view of the Unique; the Eastern reader discerns the spiritual intention without balking at the implausibility of the images, whether on the level of facts or that of simple psychology. Then there is the exaltation of poverty and generosity; here once again one must look beyond the "hyperdulia" of the poor—and the corresponding anathematization of the wealthy[8]—to find the underlying purpose, which is the moral and contemplative quality of poverty: the detachment of soul in the face of the world and its multiple seductions. As for generosity, it is most commonly represented by often unimaginable examples of almsgiving; but its spiritual meaning remains nonetheless intelligible, and even morally moving for the reader to whom it is addressed, and this is what matters. All of the virtues, whose problematical depiction is found in Muslim hagiography, take their root in the single sincerity of unitary faith: one must believe that God "is", and that, in being, He "is One"; one must accept this truly and not pretend to do so; and to accept it truly is to draw every possible consequence, from legalistic scruples to sapiential monism.[9]

Muslim hagiography stylizes the facts it aims to transmit, as sometimes occurs in ancient Christian hagiography, though in that case with a more exclusively moralizing intent,: it distills the spiritual content, offering it as a quintessence, an elixir, a pearl; and in so doing, it intends to serve as truth. This amounts to saying that the sense of truth among Easterners is focused less on the exactness of the facts or on their aspect of earthly contingence than on

---

8. All the more surprising since Khadijah, the first wife of the Prophet and his protectress in the early days of his mission, was very wealthy; but she was poor in the sense of being detached from her fortune; this nuance should suffice to spare us from the hagiographers' doubled-edged anathematization. One of the great merits of the Imam Shadhili and of his spiritual lineage was to have remained impervious to the moral automatisms dear to popular Sufism or common piety.
9. By monism, or also a "pantheism both transcendent and immanent", we mean an absolutely rigorous and thus integral metaphysical perspective such as *Advaita Vedânta*, in which the term "pantheism" is accepted according to its etymological and not its conventionally philosophical meaning; for to affirm that "everything is God" in the sense that no reality as such could be situated outside of the one Reality does not amount to reducing God to the sum total of phenomena.

their spiritual reality, whereas for Europeans the sense of truth is focused on facts as such, on their incontestable immediacy of reality; both points of view have their advantages and disadvantages, depending on the subjective as well objective conditions of their application. God, in sacred Scriptures makes use of symbols; but one could never ask the same of historians or of geographers.

Moreover, in many cases, the impression of platitude given by some accounts is due to an optical illusion: in an avid, impatient, and ambitious social setting—though noble in its way— it was necessary to insist again and again on corrective attitudes: to be content with little, to show generosity, to be patient, to fear God; in retrospect, this may seem schematic and pedantic, but for the times in question these attitudes or virtues were highly original and heroic. One must also take account of the need, in such a milieu, for setting a good example, and of doing so tirelessly and incisively, and thus inevitably with exaggeration; it was necessary to demonstrate without respite what poverty, generosity, patient and trusting resignation, faith, and sincerity are; in fact, it is this very sincerity that demands the accentuation, both excessive and monotonous, of moral intentions. We could also say that Islam prefers the risk of platitude and infantilism—since faults are humanly unavoidable— to that of philosophical, artistic, and cultural titanism; it seeks to keep men in a state of Biblical childlikeness, for which time has no meaning outside of an eschatological context. The great sinners in the Muslim world are potentates desirous in their way of anticipating on earth the joys of Paradise; they are never thinkers "of genius" wishing to put themselves virtually in the place of God.[10]

In an altogether general sense, and including prophecy itself, it is important not to be unjust out of rashness by attributing an

---

10. The creative mentality of the West—its "creative genius" if one will—goes together moreover with a singular tendency toward ingratitude, unfaithfulness, forgetfulness; if the price of this genius is a propensity to "burn what one has worshipped", it becomes compromised by that very token, for the gift of creation is a good only on condition of being accompanied by a sense of values, and thus by stability. Dynamism is a quality only on condition that it is allied with a sense of the static, and is even determined by it.

imperfection of thinking to some expressions meant to serve as symbols. "Prophets"—Ibn Arabi remarked—"use a concrete form of speech because they are addressing a collectivity and trust the wise who might hear them to understand; and if they speak figuratively, it is because of common men and because they know the degree of intuition of those who truly understand. Thus the Prophet said, when speaking of liberality, that he gave nothing to some who were dearer to him than others out of fear that God might cast them into hell-fire. He expressed himself in this way because of the weak-minded who are slaves of avidity and of passional inclinations."[11] Even a historical fact may have, in divine language, no more than the value of a sign; something that exists is sometimes denied in virtue of the meaning it takes on *de facto* for a particular collective consciousness, and something that does not exist may be affirmed for the same reason, without there being lack of veracity, since the meaning, in this case, is more real and more important than the fact proposed as a sign or symbol.[12] God never gives less than He promises; on the contrary, His gift is always greater than His promise.

But let us return to the problematical side of hagiography, with all the respect required by good intentions, but also with all the sobriety required here by truth: it is at first sight a rather curious paradox to present saintly persons by means of banal incidents or elementary virtues—though often extravagant in their depiction—while claiming that they have an unsurpassable greatness of which, precisely, no proof is offered; on the contrary, it seems that everything is done to prevent us from believing it. Islam, with its postulate concerning the uniqueness of Divine Greatness, is consistent in wishing to see on the human side nothing but a leveling out in helplessness; but this does not nec-

11. *Fusûs al-Hikam*, the chapter on Moses. This passage, which troubles itself with no euphemisms when speaking of the run of humanity, is of paramount importance for anyone tempted to overreact to a type of religious language.
12. When the Buddha rejects the Veda, he is not in fact rejecting a particular Revelation, but the "outward" form for the sake of the "inward" Reality. Zen repeats this attitude in the midst of Buddhism itself, which had become "form" in its turn. The attitude of Christianity toward the Torah is approximately analogous.

essarily entail that the greatness of saints should be presented in the form of a *petitio principii* paradoxically disguised in commonplace features—no matter how inflated with superlatives—and, if need be, denigrating any greatness foreign to its framework. What in fact proves the greatness of early Islam's most eminent figures—but not, of course, to the detriment of eminent persons situated outside of Islam—is the radiant persistence of their memory and influence, for there is no effect without a cause: if an Ali or a Fatimah has been nearly deified and if this cult, linked to a spiritual idealism extending as far as heroism, has been maintained up to our times, it is because there was a greatness in them proportioned to this prestige and radiance; and this greatness is perceivable in spite of the disservice done to it by the moralistic stereotyping of a hagiography that is wholly lacking in plausibility, meaningful contrast, and interest.

The idea of "divine jealousy"—if it is permissible to make provisional use of this metaphor[13]—permeates all of Islam and subjects it to a kind of collective humility, so that spiritual greatness is almost always no more than implicit, unless particular teachings prove it, which is scarcely the case with the Companions; sanctity is admitted by virtue of the postulate of the Divine Immanence in the hearts of the saints without wondering about its outer criteria. The cult of sincerity leads to a tendency of wishing to be more than one promises, or to be better before God than one is before men; in short, it leads one to hide a good substance—lest one appear to appropriate it to oneself—beneath displays of morality that are all the more excessive for being ordinary; hence, one neglects to give any justification for an unfavorable appearance or to explain the subtle content of something commonplace. Sincerity, the mortal enemy of hypocrisy, is all the more precious for being seen by God alone; this is the moral principle of the "men of blame", the *malâmatiyyah*, who court the scorn of men in order to feel at ease before God. To recount how an Omar neglected presiding over the Friday prayer at the mosque—he, the caliph— because he possessed only a single garment, which he was washing at the time, is doubtless one way of extolling sincerity and poverty, but it must be admitted that the argument cuts both ways.

13. Which in fact is Biblical.

Be that as it may, the tendency to show oneself before others in a manner that is beneath oneself abolishes neither the fact of human greatness nor the human need for taking note of this fact; and precisely as result of this, one finds—with the paradoxical modalities just mentioned—the Shiite hyperdulia of the Alids and the Imams, and, on the Sunni side, the glorification of the Companions and, more concretely yet, the cult of the Sheiks in the Sufi brotherhoods, which is the equivalent in practice of the cult of the Gurus in India.

Perhaps the considerations that follow will provide an adequate key to the enigma of Muslim hagiography and its precedents in the *Sunnah*: there are finally but two decisive values, faith in Unity and the sincerity of this faith. Now the sincerity of this faith can manifest itself in three dimensions: fear (*makhâfah*), love (*mahabbah*), and knowledge (*ma'rifah*). When sincerity results from fear, it manifests—or proves—itself through its scruple; if it results from love, it manifests itself through generosity; and lastly if it derives its inspiration from knowledge, or rather if knowledge is its motive force, it will produce a metaphysical monism like that of the *Vedanta*. Testimonies of this monism are encountered in the unitive exclamations of the greatest of Sufis; as for the other two dimensions, they are precisely the ones determining the didactic exaggerations that make hagiography both so tedious and so excessive. There is but one virtue, one heroism, one sanctity, and that is sincerity: the sincerity of faith, of the unique faith.

*
* *

Before proceeding further, we must in a few words call attention to an aspect of the problem which, though more contingent, is very important for a Westerner's approach to Islam: there is a body of traditions and legends, not unconnected to hagiography, whose function seems to be to blur the trail leading to Christianity by clothing its facts and illustrious persons with a kind of smallness and implausibility, or even disfigurement;[14] the reason for

14. Islam is all the more bound to do this in that its recognition of the virgin birth of Christ and the Virgin's immaculate conception constitutes a kind of opening onto Christianity. Christianity, for its part, has no need at its root of defensive measures against Islam: apart from the obvious reason

this is that a religion has a certain extrinsic right, on its periphery, to surround the positive quality of its message with a kind of protective mist, inasmuch as this message is threatened by other messages or other mythologies—threatened humanly and *de facto*, not metaphysically and *de jure*. It must be recognized, however, that this providential mist pertains to what we can term without enthusiasm the "human margin" when speaking of institutions that are substantially divine; in support of this interpretation, we shall mention the fact that commentators place largely divergent, and completely incompatible, versions of the same story side by side.[15]

Nonetheless, the humblest or most extravagant, or even the most shocking, stories can convey a profound symbolism; almost all mythologies contain such features, and the most ancient Christian hagiography is no exception, at least as regards implausibility. It should be the role—or duty—of commentators to bring out this symbolism, for what is the point of explaining obscure passages with even more obscure passages? The plurality of divergent traditional accounts moreover proves the abstract—and non-historical—character of the scriptural passage they refer to. In the same vein, many an esoterist can be reproached for grafting onto a particular story speculations that are too personal, instead of simply relating the intention belonging to the story itself.

*

* *

In Eastern thought, the indicative or suggestive association of ideas sometimes takes precedence over the logic of the facts and

that Islam did not exist in the time of Christ, there are two sayings that *de facto* and by anticipation close the door to any new religion, namely, "no man cometh unto the Father but by me" and "beware of false prophets". For centuries, however, the Christian image of Islam was a jumble of calumnies; but this was not situated—and could not be so—at the canonical level; nonetheless this proves that there is a need for self-defense that belongs to every extrinsic religion, and a choice of means that is all too human.

15. In describing Christ, the Prophet, is actually describing Christianity as it appears in relation to the dryness of Islam: if the Prophet Isa is "of a ruddy complexion as if he had just come from a hot bath", this refers, not to the person of Jesus, but to the character of "love", hence of "warmth", of Christianity. Many paradoxes in Muhammadan lore must be interpreted in an analogous fashion.

thus over the coherence of the symbol;[16] yet such an explanation is not always complete, all the more so as the dialectical means may be the result of a reflex rather than a conscious intent. The Muslim is on average a hasty and careless writer out of religious sincerism and inspirational impulsivity; thus it is hardly surprising that his productions are filled with all sorts of unconsidered thoughts; books are rough drafts written under God's sight, and it is for the reader to sift out the pearls and to forgive the weaknesses made public with pious immodesty. "Better to blush in this world than in the next"; this principle can turn into a real obsession, and applying it too automatically can clash with critical sense and good taste. What strikes a Western reader as a crime may be no more than a forgivable accident of human nature in the eyes of an Easterner in accordance with the Muslim axiom—always strongly emphasized and double-edged—of human smallness, and the overriding importance also of the moralizing intent.

To affirm that man is free is to say that he can, and must, place himself in harmony with total Equilibrium. Moralities, whether they are subtle or expeditious, do not aim beyond this; it is absurd to seek to escape from the cosmic mechanism of Existence by mocking the anthropomorphic imagery describing it, awkwardly no doubt but adequately, and to let oneself slide into a precipice because prudence was presented in pedantic or childish terms. An elementary sense of proportions should allow us to sense at once that the men before us who conformed themselves to the requirements of the great Equilibrium could not all have been as ingenuous as some of the intellectually minimal imagery they accepted or proposed; we are well aware of the double-edged sword presented by religious anthropomorphism and the naivety it occasions, but our sense of the real compels us to prefer these imperfections—since, in spite of everything, they

16. For instance, Rumi relates in his *Mathnawî* how the Prophet recommended to Ali that the best means to attain the goal is to seek the enlightening counsel of a wise man; this is absurd if one takes into account the quality of each of the characters and of the bond uniting them, but it can be understood by way of association of ideas: in order to exalt the relationship between master and disciple, Rumi bases his teaching on the image of their paradigms; he strengthens the abstract principle through the evocation of the concrete phenomenon.

convey grave truths—to a critical intelligence vituperating brilliantly in the void.

*
* *

There remains the disconcerting enigma of necessary absurdity: the question is to know where its limits are, which amounts in practice to asking how far the right of human incapacity to exercise intelligence on all planes at the same time extends. If there were in the world no element of absurdity, of unintelligibility, the world would not be the world; it would be a system of crystalline cells and mechanical rhythms. There is no religion that does not carry on its periphery some painful dissonances, and it is at least plausible to assume that without them religion would be ineffective; one must make allowance for the principle of necessary dissonance without feeling obliged to resort to euphemisms nor *a fortiori* to iconoclasm. The origin of these dissonances is above all an intrusive emotivity, which by definition disturbs thought: there is no fanaticism without some stupidity. Let a spiritual idea be launched with the vehemence required to make it psychologically effective, and it will inevitably end up being accompanied by a train of pious absurdities; it is for the wise man to discern the essential without letting himself be discouraged by the accidental, detestable though it may be. However necessary emotional dynamism is at a certain level, it nonetheless harms intelligence.[17]

From the simple point of view of the psychological phenomenon, one must note that, on average, man is incapable of correlating a fact by which he is hypnotized with the complementary and corrective facts lying outside of his field of vision; scientism is just as much an example of this as any naïve fanaticism, since it is refractory to facts which are excluded by its viewpoint, but

---

17. This is totally unrelated to the modern idea which holds that indignation or keen approval denotes a lack of "objectivity", and that it would suffice to be cold and soft to be "objective". In reality, there are emotions which, far from being sentimental assumptions are on the contrary the response to perfectly objective knowledge; in that case, man becomes indignant or rejoices because of a certitude, depending on whether this certitude is flouted or, instead, defended by others.

which are fundamental for the perception of the real in all its ramifications. With respect to the religious or spiritual domain, we have in mind here, not error pure and simple, but the narrow points of view found in the midst of a truth which, though stylized, is nonetheless sufficiently adequate to be effective; it is as if one were to reason only on the basis of the elements of space, forgetting those of time. Average man—including the average man of genius—is a strangely unilateral being; and what makes him thus is first the unevenness of the human mind, which cannot exert itself everywhere with equal perspicacity, and then a passional element rooted in his subconscious—whether it be hot or cold, positive or negative—having the effect of singularly impoverishing his imagination; lack of imagination seems to be one of the distinctive traits of the human species, be it said *cum grano salis*.[18]

The element described is, in the final analysis, self-interest, rooted in a poorly understood instinct of self-preservation; as a result, thinking is from the start not disinterested—in some respect or another—and deficient in its exercise. Perfect objectivity is a kind of extinction, and thus a kind of death, given that the nature of things so often contradicts, not indeed our ultimate interest, which coincides with the Real, but our illusory interests or our superficial sense of selfhood.[19]

In conclusion, let us return to the *de facto* ambiguous character of intelligence mentioned above. That intelligence should be preferred to stupidity is only too obvious, for one must opt for truth against error, and because truth is addressed *a priori* to the intelligence; however, since the choice between an intelligence with a satanic function and an unintelligence with an angelic tendency is practically unavoidable at a certain level, one must be resigned to tolerating unintelligence in the sector where such a question arises. Religion will have nothing to do with a proud and titanic intellectualism; thus it proposes the contrary, which is the

---

18. It would be tempting to state the contrary, but the fact is that the excess of imagination deploys itself in only one dimension.
19. Once again, one must take care not to confuse "partiality" with mere mental unevenness or asymmetry, which is a matter of cerebral economy, or even of dialectic, and not of willful or emotional subjectivity.

norm,[20] namely pure and calm understanding, which morally implies self-effacement, or near impersonal virtue; but since this is psychologically insufficient for the general run of men, religion must furthermore counter intellectualist pride with its opposite fault, which is pious stupidity, for it is constrained by the demands of human weakness to add to the good a lesser evil; in other words, it must add a good capable of taking on the color of our infirmity. The strange ambiguity of intelligence results from the fact that it is good only through truth, and this opens the way for the paradoxical compensation we have just mentioned; truth, even when poorly assimilated, is superior to aberrant intelligence, even when brilliant; but, precisely, an intelligence that is deprived of truth remains beneath its possibility, a stranger as it were to its own nature, since truth is immanent in intelligence as such.

20. Even though the norm is in fact opposed to nothing; on the contrary, deviations are what oppose the norm.

The Human Margin

Christ, in rejecting some rabbinical prescriptions as "human" and not "divine", shows that according to the measures of God, there is a sector which, while being orthodox and traditional, is nonetheless human in a certain way; the divine influence, in other words, is total only for Scripture and the essential consequences of the Revelation, and it always allows for a "human margin" where it exerts itself only in an indirect fashion, yielding to ethnic or cultural factors. The speculations of exoterism pertain largely to this sector or margin; orthodoxy is, on the one hand, homogeneous and indivisible and, on the other, contains degrees of absoluteness or relativity. We should therefore not be too scandalized at the anathemas which Dyophysites, Monophysites, Aphthartodocetae, Phthartolatrae, Agnoetae, Aktistetae, and Ktistolatrae hurl at one another over the question of knowing whether Christ is of an incorruptible substance or whether, on the contrary, his body was similar to other bodies, or if there was in the soul of Christ a measure of human ignorance, or if the body of Christ is uncreated while being visible, or if on the contrary it was created, and so on and so forth.[1]

---

1. Worthy of note is the following divergence concerning the Blessed Virgin: was Mary *a priori* free from the capacity to sin, or was she without sin out of the superabundance of her virtue? In other words, was she impeccable owing to the absolute holiness of her nature or was she holy in virtue of the absolute impeccability of her intelligence and will? Those who maintain the first thesis seek to avoid attributing to Mary an imperfection of substance; those of the second seek to avoid depriving her of the perfection of merit; both parties, however, seem to lose sight of the fact that at the level of the Blessed Virgin the alternative becomes wholly

What is surprising in most cases, and in different degrees, is this vehement desire to become fixated on questions that hold no crucial importance, and the incapacity to allow for a certain measure of latitude on matters which, precisely, Revelation did not deem it indispensable to specify; yet it would have been enough, from the mystical as well as from the dogmatic point of view, to admit that Christ, as the living form of God, would have to display in his humanity supernatural prerogatives that it would be vain to enumerate, while, being incontestably human, he would have certain limitations as is proven by the incident of the fig tree, whose sterility he did not discern from afar. The question of the *filioque* is a patent example of this tendency to unnecessary precisions, and of a dogmatization that produces a plethora of divisions and anathemas.

One fact that inevitably imposes itself, when considering ideas along these lines, is that fallen or post-Edenic man is a quasi-fragmentary being; thus we must face the fact that the holiness of a man does not prevent him from being a poor logician or from having an outlook that is more sentimental than intellectual, and that, in spite of this, he have the calling to be a teacher, not out of pretension, certainly, but out of "zeal for the house of the Lord". Inspiration by the Holy Spirit does not mean that It is to replace human intelligence and free it from all its natural limitations, for that would be Revelation; inspiration simply means that the Spirit guides man in accordance with the divine intention and on the basis of the capacities of the human receptacle. Were this not so, there would be no theological elaboration, nor any divergences within orthodoxy, and the first Church Father would have written a theological treatise that would have been unique, exhaustive, and definitive; there would never have been either a Thomas Aquinas or a Gregory Palamas. As to the rest, there are men who are inspired by the Holy Spirit because they are saints and inasmuch as they are, whereas there are others who are saints because they are inspired by the Holy Spirit and inasmuch as they are.

meaningless. The Immaculate Conception—attributed to Mary also by Muslim tradition—comprises by its very nature all meritorious attitude, somewhat as a substance synthesizes all of its possible accidents; and, conversely, perfect impeccability—which is excluded in the case of ordinary man—is *ipso facto* equivalent to the absence of "original sin".

*

* *

The most ordinary examples of the "human margin" conceded by Heaven to traditions are provided by the scissions found within the intrinsically orthodox religions; and this has nothing at all to do with the question of heterodoxy, because intrinsic heresies are situated precisely outside the margin in question. It is a fact that collective human thought is not able to conceive easily of the fluctuations between different points of view, on the one hand, and the aspects to which they correspond, on the other hand, or between different modes of the subjective and the objective; consequently, there are polarizations and scissions which, however inevitable and providential they may be, are nonetheless dangerous imperfections. Heaven allows man to be what he is, but such condescension or patience is not to be understood as a full approbation on the part of God.

Regarding the question of ecclesiology, the most ancient Christian texts sometimes uphold the Latin thesis and sometimes the Greek; as a result, the ideal, or rather the normal situation, would be an Orthodox Church recognizing a pope who was not totally autocratic, but in spiritual communion with all of the bishops or patriarchs; this would then be a pope without *filioque*, but having nonetheless the right, in theology, liturgy, and other domains, to certain particularities that are opportune or even necessary in a Latin and Germanic setting. The present-day disorders in the Roman Church—of a gravity without precedent—prove that the Latin conception of the Church is theologically narrow and juridically excessive; were it not so, such disorders would be inconceivable.[2] Besides, there seems to be something tragically insolvable in the very structure of Christianity: grant total supremacy to the pontiff, and he will become a worldly and conquering caesar; grant supremacy to the emperor, and he will make of the pontiff his

---

2. Moreover, the advent of Protestantism in the Latin West contains the same proof. Psychologically—not doctrinally—Protestantism in fact repeats, though clearly in a much more extreme form, the protest of Arianism which contained, in spite of everything, a bit of truth and an element of equilibrium.

pawn and tool.[3] But one must admit that we have here a vicious circle, traces of which are to be found wherever there are men.

*

* *

The "fathomless mystery" of the theologians is sometimes no more than the expression of a metaphysical insufficiency, unless it refers to the obviously unfathomable Divine Subjectivity: this is mysterious for objectifying and separative thought in the way the optic nerve is for vision, but there is absolutely nothing mysterious about the impossibility of the eye to perceive the optic nerve. Very often the thesis of a "mystery" is either a gratuitous affirmation meant to veil a theological contradiction, or purely and simply a truism if we understand what thought is and what its obvious limits are.

The whole drama of theologies is the incompatibility of their simplifying sublimism with the idea of *Mâyâ* at the divine degree, or of divine Relativity; because of this, they are constrained to offset the deadlocks of their fundamental voluntarism with "providential" philosophical expedients, which are "providential" insofar as they are psychologically opportune for a particular collectivity. One of the greatest difficulties of Sufism is that the highest metaphysics is inextricably mixed with theology, which tarnishes it with its habitual confusions concerning "All-

---

3. Most paradoxically, the one does not prevent the other. This is what has happened in the Latin West, where the papacy became the prey finally, not of the emperor of course, but of politics and consequently of democracy since democracy determines politics. Since the French Revolution, the Church has been substantially at the mercy, so to speak, of secularizing republics—including pseudo-monarchies that are in fact republican—for it is their ideology that decides who is worthy to be a bishop; and owing to a particularly favorable historical juncture, politics has succeeded in pumping into the mold of the Church human material that is heterogeneous to the Church. The last Council was ideo-political and not theological; its illegitimacy results from the fact that it was determined, not by concrete situations evaluated from the point of view of theology, but by ideo-political abstractions opposed to theology, or more specifically by the democratism of the world operating monstrously in the role of Holy Spirit. "Humility" and "charity", manipulated as suits the occasion and henceforth one-sided, are there to ensure the success of the enterprise.

Mightiness"; unless one admits that it is on the contrary sapience which, in this case, deepens theology by inculcating into it some liberating flashes of insights.[4]

Theologies, by taking upon themselves the contradiction of being sentimental metaphysics, are condemned to a squaring of the circle; they are oblivious to the differentiation of things into aspects and points of view, and consequently they operate with arbitrarily rigid elements whose antinomies can be resolved only beyond this artificial rigidity; moreover, they operate with sentimental tendencies, which is described as "thinking piously".[5] In Christianity, there is the purpose to admit some differentiation within Unity and the equally imperious purpose not to admit that this amounts to any differentiation in practice—the Hypostases being "no more than relations"—as if one were attempting to force the three dimensions of space into a single one; in Islam, a stubborn unitarianism runs up against the existence of the world and its diversity, whereas there would be no conflict if the unitarianism were metaphysical, hence transparent and supple, as its nature requires. In Christianity, there is a certain dispersion in the object of worship: God, the Persons, Christ, the Eucharist, the Sacred Heart; in Islam, there is on the contrary an excess of centralization on a level where it should not apply: to admit no other cause outside of God, to want to depend upon Him alone, even against the direct evidence of facts, when these facts in no way prevent everything from depending on God, and when it would suffice to be aware of this to be in conformity with the truth. There is a zeal that readily replaces thought with virtue, and virtue

---

4. The deterioration in question is detectable, not only on the speculative plane, but also on the operative plane, where the volitive element too often confers a somewhat violent tone on the method, in the stead of a more intellectual alchemy; this produces accidental ruptures, for the gates of Heaven cannot be breached with unintelligent excesses, however heroic they may be. There needs to be a balance between the quantitative and the qualitative, the volitive and the intellective, something that moralizing vulgarization readily loses sight of. Moreover, it is this vulgarization that brings about the imagery of extravagant marvels and, by repercussion, the equally unfortunate depreciation of true miracles.
5. The Councils would sometimes degenerate into brawls, which is not very metaphysical, but is better than laxity toward manifest error on the pretext of "charity" or "humility".

with heroism; in saying this, we are well aware that a devotional attitude is normal, and thus normative, and that there is no balanced intellectuality without it; but everything needs to be put in its proper place, and this has become particularly difficult for the passional humanity of the "age of iron". What matters to be understood, is that a soul filled with piety is capable of thinking with detachment, in perfect harmony with piety and not in opposition to it, all the more as the instinct of worship is profound in the very measure that truth permeates it.[6]

For extreme trinitarianism, God is certainly One, but He is so only in being Three, and there is no God-as-One except within and through the Trinity; the God who is One without the Trinity, or independently of any question of hypostatic deployment, is not the true God, Unity being meaningless without this deployment. Now this is where the full gravity of trinitarianism becomes manifest: there are Christians—though, as a matter of fact, in disagreement with the impression of most theologians—who are incapable of seeing any value whatsoever in Islam; from their point of view, Islam and atheism are equivalent; if they do not level the same reproach at Judaism, it is for the sole reason that they project onto it their trinitarianism as an axiomatic implication. Because of this, the Muslim reproach of "tritheism" is justified; he who is unable, on the strength of his trinitarianism, to see that the Koran speaks of the God of Abraham—even supposing that it does so imperfectly—and that Muslims worship God and not something else, truly deserves such a reproach. Christ, in speaking of the supreme Commandment or in teaching the Lord's Prayer, did not speak of the Trinity, any more than did the God of the Sinai, who deemed it sufficient to define Himself in these words: "Hear, O Israel: the Lord our God is one Lord".

As we have had occasion to remark more than once, trinitarianism is a conception of God that is determined by the mystery of divine manifestation: if we seek the prefiguration of this mystery in God, we discern the Trinity. This idea, when applied to any religion, whether monotheistic or not, presents itself as follows: the Essence has become form in order that the form may become

---

6. Vedantin texts confirm this, and so-called monotheistic theologies clearly contain sectors that attest to the same quality.

Essence; each Revelation is a humanization of the Divine in view of the deification of the human.

*

* *

Judaism and Islam make the following objections to trinitarianism: you say that the Son is begotten and that he is God; now God is not begotten, He is absolute. You say that the Holy Spirit emanates and that it is delegated and that it is God; now God does not emanate from anything, nor is He sent. And you say that the Father is God and that he begets; now God creates but He does not beget, otherwise there would be two Gods. Moreover, how can the Son and the Spirit each be identical with God without being identical with each other?

A Christian might respond to these objections by saying that in Judaism as well as in Islam, Divine Mercy is not identical with Divine Vengeance but that both are identical with God; Jews and Muslims will reply that there is in this a serious nuance, for while Mercy and Vengeance are indeed divine, it would be false to affirm that God can be reduced to one or the other.[7] The equation is only relative, and therein lies the root of the problem: Judaism and Islam admit in a certain sense relativity *in divinis* by making a distinction between the Essence and the attributes, the qualities and the functions, whereas Christianity, at least at the theological level, seems to want to reduce everything to absoluteness, whence the problematical ellipses of trinitarian theology.

"I am in the Father, and the Father is in me": this is the identity of essence. But "my Father is greater than I": this is the difference in degree within Principial Reality, namely that is yet uncreated or metacosmic. The meaning of an absolute equation has been ascribed to the first phrase, while the second has been relativized; instead of combining both phrases to explain the one in terms of the other, the second phrase has been arbitrarily attributed to human nature alone.

---

7. Mercy is God, but God is not Mercy only. Nonetheless, God is much more directly Mercy—the verb "to be" indicating an identity of essence and not just an equation as such—than He is Vengeance, which is extrinsic and conditional, whereas Mercy is intrinsic, and thus unconditional, without therefore being identified with Absoluteness as such.

We have cited the following argument: God creates but does not beget, otherwise there would be two Gods. We shall now specify: "does not beget" unless one admits the notion of *Mâyâ*, for this notion allows one to understand that the hiatus between Creator and creature is necessarily prefigured *in divinis* by the differentiation between the Absolute as such and the Absolute that is relativized with respect to a dimension of Its infinitude; but this difference, precisely, is real only from the standpoint of Relativity. For the Vedantins, the separation between the Absolute (*Paramâtmâ*) and the Relative (*Mâyâ* = *Îshvara*) is as strict as is, for the Semites, the separation between the Creator and the creature; but by compensation, there is an aspect that allows the created to be linked to the Uncreated, for nothing that exists can be other than a manifestation of the Principle or an objectification of the Self; "everything is *Âtmâ*".[8]

In other terms, there is *Âtmâ* and there is *Mâyâ*; but there is also *Âtmâ* as *Mâyâ*, and this is the personal Divinity, manifesting and acting; and conversely, there is also *Mâyâ* as *Âtmâ*, and this is the total Universe under its aspect of reality both one and polyvalent. In this case, the world will be the divine aspect of "Universal Man" (*Vaishvânara*) or, in Sufism, the aspect "the Outward" (*Zâhir*); this moreover is the profoundest meaning of the Far-Eastern *Yin-Yang*. And it is this doctrine that permits one to say that the *Avatâra* was "created before creation": in other words, before being able to create the world, it is necessary for God "to create Himself" *in divinis*, if one may put it thus—the word "create" having here a higher and transposed meaning, which is precisely that of *Mâyâ*.[9]

8. Had philosophical pantheism taken into consideration this aspect of things—which is not the case since it has no knowledge of the degrees of reality and transcendence—it would be legitimate as a synthetic or inclusive perspective. In the polemics between theologians, these two kinds of pantheism are readily confused.

9. For Parmenides, pure Being coincides with pure Knowledge; all the rest is "opinion", *doxa*, which is not unrelated to the notion of *Mâyâ*, though with the reservation that, in Vedantin terms, the Being of Parmenides is not completely outside of *Mâyâ*, but is identified with its summit, *Îshvara*. In parallel with their cult of Perfection, the Greeks have always had a certain fear of the Infinite, which is clearly visible even in their architecture: though the Parthenon has true grandeur, it expresses the religion of the

The distinction between the human and divine natures reflects or symbolizes the distinction, within the divine nature itself, between inequality with regard to the Father and equality, or between relativity and absoluteness; on the other hand, this principial distinction is also affirmed on the level of human nature in which one dimension is marked by earthly contingence whereas the other is near-divine, whence the Monophysite interpretation. It is not surprising that this combination of three polarities—man and God, earthly man and divine man, hypostatic God and essential God—that this combination or this complexity would give rise to the diversity of opinions, either orthodox or heretical depending on the case, which we alluded to above; it is the fundamental polarity of *Âtmâ-Mâyâ* which is repeated or reverberates in countless modalities, of which the most important for man is the confrontation between God and the world. The Prologue to the Gospel of St John enunciates this polarity as applied to Christ by juxtaposing two affirmations: *Et Verbum erat apud Deum, et Deus erat Verbum*: the dimension of subordination, then the dimension of equality or identity.

All of Arianism, without knowing it, can be explained by the concern to account for the principle of relativity *in divinis*, hence of *Mâyâ*: if Arius teaches that the Son, without having been created "in time" like the rest of creation—for time begins only with creation—is nonetheless "drawn out of nothingness", but that the Son is Divine in the sense that he is the principle of cosmic creation, hence of creation as such, he wishes to say that the Word, while being Divine, nonetheless has an aspect of relativity. It is true that Arius spoils his thesis with some aberrant speculations concerning the person of Christ; yet one has to acknowledge that there is in his doctrine a correct and profound intuition, though it is awkwardly formulated in terms typical of Semitic and creationist anthropomorphism. Instead of rejecting Arianism altogether, one could have appropriated its positive theological intention, that of divine Relativity, which is the prototype for cosmic limitation: the Word is neither wholly other than the Absolute, as Arius maintains, nor wholly—or in all cases—identical

finite and rational Perfect, which opposes itself to virgin nature by confusing the unlimited with the chaotic, the Infinite with the irrational.

to the Absolute, as the Homousiasts maintain; if ever there was a need for antinomism in metaphysical dialectics, it is here. The very expansion and tenacity of Arianism, in an epoch so close to the origin, proves that there was more to it than a mere human error; thus the Council of Nicaea marks, not the victory of truth as such, but the victory of the most important truth to the detriment of essential metaphysical nuances; there is no doubt that dogmatic theology must simplify, but a unilateral and fragmentary view is what it is: in the measure that its content requires multi-dimensional explanations, it cannot but give rise to disequilibria.

Be that as it may, it must be admitted that the theological formulation of the Trinity constitutes, in a given milieu, a providential form destined not only to transmit the mystery while protecting it, but also to provide by its very paradox a point of reference for the doctrine as a totality, and hence necessarily multidimensional.

*
* *

It is necessary to make a distinction between metaphysical knowledge and the capacity to express it: Greeks and especially Hindus have long possessed the instrument of dialectic, for it corresponds to their sense of objectivity,[10] whereas it was missing among the early Semites, as well as for nascent Islam; however, it goes without saying that this has no bearing on the degree of wisdom of particular individuals, all the more as the profoundest metaphysics can be found in a condensed form in various Biblical and Koranic sayings or in various sayings of saints who drew their inspiration from these Scriptures, early on and outside of any possible Hellenist influence. These remarks, and still more our preceding considerations about the metaphysics underlying

10. As to Far-Easterners, they are contemplative, but symbolists and not logicians; they are above all visual in their outlook. The purely Mongol traditions are those of Fu-Hsi with its Taoist and Confucian branches, then Shinto, without forgetting the various Far-Eastern and Siberian shamanisms; but the Mongol soul has also set its imprint on Buddhism, which has thus become partially representative of the spiritual genius of the Yellow Race, notably in the case of Zen, and, in a more general way, in all of sacred art.

210

theologies, prompt us to return to some fundamental facts of the *sophia perennis*, at the risk both of straying from our subject and of repeating things that have already been said. It is always a question of the notions of absoluteness and relativity, which are so important or so fateful in the context of the "human margin".

The Islamic Testimony that "there is no divinity save the One Divinity" has first of all, metaphysically speaking, the objective meaning of a discernment, that is, of a separation between the Real and the illusory or between the Absolute and the relative; it also has the subjective meaning of a spiritual distinction between the worldly outward and the divine Inward, in which case the objective and transcendent Divinity appears as immanent and therefore subjective, but subjective in a transpersonal sense, the subject being, not the human ego, but the Intellect in its purity, with the purified ego being no more than the means of access. In order to be total, the doctrine still has need of a unitive dimension, expressed in Islam through the second Testimony: to say that "the Praised (Muhammad) is the Messenger of the (sole) Divinity" means that the relative, inasmuch as it manifests the Absolute directly, is not other than the Absolute; and according to the subjective application, one will say that the outward, the world, is not other than the Inward, the Self.[11]

If the relative, however, can have this aspect of absoluteness that reintegrates it into the Absolute—for the Universe cannot rest on a radical duality—it is because the relative must be prefigured in the Absolute Itself; *Mâyâ* has its origin in *Âtmâ*, otherwise the subsequent relationship between God and the world would be inconceivable. It is for this reason that Creation as a whole, while being on the one hand separate from the Creator, is on the other hand a prolongation of Him and a "divine aspect": this is what is expressed by the divine Name "the Apparent" (*Az-Zâhir*) by opposition to the "Hidden" (*Al-Bâtin*), and this is what permits some Sufis to affirm that "all is God", in conformity with the Koranic

11. The fundamental Testimony, or the First *Shahâdah*, contains a negative part, which rejects false divinities, and a positive part, which affirms the true God: the first is the "negation", the *nafy*, and the second, the "strengthening", the *ithbât*; this is the distinction between *Mâyâ* and *Âtmâ*. The Second *Shahâdah*, that of the Prophet, adds that *Mâyâ* is not other than *Âtmâ*, in its "not unreal" substance.

211

verse: "Wheresoever ye turn, there is the Face of God". One particular manifestation of the relative reintegrated into the Absolute, or more exactly the Absolute manifested as relative, is the Logos, the Prophet; another is the Heart, the place of the inward and transmuting theophany.

The relationship of identity is expressed in the most direct manner possible by quintessential Christianity: the Son is united to the Father; Christ is God. That man, who is relative, could be identified with God, who is the Absolute, presupposes that relativity have an aspect of absoluteness and that therefore relativity be prefigured *in divinis*: whence the doctrine of the Word; "God became man that man might become God": the Absolute comprises relativity and thus relativity can be reintegrated into the Absolute; the Patristic formula just paraphrased thus signifies, on the one hand, that the human Logos directly manifests the Absolute and, on the other, that man can be reintegrated into the Absolute by uniting with the human Logos, in and through whom he is virtually identified with this Absolute.

The objection that Paradise is not the Absolute and that in no religion is man meant to become God literally in no wise compromises what we have just outlined; for it is not a question of a transmutation of the individual as such into the divine Essence, but to begin with an "adoption" of man by God: man is then situated on the divine axis; he is open in his innermost self to the Infinite, he "wears a crown of uncreated light". There is no common measure between his spiritual secret, the mystery of identity or absoluteness, and the existence—or subsistence—of the individual form, though the one does not preclude the other; man remains man notwithstanding the reality of absoluteness penetrating him. *Nirvâna* did not destroy the Buddha: it made him immortal; otherwise it would never be possible to speak of a human manifestation of the Logos. If God can "become man", it is because there is no possible concurrence between the divine and the human.

God and the world: each of these terms comprises the polarization into absoluteness and relativity, and the two terms themselves represent this polarization. There is in God the Essence together with the Attributes and their shared Life; and in the world there is Heaven, which serves as the Absolute, and earth,

212

which represents the relative as such. Here, as *in divinis*, the Holy Spirit is the unifying Life.

The theological equation between the Uncreated and the Absolute, on the one hand, and between the created and the relative, on the other, is altogether insufficient: for if it is true that the created pertains by definition to relativity, it is false to admit that the Uncreated pertains by the same token to Absoluteness; it is the Essence alone that is the pure Absolute, though it is clear that divine Relativity serves as the Absolute in relation to the created. The manifested Logos also has this aspect or function, though without being able to be the "absolutely Absolute"; if Christ addresses a prayer to his Father, it is not only by reason of his human nature, it is also by reason of the relativity of the uncreated Logos. If the Son were merely an abstract "relationship of origin", it would be impossible for him to assume the nature of man.

The dogma of the Trinity existed before trinitarian theology; the latter pertains to the "human margin" and the former to Revelation. The dogma lays down metaphysical facts; theology, by combining them, makes them Western.

*
* *

A religion is not limited by what it includes, but by what it excludes; doubtless, this exclusion does not harm the most profound content of religion—for each religion is inherently a totality—but it will take revenge all the more surely on this intermediary level that we call the "human margin" and which is the arena of theological speculations and of moral and mystical ardors. It is certainly not pure metaphysics or esoterism that should compel us to pretend that a flagrant contradiction is not a contradiction; all that wisdom permits—or, rather, obliges—us to do is to acknowledge that outward contradictions can conceal an intrinsic compatibility or identity, which in fact amounts to saying that each of the contradictory theses contains a truth and, thereby, an aspect of total truth and a means of access to it.

When one religion places the human Logos of another religion in hell, or one confession does the same with the saints of another confession, it is too much to maintain, on the pretext

213

that the essential truth is one, that there is no flagrant contradiction in this, and that such a contradiction is not by definition a serious infirmity on its own level; all that one can propose, by way of mitigating circumstance, is that the level in question is not an essential one for the tradition which is mistaken and that, as a result, the error does not inevitably impair essential spirituality, all the more so in that contemplatives are not necessarily preoccupied with the extrinsic anathemas of their religion; and one could also maintain that the people who are the object of these anathemas become negative symbols, so that there is merely an error in attribution and not in the idea as such; hence the error is one of fact and not of principle.

As for ordinary theological ostracisms—whether of the West or of the East—there is a profound wisdom in the fables of Aesop and Pilpay; the story of the fox and the grapes which were too high for him to reach, and which he therefore declared to be sour, is repeated in all sectors of human existence. In the name of wisdom, one reviles the wisdom of one's neighbor to console oneself—or to take revenge—for not having discovered it oneself: some eminent theologians have had no qualms in associating the inner voice of Socrates with the devil and in declaring diabolic all the wisdom of the Greeks—a gratuitous luxury, to say the least, seeing that Christianity, even in its Eastern branches, finally could not quite renounce from appealing to this wisdom.

In the enclosed space of theology, there are two openings: gnosis and liturgy. The opening of gnosis toward the Unlimited is immediately clear; but one also needs to know that the formal language of the sacred, whether it be the language of sanctuaries or of nature, is like the complement or prolongation of sapience. For beauty, like pure truth, is calm and generous; it is disinterested and free from passional suffocations and disputes over words; and one of the reasons for sacred art—as paradoxical as this may seem—is to speak to the intelligence of the sage as also to the imagination of the simple man, satisfying both sensibilities at the same time and nourishing them according to their needs.

*

*   *

There are dialectical excesses which are not to be found in divine language; but human language does not recoil from such audacities, which leads one to conclude that man must find in them some purpose or that his zeal is thereby satisfied. We have read in a Buddhist text: follow a master, even if he leads you into hell; an analogous expression is found in Muslim texts: be happy with God's Will, even if it destines you for the eternal fire. Literally, such expressions are contradictory, for the sufficient reason for having a master is that he should lead you to Heaven, and happiness in God and through Him coincides with salvation; but these expressions nonetheless have some meaning, and even obviously so, otherwise they would not exist in spiritual contexts. What is at stake is the perfect detachment of the ego; the absurdity of the image guarantees the effectiveness of the shock. One must act "as if the situation were so", though it could not be so; and the purpose of this is only to obtain a radical inner attitude which, from the point of view of sentimental voluntarism, would be difficult to obtain by other means. This last explanation provides the key to the enigma; voluntarist mysticism frequently operates by means of expedients, catapult-arguments, or surgical violence, for no other reason than that, at this level, pure and simple truth appears as an inoperative abstraction. For the "gnostic" or the "pneumatic", the effect is the reverse: indifferent to exaggerations and to other types of pressure tactics, he is immediately receptive to the truth as such, because it is the truth and because the truth is what convinces and attracts him.

However, it is true that there is not a strict separation between the two languages: gnosis also may use absurd formulations, but it does so by way of ellipses or as catalysts, and in presupposing intellectual intuition; thus when it is said that the sage "is Brahma", an impact-image is proposed to isolate—in view of highlighting it— a relationship that is metaphysically essential and humanly decisive, but not phenomenologically exhaustive since there are other relationships.

The dialectic of the Sufis can readily be likened to a "dance of the seven veils": in starting with the idea that nothing should be shared that might be neglected, misused, desecrated, and then scorned, and that it is essential to preserve a balance between doctrinal knowledge and methodical realization, this dialectic likes to envelop spiritual truths in abstruse complications; to accept them, or to accept their existence, we need only know the motive behind them.

A consideration which might not be out of place here is the following: one must react against the abusive opinion that attributes to sanctity as such—not to a particular type of sanctity—every imaginable quality and, consequently, all possible wisdom; in this way, the "wisdom of the saints"—no matter what saints—has been opposed to metaphysics as such, which is merely a matter of "natural intelligence", it is claimed. Now the phenomenon of sanctity consists of two things: the exclusiveness, on the one hand, and the intensity, on the other, of thought and will in view of the transcendent and of the next world, or of "God" and "Paradise". Thus sanctity, in its most general meaning, is essentially a matter of exclusivity and intensity on the basis of a religious credo; and it is on these two supernaturally inspired qualities that the gift of miracles depends. In the case of wisdom, it is the depth and scope of intellective knowledge that determines the exclusivity and intensity of the spiritual behavior, though both modes of perfection can meet and interpenetrate; there is no incompatibility, nor strict separation here, for if on the one hand "the Spirit bloweth where it listeth", on the other man always remains man.

*

* *

The human margin, needless to say, does not deploy itself on the doctrinal or dialectical level only, and we have already alluded to this when discussing the rabbinical exaggerations stigmatized by Christ. Similar in kind are some excessive practices that are consecrated or tolerated by tradition, notably in Hinduism, where particular opinions or attitudes, while not being in general totally unintelligible, are definitely disproportionate, to the point of being actually superstitious. These things can be explained, on the one hand, by the constant scruple of preserving the tradition in its original state of purity—in which case abuses are opposed to other abuses—and, on the other, by a certain totalitarianism typical of human nature; the concern for purity is obviously combined with the recognition that collectivities need a language that is precise, thus incisive and in practice immoderate, otherwise teachings fade and disappear.

Yet perhaps there is in some of these excesses a realism that tends to want to exhaust negative possibilities within the framework of tradition itself, as is somewhat the case of sacred Scriptures which contain wisely providential imperfections, or in sacred art where monsters are found next to divinities, or demons side by side with angels, in order to reduce to a minimum, by a kind of preventive and disciplined anticipation, the inevitable reactions of the powers of darkness.

*

* *

If there are variations, or even divergences, that are legitimate or spiritually and traditionally permissible, it is finally because there are three fundamental human types together with their diverse combinations: the passional, the sentimental, the intellectual.[12] Every man is a "self" placed in the "world"; this world contains "forms", and the "self" contains "desires". Now the great question is to know how a man, depending on his nature, senses or interprets at the outset these four facts of human existence; for it is this spontaneous conception that marks his spiritual type.

For the passional man, the contingent facts of existence, the world and the self with their contents, men and things, good deeds and sins, have something practically absolute about them; God appears to him as a kind of abstraction, a background that is not *a priori* relevant. Passion dominates him and plunges him into the

---

12. The trivialization of certain terms obliges us to specify that we use the words "sentimental" and "intellectual" in their proper and neutral meaning, without applying to "sentimental" the pejorative and to "intellectual" the profane and banal nuances that conventional language lends them. "Sentimental" is that which pertains to sentiment, whether base or lofty, stupid or intelligent, worldly or sacral; "intellectual" is that which pertains to the intellect, whether doctrinal or methodical, discriminating or contemplative. Thus the term "intellectual" does not have the same ambivalence as the term "sentimental", for the simple reason that sentiment is a horizontal and ambiguous faculty, whereas the intellect—not just intelligence or reason alone—is by definition a vertical and ascending faculty.

world of appearances;[13] thus his path is first and foremost a penitential one: he either redeems himself through violent asceticism or sacrifices himself in some holy war, or in servitude offered to God. The passional man can never be an intellectual in the full sense of the word; the doctrine that applies to him is made up of threats and promises, and of the metaphysical and eschatological minimum required by an intelligence mixed with passion.

For the man of the intellectual type, on the contrary, the contingent facts of existence appear at the outset as they are, in a near transparent mode: before asking "what do I want", he will ask "what is the world" and "what am I", which from the beginning determines a certain detachment with regard to forms and desires. It is true that he can be subject to attachments in relation to the heavenly realities shining through their earthly reflections; the most contemplative child can become strongly attached to things that, in the human desert he may be surrounded with, appear to him as memories of a paradise both lost and immanent. Be that as it may, for the fundamentally contemplative man, it is the invisible that is reality, whereas "life is a dream" (*la vida es sueño*); brute passion is replaced in him by the Platonic sense for beauty.

The third type is the emotional man, who might also be called the musical type; he is an intermediary possibility, for he can tend toward the passional type as well as toward the intellectual type, and in fact is reflected in both of them.[14] It is love and hope that constitute in him the dominant and operative element; he will readily place the accent on devotional manifestations, with a predilection for musical liturgy. This is the spirituality of happiness, yet also that of nostalgia.

---

13. Moreover, be it said in passing, this is the role of a large part of "culture": to pull man into the blind alleys of poisonous dreams and mental passions; to draw him insidiously away from the "one thing necessary"; to make him lose the taste for Heaven. The great novels of the nineteenth century, notably, exist for that purpose; they are the modern and centrifugal substitute for the Golden Legend and the romances of Chivalry.
14. The purely profane mode is, in this case, individualist lyrical poetry; it is in principle less harmful than the novel—provided it is authentic and natural and neither decadent nor subversive—first because its mode of expression is brief and then because it can be inspired by a cosmic beauty that transcends the poet's individuality; the case of music is analogous.

218

All this amounts to saying that there are three fundamental ways of transcending terrestrial *Mâyâ*: firstly, the penitential crushing of the ego; secondly, the conversion of passional energy into celestial music; and thirdly, intellectual penetration which turns illusion to ashes, or which brings it back to its quintessence.

These three modes or these three human types, needless to say, give rise to various combinations, made even more complex by the intervening influence of ethnic, cultural, and other factors; thus we need to take into account not just the three types insofar as they characterize different individuals, but also their presence in the same individual, and even, in a certain way, in every individual.[15] What interests us here, however, is not the complexity of the human being, but differences between men: it is the diversity of spiritual gifts, and especially the fragmentation of primordial man, that makes necessary the play of veiling and unveiling that constitutes traditional thinking.

*
* *

It is very tempting to attribute to the human margin, which develops in the shadow of divine inspirations, the seeming naiveties found in holy Scriptures; it goes without saying that there is no connection between the two, unless this margin is to be understood in a transposed and wholly different sense, as we shall propose later; but it is obviously no such transposition that modern critics have in mind when they believe it possible to draw arguments against the sacred Books from the apparent scientific errors found in them. Now the facts—assumed to be naïve—in the Book of Genesis, for instance, prove, not that the Bible is mistaken, but that man is not to know more, and this for the simple reason that he cannot bear it; certainly, no knowledge is harmful in itself, and in the nature of things there are always men capable of integrating spiritually all possible knowledge; but for the

---

15. The types in question, which refer to the ternary "fear", "love", "knowledge", hardly coincide with the three types of gnosticism: the hylic, the psychic, the pneumatic. The hylic is never a spiritual type; the passional is always a psychic type, whereas the sentimental can be a pneumatic, but is more normally to be found in the psychic category.

average man, only the knowledge provided by elementary experience, universal and age-old, hence normal, is bearable, as the history of these last centuries clearly proves. It is a fact not only that
scientific man—whose possibility was outlined in classical Greece
and developed in the modern West—loses religion as he plunges
into physical science, but that by the same token he closes himself
to the infinite dimension of supra-sensorial knowledge—the very
knowledge that gives meaning to life.

Paradise is presented in the Scriptures as being situated "up
above", "in heaven", because the celestial vault is the only height
that can be grasped empirically or sensorially; for analogous reasons, hell is "down below", "underneath the earth", in darkness,
heaviness, imprisonment. Similarly, for the Asiatics, samsaric
rebirths—when they are neither heavenly nor infernal—take
place "on earth", that is, on the only level that can be grasped
empirically; what matters for Revelation is the effectiveness of the
symbolism and not the indefinite knowledge of insignificant facts.
Now it is true that no fact is totally insignificant as such, otherwise
it would not exist; but the countless facts that elude man's normal
experience and that scientism accumulates in our consciousness
and also in our life, are spiritually intelligible only for those who
have no need of them.

Ancient man was highly sensitive to the intentions inherent in
symbolic expressions, as is proven, on the one hand, by the effectiveness of these expressions for many centuries and, on the
other, by the fact that ancient man was by any standard a perfectly
intelligent being; when he was told the story of Adam and Eve, he
grasped so clearly what the story was about—the evidence is in
fact dazzling—that he did not dream of wondering either "why"
or "how"; for we carry the story of Paradise and of the Fall in our
soul and in our very flesh. And similarly for all eschatological symbolism: the "eternity" of the hereafter denotes above all a contrast
in relation to the here-below, namely, a dimension of absoluteness
standing in opposition to our world of fleeting, and hence "vain",
contingencies; this is what matters, and nothing else, and this is
the divine intention of the image; in transmigrationist symbolisms, on the contrary, this "vanity" extends also to the hereafter,
to some degree at least and by reason of a profound difference in
perspective; here too no one is concerned with the "why" or the

"how" from the moment that the striking intention of the symbol has been seized as it were in one's own flesh.

In the man marked by scientism, the intuition for underlying intentions has vanished, and not only that: scientism, which is axiomatically closed to the supra-sensorial dimensions of the Real, has furnished man with a crass ignorance and, as a consequence, has falsified his imagination. The modernist mentality wants to reduce angels, demons, miracles—in a word, all phenomena that are non-material and that cannot be explained in material terms—to something purely "subjective" and "psychological", when there is not the slightest connection here, unless it is the fact that the psychic is also made—but objectively so—of an extra-material substance; a contemporary theologian, when speaking of the Ascension, mockingly asked, "And where does this cosmic journey end?", a comment that serves as a measure for the degree of self-satisfied idiocy of a certain type of mentality that wants to be "of our times". It would be easy to explain why Christ "was taken up" into the air and what the meaning is of the "cloud" that hid him from sight,[16] and also why it has been said that Christ "will come after the same fashion"; each detail corresponds to a precise reality, which can be easily understood in the light of traditional cosmologies; the key lies in the fact that the passage from one cosmic degree to another is heralded in the lower degree by modalities that are both "technical" and symbolic and which therefore reflect, in their way, the higher state; and this takes place according to an order of succession inherent in the nature of things.

Whatever the case may be, the deficiency of modern science is essentially related to the question of universal causality; it will no doubt be objected that science is not concerned with philosophical causality but with phenomena, and this is false, for all of evolutionism is nothing but a hypertrophy imagined as a result of denying the real causes; and this materialist negation as well as

---

16. It was not a cloud made of oxygen and hydrogen, but an extra-material substance that had become visible in order to receive the body that was about to penetrate into the higher cosmos. The "chariot of fire" of Elijah has the same meaning, as does the "sphere of light" observed during certain apparitions of the Virgin. All of this has absolutely nothing to do with fairy tales, nor above all with "depth psychology".

its evolutionist compensation pertains to philosophy and not to science.

From an altogether different point of view, it must be said that progressivists are not completely mistaken in thinking that there is something in religion that no longer works; the individualistic and sentimental argumentation with which traditional piety operates has all but lost its ability to grip consciences, and this is not simply because modern man is irreligious, but because normal religious arguments—not being able to go deep enough into the core of things and in fact not having had to do so previously—are somewhat blunted, psychologically speaking, and fail to satisfy certain needs for causality. It is a paradoxical phenomenon that human societies, if on the one hand they degenerate over time, also accumulate on the other experiences as they age, even if these experiences are mixed with errors; this is what any "pastoral", anxious to be effective, should take into account, not by seeking new directives from common error, but on the contrary by making use of arguments taken from a higher order, an order that is intellectual and not sentimental; by such means, some, at least, would be saved—and a far greater number than might be supposed—whereas with the scientistic and demagogic "pastoral", no one is saved.

The notion of the "human margin" can be understood in a higher sense which is free from all psychological and earthly connotations; in this case, we are entering into an altogether new dimension which one must be careful not to confuse with the vicissitudes of thought. What we want to say is that this notion can apply equally to the divine order and to the level of the Logos, inasmuch as certain human divergences are providentially prefigured in the Divine Intelligence; in this case, it is a matter, not of a superfluity of divergences, deriving in fact from human weakness, but of adaptations willed by Divine Mercy. No doubt there is not a total difference of principle here, but there is an eminent difference of dimension, similar to the difference between the square and the cube, or between whiteness and light.

When it is said that religious differences are no more than differences in formulation, this may be provisionally sufficient for those who are convinced in advance and in the abstract, but it is not sufficient the moment one has to enter concretely into details, for one also needs to know why these formulations are manifested as so many mutually incompatible affirmations, and not simply as differences in style. It is not enough to tell oneself that the various traditional doctrines express "points of view", and therefore different "aspects" of the One Truth; one needs to know that it is necessarily thus, and that it is impossible that things would be otherwise, for expression could never be exhaustive, while providing a perfectly sufficient key for total Truth. The same applies to physical experience: it is impossible to give of a landscape a description whose validity would be exclusive, for no one can see the landscape in all of its aspects at the same time, and no vision can prevent the existence and validity of other visions that are equally possible.

For man, the historical facts upon which his religion is established proves its exclusive validity precisely because they are facts, and thus realities; for God, these same facts have no value beyond that of a symbolist and logical demonstration, and are therefore replaceable with other facts just as a demonstration or a symbol is replaceable—though not without sufficient reason—with another demonstration or another symbol: the essential content is always the same truth, at once heavenly and salvific, but approachable in different ways since no angle of vision is the only one possible. This is what is indicated by the contradictions contained in the holy Scriptures, and also, to a lesser degree certainly, by the divergences in the visions of the saints.

Every religious belief is founded on a point of view from which this belief alone seems sublime and irrefutable; not to be of this persuasion appears not only as the worst of perversities, for it is to oppose God, but also as the worst of absurdities, for it is not to see that two plus two equal four. Everyone in the West knows what grounds there are for the sentiment that Christianity is true; but it is far less known why other religions resist that sentiment. Christianity in its immediate and literal expression—not in its essence, which is necessarily universal and hence polyvalent—is unquestionably directed toward sinners, those "who have need of the physician"; its point of departure is sin,[17] just as that of Buddhism is suffering. In Islam as in Hinduism—the most ancient religion and the most recent paradoxically meet in some features—the point of departure is man as such; the Christian perspective—whose literality, when seen from the outside, is the best "piece of evidence"—will thus appear as limited to a single aspect of man and of human nature, an aspect that is certainly real, but neither unique nor exhaustive. The marvels, whatever they may be, are not of a kind to invalidate this conviction, since it refers to the nature of things and that nothing phenomenal can take precedence over the Truth.

However it is not separative diversity that matters, but unanimity, and it would be of little avail to speak of the first without bearing in mind the second. If by "science" one means a knowledge with respect to real things—whether these can be directly controlled or not—and not exclusively a knowledge determined by such a program or such a method, narrowly limiting and philosophically abusive, then religion will be the science of total hierarchy, equilibrium, and of the rhythms operating on a cosmic scale; it gives account of both the exteriorizing Manifestation and the interiorizing Attraction of God, and it is alone to do so and to be able to do so *a priori* and spontaneously.

There can be no doubt that the Epistles of the New Testament are divinely inspired, but they are so to the second degree, which is to say that they do not pertain to direct Revelation like the words of Jesus and Mary or like the Psalms; and this explains why there can be in this secondary inspiration a new differentiation in degree depending on whether the Spirit speaks or whether it lets man almost entirely be the one who speaks; now man is in this

17. Apart from the fact that the notion itself of sin is susceptible to being transposed onto a higher plane—sin being then identified with the existential disequilibrium that the empirical ego represents or with a particular aspect of the ego—the Gospels contain many a saying which goes beyond the moral alternative and whose universal import is readily understandable; nevertheless, the Christian religion as such is based, practically speaking, on the notion of sin.

case a saint, but he is not the Holy Spirit. The apostle recognizes this himself by specifying, when giving certain counsels, that he does so on his own and not under the influence of the Paraclete. "And unto the married I command, yet not I, but the Lord." Here it is clearly the Spirit who is speaking. "Now concerning virgins I have no commandment of the Lord: yet I give my judgment as one that hath obtained mercy of the Lord to be faithful." Here it is man who is speaking. And likewise: "To the rest speak I, not the Lord." And again: "She is happier if she so abide, after my judgment: and I think also that I have the Spirit of God" (1 Cor. 7:10,12,25,40).

We find ourselves here in the presence of the "human margin", but it contains yet another degree: following the apostle, who gives his counsel, Roman theologians intervene, belatedly deducing—not without unrealistic idealism and in fact confusing asceticism with morality—the rule of celibacy for all priests,[18] a measure that goes hand in hand with placing too outward a motivation on the sacrament of marriage, thus forgetting the spiritual aspects of sexuality.[19] The result, positively, was the flowering of specific type of sanctity and, negatively, an accumulation of tensions that were the cause of all kinds of disequilibrium, culminating in the Renaissance and in its repercussions; this is not to say that the morally unrealistic and spiritually narrow angelism of a certain type of Christianity was the sole cause for the subsequent

18. Whereas the Orthodox, who are no less Christian, did not draw such a conclusion. Until the tenth century, most Catholic priests were married; Gregory VII, renewing the anathemas of Nicolas II and Alexander II, finally managed to impose sacerdotal celibacy after violent resistance which went as far as riots and the mistreatment of bishops and pontifical legates.

19. "So that they shall no longer be two, but of one flesh," declares the Gospel, placing the emphasis on the mystery of union—symbolized in a certain fashion by the miracle of Cana—and not on the two Pauline motivations, namely, the appeasing of the flesh and procreation, reserved for those who are incapable of abstaining. If it is important to avoid the pitfall of a moral automatism that is both prudish and hypocritical, it is even more important to reject the opposite pitfall, that of a loose sexualism, naturist and vitalist, and which, because of its insolent and desecrating casualness, is contrary to man's spiritual dignity. Sexuality is sacred, or else it is subhuman.

naturalist explosions, but it strongly contributed to them and is suffering the consequences today in its own flesh.

Generally speaking, when it is simply the nature of things that is being considered, but without thereby underestimating theological intentions or mystical values, one has the impression that Christianity—inasmuch as it is based on the consciousness of sin and on the sinful nature of man—has a need for sin and even creates it, in some measure, through an appropriate moral theology, when one takes account of the fact that, in such a perspective, sin is sexuality.[20] In other traditional perspectives, sexuality, in itself neutral, becomes intrinsically positive through a certain spiritual conditioning: obviously, sin is always the harmful and forbidden act, whether sexual or not; but it is also, more fundamentally, profane distraction in itself, pleasure for the sake of pleasure, hence forgetfulness of God and worldly exteriorization.[21] Piety, whether it excludes nature-as-sin or includes nature-as-sacrament, is not without a certain monotony; the guarantee of salvation lies essentially in the fixation of the heart in the consciousness of God, with all that this entails depending on circumstances and vocations, and whatever the supports in the natural order may be.

It is well-known that Judaism, which grants David and Solomon hundreds of spouses, and that Islam, which grants nine to its Prophet, are far from sharing the Pauline perspective; in general, Christian theologians have no plausible explanation for Semitic polygamy—though inadmissible opinions are not lacking[22]—which indicates that there is a dimension here which escapes, not every Westerner, certainly, but the characteristic and

---

20. Quintessentially, but not theologically. The Church is not Manichean: it blesses marriage, but marriage is considered to be both a lesser good and a lesser evil, which justifies—when looking at things in depth—the association of ideas with the notion of "sin".
21. There are religious authorities, in whom a complex of complicity toward the Renaissance is combined with a complex of inferiority toward the world of science, who show an astonishing indulgence for profane distractions which they term "innocent". Scientific progress, and the irreversible turmoil resulting from it, is fine, so long as one doesn't lose one's faith; to jump in the water, is fine, so long as one doesn't get wet.
22. It is inadmissible for instance to attribute to the author of the Psalms an insurmountable weakness of the flesh and to attribute the opposite virtue to any and every priest.

thus average perspective that has dominated the West for many centuries. Highly effective as it is on its level, this unilateral vision of natural things brings in its wake very unfortunate misinterpretations concerning not only Islam—which in any case is hardly surprising—but also the old Biblical world.

*

* *

The Mosaic Law has been given for all of time, right until the end of the world; nothing can be added to it, nothing taken away. This is the thesis of Judaism, and it is irrefutable. Nonetheless, Christianity has practically speaking abolished the Law, since according to it "the Spirit giveth life, the letter killeth"; this amounts to saying—since Christianity is, in its turn, intrinsically orthodox—that the thesis of Judaism has unconditional import only in the dimension that it represents, which is religious legalism.[23] The negation, by Christians, of the esoteric dimension is strictly speaking an inconsistency, since without the esoteric point of view Christianity would be inconceivable; if there is no esoterism, the argument of Judaism takes on absolute import and Christianity is the transgression that it appears to be from the Jewish point of view. Moreover, if the Spirit "giveth life" and the letter "killeth", this concerns only Judaism: if the "letter" of Judaism can become quite relative from a certain spiritual point of view, then the "letter" of Christianity falls under the same law, all the more since the "Spirit" that vivifies "bloweth where It listeth", which opens the door, not only to a Christian gnosis, but also to the acceptance in principle of non-Christian religions. Christianity was born of the distinction between form, which by definition is relative, and essence, which alone is absolute; if Christianity abolishes this distinction in favor of its own form, it robs itself, as it were, of the whole reason for its existence.

---

23. We have been assured that there could be no question in Judaism of practicing prescriptions mentally or of making up for them in some way, in a word, of interiorizing practices become impracticable and that all the rules remain obligatory without exception. Yet it seems to us that a religion could never prescribe what is impossible; the very fact that an observance is really impossible proves that it can be compensated for, even apart from all question of esoterism.

Without these subtle truths of principle, the Christian contradiction with regard to Judaism remains unintelligible, at least if one is aware, as one should be, of the argument of Judaism; but these truths obviously do not account for all of the concrete reality of Christianity which, being a religion, cannot possibly put into doubt its "letter" or its form on pain of abolishing itself. What needs to be specified is that the Christic message has a character of esoterism inasmuch as it is a perspective of inwardness or essentialization; but this message nonetheless is clad in an exoteric form owing to its voluntaristic and thus *de facto* individualistic character and the dogmatizing tendency that results from its urge to expand, or from the necessity for this expansion.

If on the one hand Christ is the founder of a world religion, he is on the other a Jewish prophet sent to Israel and addressing himself to it; in this second aspect—mentioned in fact by the Koran—Jesus has the function of a regenerator: he is the great prophet of inwardness, and as such he should have been accepted by Israel as Isaiah was;[24] however, this acceptance presupposed a spiritual suppleness more fitting of India than Judea. In theory, Judeo-Christianity ought to have perpetuated itself within the fold of Judaism—in parallel to its role as a world religion—as an esoteric community not unlike that of the Essenes; in practice, various aspects of the human margin precluded this possibility of principle.

Genesis relates how God "repented" when He saw the corruption of mankind: "And it repented the Lord that He had made man on the earth and it grieved Him at His heart";[25] in an analogous manner, there is something akin to a "divine repentance"

24. Christ, paraphrasing Isaiah, expresses himself thus: "This people honoureth me with their lips; but their heart is far from me. But in vain they do worship me, teaching for doctrines the commandments of men" (Matt. 15:8-9). And likewise: "Why do ye also transgress the commandment of God by your tradition?" (Matt. 15:3).
25. "If so be they will hearken, and turn every man from his evil way, that I may repent me of the evil, which I purpose to do unto them because of the evil of their doings" (Jer. 26:3). Likewise: "And God repented of the evil that he had said the he would do unto them" (Jon. 3:10), and other passages of this kind.

from one Revelation to another, in the sense that God manifests an aspect of Truth that corrects, not the aspect manifested previously, but human insistence on that aspect, or the unilateral development given by the human receptacle to an aspect which, in itself, is far less limited.

The characteristic—and inevitable—mistake of all exoterism is to attribute a human subjectivity to God and consequently to believe that any divine manifestation refers to the same divine "I", and thus to the same limitation. This is to fail to realize that the Ego that speaks and legislates in Revelations is no more than a manifestation of the Divine Subject and not the Subject Itself; in other words, one must distinguish in God—always from the point of view of Revelation—first of all the one and essential Word, and then the manifestations or actualizations of this Word with regard to particular human receptacles. The divine "I" that speaks to men—and of necessity to a "particular collectivity of men"—could never be the Divine Subject in a direct and absolute sense; it is an adaptation of this "I" to a human vessel and, as a result, takes on something of the nature of this vessel, failing which all contact between God and man would be impossible and failing which it would be absurd to admit that any Revelation, Hebrew, Arabic, or other, could be word-for-word of divine origin.

God cannot contradict Himself, certainly; but this axiomatic truth concerns essential, unlimited, and formless Truth, the only one that counts *in divinis*; relative enunciations may perfectly well contradict themselves from one Revelation to another—exactly as human subjects or material forms mutually exclude and contradict one another—so long as essential Truth is safeguarded, and made as effective as possible. The particular divine "I" of a Revelation is not situated in the Divine Principle Itself; it is the projection, or emanation, of the Absolute Subject and is identified with the "Spirit of God", that is, with the cosmic Center of which it could be said that it is "neither divine nor non-divine"; this revelation-giving "I" "is God" in virtue of the ray attaching it directly to its Source, but it is not God in an absolute way, for it is impossible that the Absolute as such would start speaking in a human language and say human things. This is the meaning of the doctrine of the "descent" of the Koran by successive stages, and this is what accounts for discussions concerning whether it is "created" or "uncreated", or in what way and in what respect it is or is not so; but this does not open the door to any naturalism, or to any humanism, for the earthly wording of a sacred scripture, while being determined from a certain point of view by human contingencies, remains divine through its heavenly origin and also through its as it were theurgic substance.

*

* *

When approaching Islam, a particularly serious difficulty is the accusation—leveled by Muslims against Jews and Christians—of "falsification of the Scriptures"; this accusation is aimed chiefly at what Islam considers to be a lack of due receptivity toward the totality of the Revelation, which is *a priori* as if suspended between God and man, its manifestation being determined by the human receptacle. Since Jewish and Christian theologies, when seen from the point of view of Islam, contain restrictive crystallizations, Islam will present these restrictions of perspective as "falsifications", in which case the "Scripture" is implicitly considered in its non-manifested and still heavenly totality.

Islam would readily accept the concepts of "Chosen People" and "God-Man" in a compensatory metaphysical context that would re-establish the equilibrium of total Truth; however, such a context, precisely, would appear to Jews and Christians as a nullification of their respective positions. Once again it must be emphasized here that every revealed and traditional symbolism is a key for the totality; but this does not abolish the distinction between spiritual forms opening more particularly onto a path either of works, or of love, or of gnosis, in other words, onto a path that is fundamentally determined by one or the other of these elements, although none of these determinations need have an exclusive character. In the economy of Revelation, spiritual opportunity, depending on its human receptacles, requires limitations and therefore negations; more specifically, it is necessary sometimes to deny things on the plane of formal expression, without ever having to call into question essential Truth.[26]

26. The ostracism between confessions is repeated within the same orthodoxy: when St Benedict condemns outright the Sarabaite and gyrovague

The "falsification of the Scriptures"—which Islam reproaches the two earlier monotheisms for—may also be reduced to a simple question of interpretation; thus Ibn Taymiyyah, Hanbalite protagonist of an extreme literalism, reproaches Jews and Christians for having falsified the meaning of several passages in their Scriptures—the meaning and not the text itself. A given spiritual mentality may feel the need to fix dogmatically, and to develop theologically and liturgically, a specific aspect of the truth to the detriment of another that may be more important, though not absolutely indispensable; we have in mind here Talmudic speculations and the vicissitudes of trinitarian theology, and also the factors that provoked the Christian schisms and the split between Sunnite and Chiite Islam.[27]

We do not intend, with these rather general interpretations, to settle the whole problem of the divergences between the Bible and Koran. We shall simply add that Muslims think it strange that the Bible should attribute the golden calf to Aaron without drawing any consequences from this, and that it should make grave accusations against both David and Solomon; or again that it says that the hand of Moses became leprous, by way of a sign, when he withdrew it from his bosom, when according to the Koran it was made luminous "without any hurt".[28]

---

monks, he does so above all in the name of a methodological and disciplinary perspective, for it is impossible to accept that the situation of these monks—some living in their houses and others wandering—did not correspond to real vocations, despite all the real abuses, though occurring more or less in the later stages. An analogous remark could apply to quietism—to cite but this one example—whose abuses in the seventeenth century do not invalidate the principle of quietude.

27. The suppression of all gnosis, the condemnation of Origen, and then the immense success of Arianism—not to mention the excessive influence of that two-edged sword of Aristotelianism—in a Christianity that was still relatively young, proves how difficult assimilation was for a human receptacle that was both too heterogeneous and too narrow.

28. When one reads the predictions of Christ concerning the latter times, one is struck by the fact that they refer in part to the ruin of Jerusalem, though distinctions between the various applications are not to be found in the speech itself; as is seen already in ancient prophecies predicting the advent of Christ, it happens in fact that prophetic language compounds two or more completely different, but obviously analogous orders; now analogy is a certain mode of identity, metaphysically and "divinely" speaking. There are similar coincidences—or cumulations—in

Certain religious theses, polemical in their tone, may seem unjust or crude; but they conceal under the very excess of their appearance a "divine point of view" that goes beyond dogmatism as such. Moreover, the reproach of "falsification of the Scriptures" can have for its aim the liberty that Revelation sometimes takes with words: an example is the manner in which some passages of the Old Testament are reproduced in the New; there is no doubt that in the eyes of the rabbis these are genuine falsifications,[29] when in fact, in cases of this kind, the same idea is divinely "re-thought" in relation to a new human receptacle.[30]

*

* *

To return to the Muslim point of view, the core of the issue is this: if we start with the idea that "Scripture" is the "uncreated Koran" that is with God, thus the Divine Word Itself or the Logos, vessel of all truth, then these Revelations, which are adapted in their expression to a particular collective human receptacle—for "water takes on the color of its container", as Junayd said—are, extrinsically, restrictions in relation to the uncreated Word; therefore, they "falsify" it in some fashion, if we can make use of this term here to highlight an analogy; hence the "falsification" considered by the Muslim reproach is above all, from the point of view of totality and universality, a restriction of perspective and a limitation.

the prophecies of Isaiah concerning Cyrus, the liberator of Israel (44:28, 45:1-6, and 63:1-3), if one applies them to the Prophet of Islam as do Muslims, basing themselves on the fact that the name of Cyrus—*Kôresh* in Hebrew—evokes that of *Quraysh*, the name of the tribe of Muhammad. We shall note that in Persian the name Cyrus, *Kurush*, means "sun", whereas in Elamite *kurash* means "shepherd", a meaning taken up by Isaiah; now both meanings equally suit the founder of Islam, who was first a shepherd before becoming a sun for a whole sector of the world.

29. And Christian theologians would doubtless be of the same opinion as the rabbis if it were a question of a non-Christian Scripture.

30. The divergences between the Hebrew text and the Septuagint translation occasion the same remark. According to St Augustine, the Septuagint translators benefited in their turn from the revelational breath, and the divergences between their translation and the Hebrew text had in each case a meaning implicitly contained in the original.

There are three aspects to be distinguished in Revelation: namely, first, the eternal Word in God; secondly, its specification—on the archangelic plane—in view of a particular human receptacle; thirdly, its manifestation on earth and in time according to circumstances that are providential, surely, but human and earthly nonetheless.[31] The second, or intermediary, degree presents two aspects, one essential and the other specific: thus the Koran, having descended to the seventh Heaven, remains on the one hand Divine Word, absolute and undifferentiated, and becomes on the other hand a specific Divine Order or particular Message. It is at the third degree that the Koran pours out into the human language and manifests its intentions of perspective, equilibrium, and salvation by means of human contingencies that determine a particular expression; the heavenly Koran, and with all the more reason the Divine Word in the absolute sense, does not speak of this or that name or incident; but it contains the intention which, on earth, can express itself through the most diverse human facts. In order to understand the nature of the Koran and the meaning of its discontinuities—but not those due to mere contingencies in compilation—it is necessary always to keep in mind these three degrees, which are intimately interwoven in the verbal crystallization of the Book and yet are recognizable by the sudden changes in level.

It results from what we have just said, not only that the revealed Book contains three degrees that are as it were hypostatic, but also, at the earthly degree, that this Book could be other than what it is; the events and words themselves have nothing absolute about them, otherwise contingency would not be contingency. The Logos in God could be compared to a formless and uncolored substance, and the Logos "descended" into the archangelic world to a religious perspective that is still superhumanly unarticulated; in which case, earthly manifestation would be comparable to the dispersion of a heavenly substance into earthly coagulations, formed by the social setting

---

31. This doctrine is moreover to be found in the theory of the "three bodies of the Buddha": "earthly" (*nirmâna-kâya*), "heavenly" (*sambhoga-kâya*), and "divine" (*dharma-kâya*).

and circumstances, which however would not affect this heavenly substance nor its divine essence. Or again: if we compare the eternal Word of God to gold as such, and a particular heavenly specification of this Word to a particular mass of gold, it will be readily seen that all the forms that can derive from this mass will in no wise affect either the weight or the nature of the metal.

This doctrine of the three hypostatic degrees of the Divine Word allows us to understand the principle of "abrogation" (*naskh*), which manifests in all sacred Scripture at the level of language, even if no practical consequences are drawn from it; now if there were no human margin, no abrogation would be possible.

Another principle, connected to the same doctrine, is that of "personal revelation", which is also directly divine, but given to a saint who has no prophetic mandate properly speaking. It is true that every spiritual truth necessarily derives from the heavenly prototype of the Book, but it does so in a manner altogether different than in the case of the "personal revelation" we have in mind here, where the wording is received, not through mere inspiration as is the case of some writings of saints and sages, but through revelation in the true sense, that is to say, in virtue of a direct divine action. A famous case is that of the Bhagavad-Gita which should logically be part of secondary inspiration (*smriti*) since it belongs to the Mahabharata, but which in fact is considered as one of the Upanishads, and thus as pertaining directly to heavenly inspiration (*shruti*); another case, found in Islam this time, is that of the chapter on Adam which Ibn Arabi declared as being derived from Divine revelation—in the manner of the Koran—and which indeed is a masterpiece from the point of view of both its form and content. Once the sage becomes, by the effect of a very special election, "his own prophet", he is thereby "his own law"; this election is at the same time a "heavenly adoption", manifested by objective signs, but of so super-eminent an order that it would be vain to hope that there could be here a spiritual degree accessible by efforts and by virtue of natural gifts. Be that as it may, it is understandable that the quality of "prophecy" (*nubuwwah*) could have been attributed to some Sufis; it is not in this case a "legislating" prophecy, but one that is nonetheless "radiant" in one way or another.[32] The objective and polyvalent revelation is repeated somehow in a particular human microcosm, not in the sense of a general and obvious analogy—every intellection being a "revelation"—but in virtue of an altogether particular possibility and of a participation, outside of time, in the "descent", or rather "reception", of the uncreated Book.

32. According to a *hadîth*, no woman was ever a prophet, but it is only a question here of legislating prophecy, this would seem obvious; thus there is no reason for thinking, Islamically speaking, that the term "prophetess" (*nabiyah*) could not suit the Virgin Maryam and should be replaced by the turn of phrase "of a prophetic nature" (*nabawiyah*), nor that the eulogistic form "upon her be Peace" (*'alayhâ as-Salâm*) should be replaced in her case by the formula, attributed to ordinary saints, "may God be satisfied with him or her" (*radhiya 'Llâhu 'anhu* or *'anhâ*); this all the more obvious in that, from the point of view of cosmic manifestation, Mary eminently surpasses all the saints.

Comments on
an Eschatological Problem

The great Revelations have, in varying degrees, a character that is at once total and fragmentary: total by reason of their absolute content or their esoterism, and fragmentary by reason of their particular symbolism or their exoterism; but even this exoterism always contains elements that make it possible to reconstitute the total truth. In Islam, for example, one of these elements is the idea, expressed in various ways, of the relativity—or non-eternity—of hell; nothing equivalent, that we are aware of, has been formulated about Paradise except—on the part of Sufis—that it is "the prison of the gnostic", and the Koran itself affirms that "everything is perishable; there remaineth but the Countenance (Essence) of Allah".[1] The profound meaning of all these allusions is as follows: toward the completion of a major cosmic cycle, in the words of a *hadîth*: "the flames of hell will grow cold";[2] correlatively, but without there being any true symmetry—for "My Mercy taketh precedence over my Wrath"—the Paradises, at the approach of the *apocatastasis*, will of metaphysical necessity reveal their limitative aspect, as if they had become less vast or as if God were less close than before; they will experience a sort of nostalgia for the One without a second or for the Essence, for proximity is not Unity and comprises an element of otherness and separativity. Without involving suffering of

---

1. The Gospels: "Heaven and earth shall pass away, but my Words shall not pass away" (Luke 21:33).
2. Abdul-Qadir al-Jilani states that in the place of hell, when it is extinguished, there will spring up a green tree called *Jarjîr*, "and the best of the colors of Paradise is green", opposed to the red of fire.

any kind, which would be contrary to the very definition of Heaven, the aspect "other than God" will manifest itself to the detriment of the aspect "near to God". This will be no more than a passing shadow, for then will come the *apocatastasis* whose glory will surpass all promises and all expectations, in conformity with the principle that God never fulfills less than He promises, but on the contrary always more.[3] At the very moment when, perhaps, one of the blessed will ask himself whether he is still in Paradise, the great veil will be torn asunder and the uncreated Light will flood all and absorb all; the "garden" will return to the "Gardener";[4] universal Manifestation will be transmuted and everything will be reintegrated within the ineffable Plenitude of the Principle; Being itself, together with its possibilities of creation, will no longer be detached from the indivisible Self; its possibilities will be dilated into what might be called, notwithstanding a certain inherent absurdity in the expression, the "absolute Substance". Sufis already perceive this aspect of Paradisal "twilight" in the contingency of the celestial states themselves, and with the help of the *Shahâdah*—the testimony of Unity—the key to discernment between the Absolute and the contingent;[5] it is this discernment that allows them to compare Paradise—or the Paradises—to a "prison"; in other words, they see the effects in the causes and perceive a priori the limits of all that is not God, while at the same time—and from another standpoint—they see God through phenomena. On the other hand, the Sufis rejoin the Buddhist perspective analogically when describing the Divine Beatitude as the "Paradise of the Essence", which corresponds directly to *Nirvâna*;[6] the latter is in fact "God" considered

---

3. This explains an apparent contradiction in the Koran which, having limited Paradise to "so long as the heavens and the earth endure", immediately adds that Paradise is "a gift that shall not be cut off".
4. Sufi expressions, the Koranic term for "Paradise" being "Garden" in either the singular or the plural (*Jannah, Jannât*).
5. Christianity possesses the same key in this saying of Jesus "There is none good but one, that is, God" (*Nemo bonus nisi unus Deus*) (Mark 10:18). This sentence contains the whole doctrine of the relationship of the contingent to the Absolute and consequently enunciates the non-eternity of created states: Heaven, not being God, could not be "good"; it is thus of necessity ephemeral when considered on the scale of the "Lives of *Brahmâ*" and with respect to the contingent nature of "ex-sistence".
6. This term has in itself a total and unchanging value that is independent not only of the secondary and contingent distinction between *Nirvâna*

from the standpoint of Beatitude and Permanence. All these considerations reveal an important point of contact between the Semitic and Brahmano-Buddhic eschatologies,[7] and illustrate the crucial idea of the "impermanence of all things".

We have just seen that at the approach of the final absorption of the Paradise into the Essence, the aspect of separativity will be accentuated at the expense of the aspect of nearness, at least in a certain measure. The case of hell—or the hells—is however analogically inverse, in the sense that they comprise on the one hand an aspect of remoteness, which is their reason for being, and on the other hand an aspect of necessity or existence, which perforce attaches them to the Will of God, and thus to Reality as such; at the beginning the first aspect will predominate, but the second aspect is bound to assert itself toward the end of the cycle, whence precisely the "cooling"—as a *hadîth* expresses it—of the infernal flames. God being Love or Mercy—more essentially than Justice or Rigor—His Goodness is included in Existence and in all existential substances, and it will take possession finally of everything that exists; in each thing and in each creature, that which is good is firstly its pure and simple existence, then its deiformity, even the most indirect, and lastly its particular qualities; these positive aspects, without which nothing can exist, will in the end triumph over the negative accidents, and they will do so in virtue of the universal law of equilibrium with its twofold aspect of exhaustion and compensation.[8] Considerations of this kind, whether relating to Heaven or hell, can only be schematic, and cannot take

and *Paranirvâna*, but also of the different cosmic degrees of "extinction".

7. Here is another analogy: the Samyaksam-Buddha, thanks to the immensity of his merits and his knowledge, produces a Paradise situated on the fringe of transmigration, on the nirvanic axis; Christ, before leaving the world, speaks to the apostles of the "place" that he will prepare for them "in his Father's house".

8. A Hindu text describing the *apocatastasis* says that *tamas* will be converted into *rajas*, and *rajas* into *sattva*. In the Apocalypse of St Peter, the risen Christ speaks of the *apocatastasis* while at the same time forbidding the disclosure of this doctrine, in order that men may not sin the more; thus it is indeed only logical that it has not been retained in the general teaching of the Church. But in our days the situation is quite different, at least as regards the opportuneness of certain truths, though not as regards the dogmas.

account of all possible modalities, which in the nature of things are unknown to us; Revelation teaches us directly or indirectly that Paradise and hell comprise regions and degrees—in both the "horizontal" and "vertical" dimensions[9]—but the "life" or "movements" in these abodes scarcely unveils itself to earthly understanding, unless it be through rare and fragmentary images. In any case, the metaphysical basis of the whole of this doctrine rests on the most solid of foundations, for it coincides with the very notion of contingency.

To speak of existence is to speak of particularity and change; this is demonstrated by space and time on the plane of corporeal existence, and by the worlds and the cosmic cycles on the plane of universal Existence. Existence is, analogically speaking, both a "form" and a "movement"; it is at once static and dynamic, but at the same time comprises alternations of unfolding and crystallization; the transmigration of souls has no other significance.[10] At the summit of universal Existence, this "migratory vibration" comes to an end, because it turns inward in the direction of the Immutable; there remains only a single movement, a single cycle, that of Paradise, which opens onto the Essence. In God Himself, who is beyond Existence, there is an element that prefigures Existence, and this is the Divine Life, which the Christian doctrine attributes to the Holy Spirit and which it calls Love; toward this Life converge those existences that are plunged in the light of Glory and sustained by it; and it is this Light, this "Divine Halo", which keeps the Paradises outside the "migratory vibration" of existences that are still corruptible. The sage is not strictly speaking separated from his existential movement—although from the standpoint of the cosmic wheel he is so—but turns it inward: the movement becomes lost in the Infinite or is dilated, as it were, into the "immutable movement" of the "Void".

9. "There are many mansions in my Father's house," said Christ. St Irenaeus refers to this saying when echoing a doctrine according to which some will enter Heaven, others the earthly Paradise, and others again the celestial Jerusalem; all will see the Savior, but in different manners according to their degree of dignity.
10. The meeting point between the monotheistic eschatology and Indian "transmigrationism" lies hidden—in Monotheism—in the concepts of limbo and hell, not to mention the "resurrection of the flesh", in which the being is not however invested with a new individuality.

Or again: to identify oneself with movement is to engender movement and therefore change, the series of movements; to identify oneself with pure being engenders being and therefore the interiorization and transmutation of movement, or the cessation of movement in the Immutable and the Unlimited. Desire is movement, and contemplation is being.

*

* *

Revelation offers truths that are not only explicit but also implicit; it presents both postulates and conclusions, ideas that are causes and ideas that are consequences; it cannot escape from reckoning with these consequences concretely once it has provided the keys to them. Now these keys necessarily imply the corresponding consequences, of which they are as it were the living anticipations: the "totality" of love in Christianity, and the "sincerity" of faith or knowledge in Islam imply the most decisive metaphysical truths—or the most subtle, if one prefers,—even were these truths to reveal the illusory nature, not of the literal interpretations which are always valid on their own levels, but of these levels themselves. It is for this reason that the criterion of traditional orthodoxy does not necessarily consist in agreement with a particular exoteric thesis, but in agreement with the principle of knowledge or realization by which this thesis is accompanied: to speak of "ice" is to speak of "water", even if from the point of view of immediate vision—which counts only at a certain level—there is opposition between solidity and liquidity. It is for this reason that it is absurd to expect from Revelation explicit teachings about every truth; it needs to be explicit in regard to those truths which necessarily concern all men, but it has no cause to be explicit in regard to truths which, being neither comprehensible nor necessary to the majority of men, should remain in a state of potentiality that only esoterism is called upon to actualize. For example, when the Scriptures proclaim that "God is Love", this implies metaphysically the relativity and even the end of hell: moreover, to speak of "relativity" is to speak of a "limit", and so an "end"; but this end derives from a "dimension" that is higher than the reality of hell; it is not therefore hell that comes to an end, but the end that seizes hell. It is as though the dimension of depth were to absorb one of the other two dimensions, or rather both of them at the same time, by dissolving or transmuting all of the planar surface; neither of the two dimensions would cease to exist in relation to their common plane, it is this plane itself that would cease to exist.

The Two Paradises

The Vedantin notion of "Deliverance" (*moksha, mukti*) evokes, whether rightly or wrongly, the paradoxical image of a refusal of Paradise and a choice of the Supreme Union, which seems to imply, according to some formulations, the dissolution of the individual and the identification of the Intellect-kernel with the Self. If such an end is presented as the object of a strictly human option, one will rightly object that the individual could have no motive for choosing anything other than his own survival and his own happiness; the rest is pretension and bookish speculation, and thus has no connection to the Vedantin notion in question.

To begin with, the following two points must be considered: first, the idea of "Deliverance" or of "Union" corresponds to a metaphysical evidence, whatever pedantic or extravagant interpretations may do, depending on the case, to alter its meaning; next, there are in man two subjects—or two subjectivities—with no common measure and with opposite tendencies, though there is also, in some respect, coincidence between the two. On the one hand, there is the *anima* or empirical ego, woven out of objective as well as subjective contingencies, such as memories and desires; on the other hand, there is the *spiritus* or pure Intelligence, whose subjectivity is rooted in the Absolute, so that it sees the empirical ego as being no more than a husk, that is, something outward and foreign to the true "my-self", or rather "One-self", at once transcendent and immanent.[1]

---

1. Although "every thing" is *Âtmâ*, this is so in an altogether different and in some way opposite respect.

243

Now if it is incontestable that the human ego normally desires happiness and survival in happiness, to the point of having no motive for desiring more than this, it is equally true that pure Intelligence exists and that its nature is to tend toward its own source; the whole question is to know, spiritually speaking, which of these two subjectivities predominates in a human being. It can be rightly denied that the choice of the supra-individual has any meaning for the individual as such, but it cannot be denied that there is something in man that surpasses individuality and can take precedence over the latter's aspirations, in order to tend toward the plenitude of its own transcendent nature.

We speak of taking precedence over the aspirations of individuality, but not of abolishing them; here we touch on another aspect of the problem, and by no means the least. When one speaks traditionally of a "dissolution" or of an "extinction" of individuality, one has in view the privative limitations of the ego, but not its very existence; if there is no common measure between the ego of the one who is "freed in this life" (*jîvan-mukta*) and his spiritual reality—so that it can be said of him that he "is *Brahman*" without having to deny that he is this particular man—the same incommensurability and, along with it, the same compatibility, or the same parallelism, present themselves in the hereafter; if this were not the case, one would have to conclude that the *Avatâras* had completely vanished from the cosmos, and this has never been traditionally admitted. Christ "is God", which in no wise prevents him from saying: "Today shalt thou be with me in paradise", nor from predicting his return at the end of the cycle.

The world is the plane of phenomena or of contingencies; the ordinary ego, the *anima*, is thus part of the world and is situated "outside" for him who is able to envisage it from the *spiritus*, which by definition derives from the *Spiritus Sanctus*; and this could never be a matter of ambition or affectation: it is a matter of true understanding and of innate perspective. This means that subjectivity can be conceived, or realized, according to three degrees, which correspond precisely to the ternary of *corpus, anima, spiritus*: the first degree is that of animality, be it human; the second is that of the microcosm of dream, in which the subject is no longer identified with the body alone, but with this ever increasing mirage that is imaginative and sentimental experience; the third degree is that of pure Intelligence, which is the trace in man of the unique and "transcendentally immanent" Subject. The soul is the inner witness of the body, as the spirit is the inner witness of the soul.

The nature of Intelligence is not to identify itself passively and quasi-blindly with the phenomena it registers, but on the contrary, by reducing phenomena to their essences, to know ultimately That which knows; by the same stroke, the sage—precisely because his subjectivity is determined by Intelligence—will tend "to be That which is" and "to enjoy That which enjoys"; and this brings us back to the Vedantin ternary "Being, Consciousness, Bliss" (*Sat, Chit, Ânanda*). In reality there is but a single Beatitude, just as there is but a single Subject and a single Object; the three poles are united in the Absolute, but are separated insofar as the Absolute enters into Relativity, according to the mystery of *Mâyâ*; the conclusion of this descent is precisely the diversification of subjects, objects, and experiences. Object, Subject, Happiness: our whole existence is woven out of these three elements, but in illusory mode; the sage does nothing other than the ignorant, that is, he lives from these three elements, but he does so in the direction of the Real, which alone is the Object, the Subject, and Happiness.

*

* *

When it is said in Sufism that "Paradise is inhabited by fools",[2] one must understand this to mean subjects who are attached to phenomena rather than to the unique Subject, who is His own Object and His own Beatitude. All paradoxical sayings referring to the distinction between the "saved" and the "elect" must be interpreted above all as metaphors affirming such a principle or such a tendency; the paradox results from the fact that the image is naively human, and thus psychological, when in fact the principle involved shares no common measure with psychology. Two subjectivities, two languages: the whole enigma of esoterism is to be found in this. A doctrine is esoteric inasmuch as it appeals to

---

2. This idea is plainly inspired by the following *hadîth*: "Most of the dwellers in Paradise are simple-minded" (*al-bulh*), that is, without guile or malice. The meaning is thus positive, whereas it is pejorative in the interpretation just mentioned, which aims at marking an opposition between two attitudes or two categories.

the "inward subjectivity" and thus puts aside the "outward subjectivity"; conversely, a doctrine is exoteric inasmuch as it accepts the empirical ego as a closed system and an absolute reality, and thus confines itself to subjecting the ego to prescriptions that are equally absolute. For the Sufis, the attestation that there is no divinity if not the sole Divinity is esoteric owing to the fact that in the end it excludes the outward egoity; "in the end", that is to say, when this attestation is understood "sincerely" (*mukhlisan*), hence totally. The traditional expression "knowing through God" (*'ârif bi-'Llâh*)—and not "knowing God"—is characteristic in this respect, the preposition "through" serving precisely to indicate the quasi-divine subjectivity within pure intellection.

The outward ego by definition nourishes itself with phenomena and is in consequence fundamentally dualistic; to it corresponds the revealed and objective religion, whose Messenger is a particular historical person. The inward ego looks toward its own Source, which is at once transcendent and immanent; to it corresponds the innate and subjective religion,[3] whose *Avatâra* is the heart; wisdom is in fact inaccessible without the concurrence of objective and revealed religion, just as the inward ego is inaccessible without the concurrence of the sanctified outward ego.

The crystallization of metaphysical truth into a religious, and thus dogmatic, phenomenon results from the principle of individuation: in falling into the human atmosphere, the Divine Truth is coagulated and becomes individualized; it becomes a point of view and is personified, such that it is impossible to reconcile one particular religious form with another on the plane itself of this personification; this is as impossible as to change from one human ego to another, even though we know perfectly well that the ego of others is not more illogical nor less legitimate than our own. In compensation, the passage from one form to another—in other words, from one metaphysico-mystical subjectivity to another—is always possible by returning to the source of the religious coagulations, for this source pertains precisely to the

---

3. "Know"—God reveals to Niffari—"that I shall accept from thee nothing of the *Sunnah*, but only that which My Gnosis bringeth thee, for thou art one of those to whom I speak." Not everyone holds this station, to say the least, and to attribute it to oneself is to risk an irremediable fall; if we bring it up here, it is for the sake of doctrine.

universal Subjectivity or, if one prefers, to Intelligence in Itself; man has access to this source, in principle or even in fact, through pure intellection; and this is the subjectivity that is concerned with "Deliverance" in the Vedantin sense of the term.

When Sufis disdain Paradise out of their desire for God alone, it goes without saying that in this case they are envisaging Paradise inasmuch as it is created, that is, inasmuch as it is "other than God", and not inasmuch as it is divine in its substance and content—notwithstanding its existential degree; this is so true that Sufis speak completely logically of a "Paradise of the Essence", which precisely is situated beyond creation. Analogously, when Sufis seem sometimes to reject works or even virtues, what they mean is these values inasmuch as they appear as "mine", and not inasmuch as they belong to God; or again, when a Sufi affirms that for him good and evil are equally a matter of indifference, this means that he is envisaging them in relation to their common contingency, which in its turn plays the role of "evil" with respect to the sole "good" that is absoluteness. If we compare good to light and evil to an opaque stone, the fact of whitening the stone does not transform it into light; the stone can be streaked with white and black by way of depicting "good" and "evil", but because of its opacity and heaviness, it will nonetheless remain a kind of "evil" in relation to the luminous ray.

The two human subjects, the outward or empirical and the inward or intellective, correspond analogically to the two aspects of the Divine Subject, the ontological or personal and the supra-ontological or impersonal; in man, as *in divinis*, duality is perceptible, or is actualized, only in relation to the element *Mâyâ*.[4] Or again, to return to the ternary *corpus, anima, spiritus*: these three subjectivities respectively reflect the three *hypostases*—if indeed this term applies here—Existence, Being, Beyond-Being; just as God is not "absolutely Absolute" except as Beyond-Being, so man is not absolutely himself except in the Intellect; whereas the empirical ego nourishes itself with phenomena, the intellective ego burns them and tends toward the Essence. However, this difference of principle does not imply an alternative of fact, pre-

---

4. In Sufism, the key notion of *Mâyâ* is expressed through the terms *hijâb*, "veil", and *tajallî*, "unveiling" or "revelation".

cisely because there is no common measure here; the norm in this case is an equilibrium between the two planes, and not a concretely inconceivable dehumanization.

The paradoxical expression "absolutely absolute" calls for some explanations. Orthodox theologians, according to Palamas, make a distinction in God between the Essence and the Energies; this is an error, say the Catholics, for the divine nature is simple; there is no error, rejoin the Orthodox, for the laws of logic do not apply to God, who is above them. This is a dialogue between the deaf, we conclude, for logic in no way prevents one from admitting that the divine nature comprises Energies even while being simple; to understand this, it suffices to have the notion of divine Relativity, which the totalitarian sublimism of theologians excludes, precisely, since it makes it impossible to combine antinomic relationships which, in pure metaphysics, are contained in the nature of things. There could never be any symmetry between the relative and the Absolute; as a result, if there is clearly no such thing as the absolutely relative, there is nonetheless a "relatively absolute", and this is Being as creator, revealer, and savior, who is absolute for the world, but not for the Essence: "Beyond-Being" or "Non-Being". If God were the Absolute in every respect and without any hypostatic restriction, there could be no contact between Him and the world, and the world would not even exist; for in order to be able to create, speak, and act, it is necessary that God Himself make Himself "world" in some fashion, and He does so through the ontological self-limitation that gives rise to the "personal God", the world itself being the most extreme and hence the most relative of self-limitations. Pantheism would be right in its own way if it could restrict itself to this aspect without denying transcendence.

Monotheist exoterism readily loses sight of the aspects of inclusiveness, but it has the advantage—and this is its reason for being—of placing man as such before this "human Absolute" that is the creator God; however, it must pay a penalty for this simplification: the theological deadlocks—which Christians justify by means of the argument of "mystery" and Muslims by means of the argument of God's "good pleasure"—testify to the need to take account in one and the same breath of both the unity of God and the antinomic complexity of the divine intervention in the world.

Now this complexity cannot be explained by unity, but it can be explained, on the contrary, by relativity *in divinis*, that is to say by the hypostatic gradation in view of the creative unfolding; and this relativity does not affect unity anymore than space affects the unicity of the center-point or the homogeneity of total space, which derives from that point and which deploys it.

In the face of the paradoxical complexity of the metaphysical Real, the situation of theologies can be summarized as follows: first of all, there is the axiom that God is the Absolute since nothing can be greater than He; next, there is the logical evidence that there is in God something relative; finally, the conclusion is drawn that since God is the Absolute, what is relative in appearance cannot be other than absolute; the fact that this is contrary to logic proves that logic cannot reach God, who is "mystery" (Christianity) and who "does as He wills" (Islam). Now we have seen that the solution of the problem rests upon two points: objectively, the Absolute is susceptible of gradation, unless one wishes to cease discussing it; subjectively, it is not logic that is at fault, but the opacity of our axioms and the rigidity of our reasonings. Certainly, God "does as He wills", but that is because we cannot discern all of His motives on the phenomenal plane; certainly, He is a "mystery", but this is because of the inexhaustibility of His Subjectivity, the only one that is, in the last analysis, and that becomes clear to us only inasmuch as it whelms us in its light.

*

* *

It is plausible that the ego, in the measure that it is determined by objects, which are "not-myself", is not entirely itself; the true ego, the pure Subject, bears its object within itself, like the Divine Essence, which "tends toward Its own infinite Center"—if this inadequate image is permissible—whereas Being tends toward creation, but obviously without "emerging from itself", and without being affected by the world and its contents. In other words: the subject-intellect, in the likeness of Beyond-Being, bears its object within itself; but the empirical or psychic ego, in the manner of Being, has its object both within itself and outside itself; and just as Existence has its object outside itself, namely in existing things, so does the sensorial ego have its object in the outward and tends toward the outward. Now God can be at the same time Beyond-Being, Being, and even Existence, if we speak according to *Mâyâ*, for in the last analysis, Beyond-Being does not Itself unfold: It contains everything within Itself in a state that is undifferentiated but infinitely real; man, who is made in the image of God, nonetheless has the possibility of being unfaithful to this image, since he is not God and is free; having committed this act of infidelity and bearing it in his inborn nature, he must, in order to become deiform, tend toward the divine Inward. The animic subject must become free from the corporeal subject, and the intellectual subject must become free from the animic subject, in conformity with this teaching: "Whosoever shall seek to save his life shall lose it; and whosoever shall lose his life shall preserve it" (Luke 17:33). And likewise: "Except a corn of wheat fall into the ground and die, it abideth alone; but if it die it bringeth forth much fruit. He that loveth his life, shall lose it; and he that hateth his life in this world shall keep it unto life eternal" (John 12:24-25).

The "life" or the "soul" to be sacrificed is, we repeat, the ego inasmuch as it is a passional nucleus and not inasmuch as it is simply a particular subjectivity; thus the criterion of a spiritual degree is not the absence of the consciousness of "self", which could never occur habitually—otherwise Christ could not have moved in the world—but the abolishing of the passional entanglement founded on desire, ostentation, and optical illusion. The first spiritual phase is isolation, for the world is the ego; the summit is to "behold God everywhere", for the world is God. In other words, there is a spiritual perfection wherein the contemplative perceives God only in the inward, in the silence of the heart; and there is another perfection, superior to the preceding one and issuing from it—for the second is conceivable only in terms of the first—wherein the contemplative perceives God also in the outward,[5] in phenomena: in their existence, then in their

5. This state corresponds to the station of the *Bodhisattva*, whereas the preceding state is that of the *Pratyeka-Buddha*. To surpass the need for solitude of the *Pratyeka-Buddha* and to become a *Bodhisattva* is to remain in the state of union as much in a harem as on a battlefield; and this quite apart from the active and creative function of the *Samyaksam-Buddha*, who represents, not a spiritual degree—he possesses by definition the supreme degree without being the only one to possess it—but a cosmic

general qualities, and then in their particular qualities, and even indirectly in their privative manifestations. In this realization, not only does the ego appear as extrinsic—which happens also in the first perfection—but the world appears as inward by revealing its divine substance, things becoming nearly translucent; it is to this realization, both radiant and inclusive, that Sufis allude when they say with Shibli: "I have never seen any thing save God."[6]

However, "to behold God everywhere" can have a more particular meaning, which in a sense coincides with understanding the "language of the birds" and at the same time brings us back to the principle whereby "extremes meet": the intelligence that is penetrated by what is most inward may thus enjoy, charismatically, the faculty of understanding the secret intentions of outward things, and so of forms in an altogether general way.

We have quoted above the saying of Christ about "life"; those who would save it, lose it, and those who of their own will lose it, save it for eternity. No doubt this teaching establishes a first distinction, entirely general, between worldly and spiritual men; but it also refers, since it is sacred and thus polyvalent, to the two subjectivities that concern us particularly, the phenomenal and the intellectual, or the empirical "self" and the transcendent "selfhood". In the latter case, the notion of "perdition" must be transposed; in other words, this notion will refer merely to the ambiguous situation of the "psychic" individual: whereas the "pneumatic" is saved by his ascending nature, his subjectivity being intellective, the "psychic" risks being lost owing to the contingent and passive character of his egoity.

phenomenon of the first order of magnitude, for it belongs to the order of divine manifestations.

6. Tradition attributes analogous words to the four *râshidûn* Caliphs: one beheld God before what had been created, the other after it, the third at the same time as it, and the fourth beheld nothing other than God. Likewise Hujwiri in his *Kashf al-Mahjûb*: "One saint sees the act with his corporeal eye and, in seeing, perceives the divine Agent with his spiritual eye; another saint, owing to his love for the Agent, finds himself separated from all things, so that he see only the Agent." This is not unrelated to this saying of St Paul: "To the pure all things are pure."

It is however in the nature of things that spiritual subjectivity give rise to an intermediary solution, more sacrificial than intellectual, in which the subject, even if it is not the microcosmic prolongation of the Shankarian "Self", is nonetheless more than the empirical "self"; and this is the heroic subjectivity of the path of Love, which tears itself free from phenomena without being able to integrate itself with the Witness who is both transcendent and immanent. In this case, a ray of Mercy enters into the subjectivity that is cut off from the world: deprived of the worldly "self", the immortal soul lives finally from the Grace that sustains and adopts it.

Since the distinction between the two subjectivities is essential, it cannot but arise in the midst of a spiritually integral tradition; if we did not know of a Meister Eckhart, we would nonetheless have to admit that this point of view is not absent in Christianity. Meister Eckhart, with characteristic audacity, prayed to God to free him from God, specifying that this applied to God as the origin of creatures and that our essential being is above God envisaged in this manner; "the Essence of God and the essence of the soul are one and the same," he would say, thus providing the key to the enigma.[7] This expression indicates a compensatory reciprocity between the Absolute and the relative or between *Âtmâ* and *Mâyâ*: for to the mystery of incommensurability (Islam: *Lâ ilaha illâ 'Llâh*) is adjoined the compensatory mystery of reciprocity (Islam: *Muhammadun Rasûlu 'Llâh*); in other words, in *Âtmâ* there is a point that is *Mâyâ*, and this is Being or the personal God, whereas in *Mâyâ* there is a point that is *Âtmâ*, and this is Beyond-Being or the Divine Essence present in the Intellect; it is the immanent absoluteness in the human relative. Once again we rejoin here the Taoist symbolism of the *Yin-Yang*: the white part contains a black dot, and the black part a white dot. The fact that man can conceive of the limitation of Being in relation to the pure Absolute proves that he can in principle realize this Absolute

---

7. One will note the analogy with the *Tat tvam asi* ("That art thou") of the *Vedânta*.

and thus transcend the Legislation emanating from Being, namely formal religion; we say "in principle", but rarely in fact, otherwise religions would not exist.

"If I were not, neither would God be," Meister Eckhart furthermore says, which becomes clear in light of the doctrine we have just expounded;[8] and he takes care to recommend, for those who do not understand this "naked truth issued from the very heart of God", that they not "beat their heads against a wall", for none can understand it except he who "is like unto it". In other words, the doctrine of the supreme Subjectivity requires a providential predisposition to receive it; we say a "predisposition" rather than a "capacity", for the principal cause of a lack of metaphysical understanding is not so much a fundamental intellectual incapacity as a passional attachment to concepts that are conformed to man's natural individualism. On the one hand, transcending this individualism predisposes man to such an understanding; on the other hand, total metaphysics contributes to this transcending; every spiritual realization has two poles or two points of departure, one being situated in our thought, and the other in our being.

*
* *

The *Sûrah* of "The Merciful" (*Ar-Rahmân*) attributes to "him who feareth the station of his Lord" two celestial gardens, and then goes on to mention two further gardens; according to the commentators, the first two gardens are destined respectively for men and the jinn,[9] or again, according to others, for each believer, but without the difference between the two gardens being explained; it is generally considered—following Baidawi—

---

8. We have no intention of denying the problematical character of such an expression; in other words, it is ill-sounding because it is too elliptical: the relativity of the "God" of the formula is not explained.

9. The jinn are the subtle or animic beings situated between corporeal creatures and angelic creatures. Each one of these three degrees comprises peripheral states and one central state; on earth there are animal species and there is man, as in Heaven there are angels and archangels; the latter are identified with the "Spirit of God" (*ar-Rûh*). Likewise, there are two kinds of jinn: those belonging to the central state can be believers and win Paradise; they are the ones the *Sûrah* of "The Jinn" speaks of.

that the two further gardens are destined for believers of lesser merit or of lesser quality.[10] In any case it seems plausible to us to make a distinction, in each of the two cases mentioned, between a "horizontal" garden and a "vertical" garden—this second Paradise being none other than God Himself as He communicates or manifests Himself with respect to the degree considered; in this we have the exact equivalent of the distinction between the "celestial body" of the Buddhas and their "divine body".[11]

In the case of the elect or those "brought nigh" (*muqarrabûn*), the vertical garden is the state of union; we have already seen that this state could not prevent the personal presence of the bodies of glory in a created Paradise, otherwise many a passage in the Scriptures and many a sacred phenomenon would be inexplicable. As for the two lower gardens, the second of the two will be a state of beatific vision, but not a state of union; now this vision, like union, will be "vertical" in relation to a "horizontal"[12] or phenomenal and specifically human beatitude. This is one of the meanings, along with other symbolisms, of the crowns of uncreated light that the elect will wear, according to a Christian tradition; and this meaning applies with all the more reason, at an unsurpassable degree of reality, to the coronation of the Virgin.

In the famous prayer of Ibn Mashish, which is concerned with the Logos or the *Haqîqatu Muhammadiyah*, mention is made of the "radiance of Beauty" and of the "overflowing of Glory": apart from other meanings, this can refer to the two heavenly degrees that we have just spoken of. In erotic symbolism, this is the difference between the vision of the beloved and union with him: in the second case, form is extinguished, just as the accidents are resorbed into the Substance and just as the divine Qualities lose their differentiation in the Essence. This extinction or this resorption, or again this indifferentiation, pertains to what we have pre-

10. According to other commentators—Qashani foremost—the two other gardens are on the contrary higher than the first two, though this question of symbolic presentation is without importance here.
11. *Sambhoga-kâya*, the "body of heavenly Delight", and *Dharma-kâya*, the "body of the Law", the Divine Essence.
12. We could just as well speak of a "circular" garden and an "axial" garden, in conformity with a geometric symbolism not at all difficult to understand.

viously called the perspective of centripetal rays, as opposed to the perspective of concentric circles:[13] according to the first mystery, that of continuity or inclusiveness—and this is infinitely more than a way of seeing[14]—"every thing is *Âtmâ*", and direct union is therefore possible;[15] according to the second mystery, that of discontinuity or of exclusiveness, "*Brahman* is not in the world", and the separation between created and uncreated orders is consequently absolute, hence irreducible. It is only on the basis of this irreducibility that it is possible to conceive adequately of the inclusive homogeneity of the Real and of its spiritual consequence, the mystery of Identity or the "Paradise of the Essence".

13. This is the complementarity between the "axial" dimension and the "circular" dimension.
14. In the principial order, a perspective is determined by an objective reality; it is not the "point of view" that as it were creates the "aspect", unless one dare speak of a "divine point of view".
15. Given that indirect union, precisely, is preexistent; in other words, it is realized in advance through the divine homogeneity of the Universe, which pantheism would account for if it had the complementary and crucial notion of transcendence. The geometric symbol of this homogeneity, which is not "material" but transcendent, is the spiral, for it combines the perspective of the concentric circles with that of the rays.

BY THE SAME AUTHOR

The Transcendent Unity of Religions, *1953*
Revised Edition, *1975, 1984, The Theosophical Publishing House, 1993*

Spiritual Perspectives and Human Facts, *1954, 1969*
New Translation, *Perennial Books, 1987*

Gnosis: Divine Wisdom, *1959, 1978, Perennial Books, 1990*

Language of the Self, *1959* Revised Edition, *World Wisdom Books, 1999*

Stations of Wisdom, *1961, 1980*
Revised Translation, *World Wisdom Books, 1995*

Understanding Islam, *1963, 1965, 1972, 1976, 1979, 1981, 1986, 1989*
Revised Translation, *World Wisdom Books, 1994, 1998*

Light on the Ancient Worlds, *1966, World Wisdom Books, 1984*

In the Tracks of Buddhism, *1968, 1989*
New Translation, Treasures of Buddhism, *World Wisdom Books, 1993*

Logic and Transcendence, *1975, Perennial Books, 1984*

Esoterism as Principle and as Way, *Perennial Books, 1981, 1990*

Castes and Races, *Perennial Books, 1959, 1982*

Sufism: Veil and Quintessence, *World Wisdom Books, 1981*

From the Divine to the Human, *World Wisdom Books, 1982*

Christianity/Islam, *World Wisdom Books, 1985*

The Essential Writings of Frithjof Schuon (S.H. Nasr, Ed.),
1986, Element, 1991

Survey of Metaphysics and Esoterism, *World Wisdom Books, 1986, 2000*

In the Face of the Absolute, *World Wisdom Books, 1989, 1994*

The Feathered Sun: Plains Indians in Art & Philosophy,
World Wisdom Books, 1990

To Have a Center, *World Wisdom Books, 1990*

Roots of the Human Condition, *World Wisdom Books, 1991*

Images of Primordial & Mystic Beauty: Paintings by Frithjof Schuon,
Abodes, 1992

Echoes of Perennial Wisdom, *World Wisdom Books, 1992*

The Play of Masks, *World Wisdom Books, 1992*

Road to the Heart, *World Wisdom Books, 1995*

The Transfiguration of Man, *World Wisdom Books, 1995*

The Eye of the Heart, *World Wisdom Books, 1997*

Songs for a Spiritual Traveler: Selected Poems,
World Wisdom, 2002